ACCLAIM FOR *HER NAME WAS MARGARET*

"Denise Davy's fascinating yet terrifying account should have everyone storming the bastions of power to demand the government deliver on a sixty-year-old promise to provide generous, robust support systems as part of its policy of deinstitutionalization. Instead it threw people out of their psychiatric beds and left them on the streets.

"Against the tragic story of a woman named Margaret, Davy applies journalistic rigour to the great taboo of our times, homelessness. She disabuses the myths and explains the complex issues that cause many to tumble into life on the street. Homelessness is never a choice; it's a desperate last resort, one that is largely ameliorated by the thankless hours, patience and kindness of doctors, health care workers and volunteers. Such compassion, however, is no solution: it effectively shields from action the political will necessary to wrestle the problem. Successful programs and solutions exist – Davy cites them – so why are they not implemented? Never has society been more prosperous; never has it been so ostrichlike when it comes to the great unnatural disaster of homelessness. Readers, be prepared to ride a wave of emotion from shame to anger to profound grief. *Her Name Was Margaret* is a reminder that the messy lives we see daily are indeed our responsibility." – Jane Christmas, author of *Open House: A Life in Thirty-Two Moves*

"Growing up in a loveless but well-intentioned family Margaret Jacobson battled lifelong symptoms of mental illness. Davy has written a devastating portrait of a woman who floundered in the Canadian medical system seeking an elixir that couldn't be distilled. Despite the ravages of homelessness, endless hospital stays and boarding houses, the reader will cheer Margaret's indefatigable will to survive, her humour, her humanity. This is a book every social worker, every psychiatrist, every caring heart will read and reread. A triumph." – Susan Doherty, author of *The Ghost Garden: Inside the Lives of Schizophrenia's Feared and Forgotten*

"Riveting and heartbreaking, Denise Davy's *Her Name Was Margaret* is a compellingly researched story of mental illness and homelessness. With brilliant attention to detail, Davy takes us inside Margaret's world, and the result is unforgettable. A must-read for all Canadians with a conscience." – Ann Dowsett Johnston, author of *Drink: The Intimate Relationship Between Women and Alcohol*

"I was moved to tears at several points. This was a very moving book for me. How little did I know of those horrible years." – David Jacobson, Margaret's brother

"*Her Name Was Margaret* is a moving portrait of a real-life human being – Margaret Jacobson – who lived with a mental illness on the streets of Hamilton. The book documents the many ways that Margaret was cruelly treated by the 'system,' and also explains in detail what public policies and programs are needed to solve the problems that people like Margaret face on a daily basis. Regrettably, governments still resist adopting these policies and programs.

    "This book is a must-read for anyone with a social conscience. Hopefully the events it describes will motivate readers to pressure governments to finally seriously address the growing problem of homelessness in Canada." – Michael Kirby, former senator and chair of the Standing Senate Committee on Social Affairs, Science and Technology

"Margaret's story chronicles bureaucratic and institutional failures to provide adequate and evidence-based solutions to homelessness and deinstitutionalization. It is also about the kindness of strangers and the opportunity to spread and scale proven solutions to homelessness." – Steve Lurie, executive director of the Canadian Mental Health Association, Toronto

"Margaret Jacobson was an icon and a mentor to those of us trying to understand mental health and women's homelessness in the 1980s and 1990s. Denise Davy has impeccably researched Margaret's life, death and legacy, and written with compassion yet also bluntness about 'victims of a plan gone mad.' *Her Name Was Margaret* reads like a mystery story even though we know the ending." – Rev. Bill MacKinnon, homeless shelter worker, chaplain at Alexander Place

"Behind every homeless person you might cross the street to avoid is an untold story. The compassion and rigour that Denise Davy brings to Margaret's story serve as both an epitaph for countless other lives of lost potential and an indictment of a system that neglects its most vulnerable." – Rona Maynard, author of *My Mother's Daughter*, mental health advocate

"Denise Davy tenderly and compassionately chronicles the painful, abusive and too often inhumane and cruel life and death of Margaret Jacobson. As I read, I was reminded of stark realities endured by those who struggle with disabling mental health, past trauma and other cognitive challenges. And so many youth, men and women I have had the privilege to know – too many of whom have also died in egregious circumstances.

"I was also repeatedly struck by the parallels between the ways the current pandemic has fully exposed racist, classist and misogynist chasms in our economic, social and health systems and the manner in which the deinstitutionalization of psychiatric hospitals laid bare the near simultaneous evisceration of community-based supports. Then and now, long-existing and horrendous realities of the inadequacy of institutional care, whether for seniors and others in long-term care or those in psychiatric facilities, exacerbated by economic, health and racial inequalities have led to many more people being forced into poverty and homelessness.

"This book makes a valuable contribution to the policy and legislative work we need to remedy systemic and ongoing inequalities – the inherent inhumanity of systems that far too often render the lives of the most marginalized and vulnerable as disposable." – Senator Kim Pate

"You will never forget Margaret's tragic story as rendered here with meticulous research and unflinching compassion. Denise Davy shines a light straight into the heart of the national disaster of mental illness and homelessness in Canada. We have to do something and we have to do it now." – Diane Schoemperlen, author of *This Is Not My Life: A Memoir of Love, Prison, and Other Complications*

"Margaret Jacobson's story is woven through this book that informs eloquently the life journey of real people who are part of our community. It lays bare the desperate need to rethink services to ensure sustainable change for everyone's benefit. Margaret and so many others deserve better. I found myself saying, 'If only . . .' so many times while reading about Margaret and hoping that many people will read this compassionately written book and commit to making change. Bravo Denise." – Honourable Paddy Torsney

"*Her Name Was Margaret* is an unforgettable chronicle of loss and neglect, and a haunting indictment of how we as a society have failed the vulnerable in our midst. We want to cheer for Margaret as she encounters continual challenges and tragedies and somehow finds a way to survive, and yet we know that there are no happy endings in store for her, and many like her. Instead, we descend with Margaret into the darkest, most neglected corners of our cities, and endure every failing attempt to force her into narrow definitions of wellness instead of helping her live with a dignity all her own. Exceptionally well researched and engaging, *Her Name Was Margaret* is a remarkable achievement that compels us to not look away." – Brent van Staalduinen, author of *Boy* and *Nothing But Life*

HER NAME

was

MARGARET

HER NAME

was

MARGARET

Life and Death on the Streets

To: Judith,

Enjoy!

DENISE DAVY

© Denise Davy, 2021

No part of this publication may be reproduced, stored in a retrieval system or transmitted, in any form or by any means, without the prior written consent of the publisher or a license from the Canadian Copyright Licensing Agency (Access Copyright). For an Access Copyright license, visit www.accesscopyright.ca or call toll free to 1-800-893-5777.

James Street North Books is an imprint of Wolsak and Wynn Publishers.

Publisher and Editor: Noelle Allen | Copy editor: Andrew Wilmot
Cover and interior design: Jennifer Rawlinson
Front cover image: Barry Gray, *Hamilton Spectator*
Back cover image: Courtesy of Jacobson family
Author photograph: Daniel Nolan
Typeset in Minion, Bodoni and Candara
Printed by Brant Service Press Ltd., Brantford, Canada

Printed on certified 100% post-consumer Rolland Enviro Paper.

Map on page xiii: Map tiles by CartoDB, under CC BY 3.0. map data © OpenStreetMap contributors under ODbL

10 9 8 7 6 5 4 3 2 1

The publisher gratefully acknowledges the support of the Ontario Arts Council, the Canada Council for the Arts and the Government of Canada.

James Street North Books
280 James Street North
Hamilton, ON
Canada L8R 2L3

Library and Archives Canada Cataloguing in Publication

Title: Her name was Margaret : life and death on the streets / Denise Davy.
Names: Davy, Denise, 1953- author.
Description: Includes bibliographical references.
Identifiers: Canadiana 20200410385 | ISBN 9781989496329 (softcover)
Subjects: LCSH: Jacobson, Margaret, -1995. | LCSH: Mentally ill homeless persons—Ontario—Hamilton—Biography. | LCSH: Mentally ill women—Ontario—Hamilton—Biography. | LCSH: Homeless women—Ontario—Hamilton—Biography. | LCSH: Mental illness—Canada—Case studies. | LCSH: Homelessness—Canada—Case studies. | LCGFT: Biographies.
Classification: LCC RC464.J33 D38 2021 | DDC 616.890092—dc23

To Margaret and every person who calls the streets their home

To my daughters, Emma and Katie, who shine a bright light on every one of my days

Contents

PART THREE: ON THE STREETS, 1985–1995

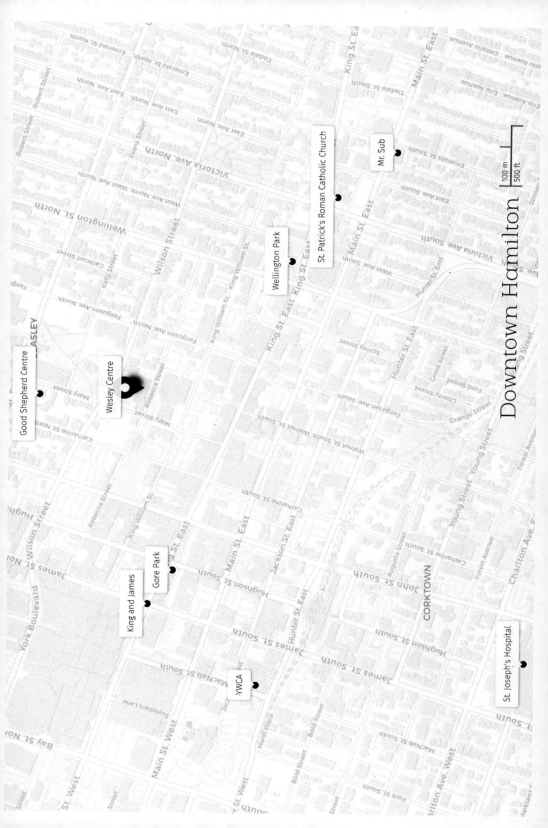

Downtown Hamilton

Margaret as a child. Courtesy of Jacobson family.

AUTHOR'S NOTE

The mysteries of Margaret's life were buried among her medical files, an adoption report, a church newsletter, a coroner's report, letters from her family and her personal diary. To fully understand what she went through, I read through hundreds of pages and talked to family, friends, social workers and shelter staff. I exchanged emails with her two nephews in the States and her brother, David, in China. I also visited the shelters where she stayed, retraced her steps from the night she died and sat in the chair where she had her last cup of tea.

The chapters on her years on the streets were pieced together with information from interviews with her friend Bob Dixon, with all facts confirmed by shelter staff. I relied on this information to weave Margaret's story together and recreate some of the more extraordinary moments in her life. Where I don't have permission from a person to quote them, I have used a pseudonym. This is a work of non-fiction; however, the views expressed in parts throughout this book are mine.

Introduction

When I began writing this book, my focus was on telling the story of a homeless woman named Margaret, who I met at a shelter one cold winter night. I sat across from her, transfixed by the broken-down woman before me and listened as she shared her story. Meeting Margaret opened my eyes to the reasons why so many homeless people on our streets have a mental illness and became the starting point for my twenty-year journey into the homelessness crisis in Canada.

Margaret is one of thousands of homeless people who have been victimized by a government plan that resulted in one of the grimmest and most shameful chapters in the history of Canada's psychiatric care. What happened to Margaret is the untold story of why so many homeless people today struggle with mental illness and why so few social services exist for them.

This book follows one woman's brutal descent into homelessness and shows how she went from hospital patient to homeless person as a result of deinstitutionalization that swept across the country starting in the 1960s and led to thousands of psychiatric patients being discharged into boarding homes and communities. It was supposed to help former patients become more independent and productive, and take them out of oppressive hospital environments.

Deinstitutionalization moved forward without opposition, and over the next many decades led to the closure of more than 80 percent of psychiatric hospital beds in Canada. The problem was in the government's failure to set up community services and provide supportive housing for the former psychiatric patients. These same people who had been receiving 24-7 care inside the hospital were moved into the community and suddenly had to fend for themselves.

The supports that were promised never materialized, nor did the services that were supposed to help former patients secure housing and find jobs. The health care workers weren't hired to make sure former patients were taking their medications, and the community treatment centres that were to open in areas close to where patients were being moved were never built. Instead of the former patients living in supportive housing and having access to a wide range of supports, they ended up sleeping in alleyways in cardboard boxes and on top of hot air grates, and begging for spare change for their next meal. Because of this rough living, they're dying at much higher rates and at much younger ages than the general population.

This book shows how deinstitutionalization was the catalyst for the crisis that exists on our streets today. While it may have successfully reduced the patient population inside psychiatric hospitals, it also created a subculture of mentally ill homeless people who wander the streets today. Most survive by relying on a network of underfunded shelters and hot meal programs that are held together by shoestring budgets and the compassion of dedicated volunteers.

MARGARET HAD THE misfortune to enter the psychiatric hospital system in the 1960s, when deinstitutionalization was in full swing. She was only seventeen, still an impressionable teenager. Caught up in the frenzy to close beds, doctors repeatedly discharged her into rundown, unregulated boarding homes that were typically operated by people with zero experience working with persons with mental illness. Although no community supports were offered, she was expected to do it all – from making bus trips to the hospital for medication to keep her schizophrenic symptoms under control to managing her finances.

In short time, she would falter. She would stop going to the hospital and, once off her medication, would begin her free fall. During the twenty-four years that Margaret spent in a psychiatric hospital, she was discharged several times, each one ending more tragically than the one before. With each move, she became sicker and sicker. But that didn't deter medical staff from releasing her again. This same process was inflicted on thousands of psychiatric patients during deinstitutionalization. Staff who worked at the hospital remember being told that the goal was to get patients out, regardless of their condition when they came back. Because there was so little, if any, follow-up on patients, their outcomes and how they fared isn't known. Their stories have never been told – until now. As a result of gaining unprecedented access to Margaret's 869-page medical file, we're being given a glimpse into what happened to one of those patients and how it led her into homelessness.

Margaret's story unfolded many years ago on the streets of Hamilton, Ontario, but similar stories have played out – and are still playing out – in cities and towns across Canada. Every year, an estimated 235,000 people are counted among the homeless population in Canada and, on any given night, 35,000 people are sleeping on our streets. The exact number who have some form of a mental illness may be as high as 70 percent.

They often fall into the group known as the chronically homeless – those who have been there the longest – and they suffer from the most severe health problems. They are more vulnerable to developing frostbite and sunstroke and other issues from exposure to the elements. Having a mental illness puts them at much higher risk to experiencing homelessness; however, some people develop a mental illness only after they become homeless. The cruel reality of sleeping rough means not knowing where you'll be sleeping each night, eating a poor diet and living in a heightened state of fear of being assaulted or raped. All of these explain why there are such high rates of anxiety and depression among homeless people.

The tragic story of deinstitutionalization's impact has never been told. Neither has any group or government body ever been held accountable for the outcome. While the closure of psychiatric beds and hospitals saved the government billions of dollars, few of those funds were rerouted into community supports. It wasn't that anyone disagreed with the concept of deinstitutionalization; it was the subsequent failure to set up adequate community supports and supportive housing that was the problem.

The truth of how Margaret's life trajectory was impacted by that flawed plan needs to be told because the reality is, we are still sentencing people with mental illness to life on the streets. Their stories are the stories of deinstitutionalization's failures. And yet today, as the numbers of homeless grow, so has our capacity to look away. Now when we see someone on the streets, we walk by and ignore them. As American psychiatrist and essayist Charles Krauthammer wrote, "Thirty years ago, if you saw a person lying helpless on the street, you ran to help him. Now you step over him. You know that he is not an accident victim. He lives there."

That's true in cities across the country. In Toronto, encampments have been built under highways where people sleep in tents, even during the winter. In Windsor, Ontario, in 2016, a woman was discovered sleeping in a dog cage on the street. The *Windsor Star* reported that by the time word of her plight spread through social media, she'd been living in the cage for eight months.

In Edmonton in 2017, city workers removed 1,690 homeless people from camps set up along Edmonton's River Valley, where people were living under tarps and in tents. One homeless man named Shane told *Global News* he had stayed in a tent with two other people in -25°C weather. Said Shane, "I don't want to spend another winter [outside]. No. My feet, my back, it'll kill me."

In 2016 in Victoria, BC, droves of homeless people camped out on the lawn of a courthouse until the province closed the tent city down. Victoria has one of the highest (per capita) numbers of homeless in Canada. According to a 2016 count, there were 1,387 homeless people, although shelter workers said that the number was closer to 1,800 as the count didn't include the hidden homeless, those people who stay with relatives, friends or even strangers because they have no other option, also known as couch surfing. Some became homeless after losing their low-rental housing to gentrification. Others may have been hospitalized for a mental illness then released under short stay policies, then because of so few supports, they ended up in a shelter. Many people who struggle with a mental illness find the loud, chaotic environment of shelters impossible to handle, and so they sleep on the streets.

But people with mental illness aren't only languishing on our streets; they're stagnating in our prisons where the numbers are so high that prisons have been called the new asylums. Inmates with a mental illness are living within these chaotic confines and are not receiving any supports. It's little wonder they're at such high risk to self-injury, premature death and solitary confinement, which involves isolation for twenty-two or more hours a day in a cell the size of two queen-sized mattresses.

With more people living on the street, it's highly likely that the number of homeless deaths has increased; however, it's impossible to know since many municipalities don't count them. BC is an exception, and in 2016, a report from the BC Coroners Services showed that the number of homeless people dying on streets across BC had steadily increased since 2011, largely due to the overdose crisis. Of the 175 deaths reported, ninety-three – more than half – were the result of drug overdoses or alcohol poisoning. That number is triple the thirty-eight homeless people who died due to drugs or alcohol the previous year. The 175 homeless deaths, including sixteen in Victoria, was more than double the seventy deaths recorded the year before. That was up from 2011, when twenty-five homeless deaths were recorded.

On the east coast, on Cape Breton Island, the Homeless Hub identified 137 homeless people. This might not seem like a high number, but consider that the island's total population sits at around 100,000. The problem is particularly serious for homeless women as there are no overnight shelters for women on Cape Breton Island. The executive director of the Cape Breton Community Housing Association told council: "Twenty-four of those individuals were sleeping outside or in a place not fit for human habitation." Many would say that we wouldn't subject dogs to the kind of treatment we deem acceptable for homeless people.

In 2016, CAEH and York University's Canadian Observatory on Homelessness released a report called *The State of Homelessness in Canada 2016*, which recommended ways for the government to start solving the homeless problem. They include expanding the supply of permanent housing by 50,000 units and creating an Urban Indigenous Housing Strategy to address the disproportionate number of Indigenous people experiencing homelessness. While Indigenous people make up around 4.9 percent of the population, in major urban areas like Toronto they comprise 20 to 50 percent of the homeless population. Other groups who experience homelessness at a disproportionate rate include LGBTQIA2 youth, new immigrants and people who struggle with mental illness and addiction.

LOOKING BACK INTO the history of psychiatric care, it's a challenge to find any period in which people with mental illness have been treated well. In the 1750s, some US asylums began allowing visitors so they could gawk at the "lunatics," a practice that became so popular it was likened to a Sunday afternoon visit to the zoo. As Robert Whitaker wrote in *Mad in America: Bad Science, Bad Medicine and the Enduring Mistreatment of the Mentally Ill*, "Philadelphians were eager to get a glimpse of these wretched creatures, with good sport on occasion to be had by taunting them, particularly those restrained in irons and easily roused into a rage."

Today, more than 260 years later, you don't have to visit the local asylum to catch a glimpse of the patients – you just have to walk down the street. There you'll see the ragged parade of men and women pushing rusty grocery carts and sleeping rough on sidewalks and in alleyways. Lest you think we've come a long way, these scenes are a testimony to how little progress has been made. As long as one person is sleeping on a park bench or struggling to find warmth over a hot air grate, we can't pride ourselves on being a compassionate and caring country. In a country where housing should be a human right, it's instead only available to some.

THIS IS MARGARET's story. It's the story of a child who showed great potential; she was an A student, played the piano and accordion, and taught Sunday school classes. Her grade school teacher described her as a "quiet, hard-working girl with a great ambition to succeed." Instead, she became a toothless, worn-down homeless woman who haunted the streets and smoked two packs a day. Margaret wasn't just a mentally ill homeless person. She was a human being and she had a name, which is the most important piece of identity anyone has. Once we know the names and stories of all homeless people, it will be harder for us to turn away.

Margaret, age forty-nine, inside the Wesley drop-in shelter. Courtesy of Barry Gray, *Hamilton Spectator.*

CHAPTER ONE
"Nobody Came"

December 6, 1995
Hamilton

The woman was dangling off the edge of her chair, arms flailing about like a wild animal. She tried desperately to grab the side of the table but wasn't strong enough to pull herself back upright. She had wandered into this sub shop about twenty minutes ago, wearing thin, tattered clothes with a blanket draped over her shoulders, perhaps placed there by a kind stranger who took pity on the homeless woman. Her brown hair was a matted mess and her face was deeply lined, like a landscape over which rough weather had passed.

She had bought herself a cup of tea and settled into the small table by the door, cupping the tea in her hands and letting the steam drift over her face. Every once in a while, she rested her weary head on the table, as if it were too heavy to hold up. From behind the counter, Claudette Gadoury could see that the woman needed to warm up and decided to let her stay. She was relieved the woman had found shelter on this wretched December night when temperatures had dipped below freezing. Then customers began complaining about the "bag lady" who was "smoking up a storm."

"She needs to go," one man sternly told Claudette.

Claudette reluctantly walked over to the woman and asked her to leave.

She was surprised when the woman refused to go. She hadn't expected such stubbornness from someone so frail. When Claudette asked again, the woman waved her away. Claudette tried one more time and this time the woman ignored her.

It was 6:48 p.m. when Claudette made the first call to 911.

"Nine-one-one, what's your emergency?"

"There's a bum off the streets who is making a nuisance of herself," Claudette told the dispatcher. "We don't keep that kind of clientele in our store."

CLAUDETTE WAS IN her early twenties, a soft-spoken young woman with an easy, forgiving smile. Later she would question why she referred to the woman as a bum, something that would haunt her long after this ordeal had ended. The sub shop was in a quiet L-shaped strip plaza in the east end of Hamilton, Ontario, a few kilometres from downtown, squeezed alongside a convenience store and a cheque-cashing business.

Fifteen minutes after Claudette made the 911 call there was still no sign of police, so she called again. The dispatcher told her there'd been a delay because of a shift change and assured her it won't be much longer. Another ten minutes passed and no one showed. Then the woman suddenly became wedged between the chair and table. Claudette thought she may have bent down to pick something up and got stuck.

Her bony body was dangling over the side of the chair, her arms and legs flying in every direction. Claudette grabbed the phone and called 911 a third time.

"The woman is now in trouble," Claudette yelled into the phone. "She is stuck in the chair and can't get up."

"Help is on the way," the dispatcher told her again.

Suddenly, the woman started to scream – loud, raspy cries that filled the shop. "Help, help," she yelled, still struggling with the table.

Just then the woman started banging her head against the window, perhaps trying to call attention to her plight. Bang, bang, bang. The disturbing sound filled the shop. No one stepped forward. Over and over she hit her head while flinging her arm up to grab the table.

There was still no sign of police. Still no offers of help.

Suddenly there was a thud. The yelling stopped. The woman had collapsed and fallen off her chair. Her head collided with the floor. Blood began oozing from her head. Claudette frantically grabbed the phone again. It was now 7:47 p.m., a full hour after the first call was placed. Where are they?

"She just bumped her head and now she's bleeding," Claudette yelled into the phone. "Blood is coming out of her nose or off her face. I don't know what to do."

Again, the dispatcher told her that police were on their way. "Don't move her."

The call should by this point have been escalated from a nuisance call to a life-and-death emergency, which requires that police act immediately. But where were they? Claudette stared at the woman's lifeless body. Blood was soaking into her matted hair and spreading across the floor. Claudette felt helpless, desperate. Oh my god, what if she dies, she thought.

Twelve more minutes passed. It was 7:59 p.m. A halo of blood now surrounded the woman's head as she lay motionless on the floor. Claudette made another frantic call.

"I have a woman lying on the ground," she screamed into the phone. "Lying in my . . . in Mr. Sub on the corner of King and Emerald. She's lying there bleeding from her head. She's been there for about an hour. We called earlier and they told us we couldn't move her. They said they'd send somebody and they still haven't sent anyone!"

By now, most people had left. Claudette feared the woman was dead. The silence in the shop was deafening. She reached for the phone just as a police car and ambulance pulled up. Claudette held her breath and watched as the paramedic knelt down beside the woman and checked her pulse. "She's alive," she heard them say. Claudette breathed a sigh of relief.

The paramedic cut through the woman's tattered red cardigan and black blouse then hooked her up to an intravenous. They wrapped a cervical collar around her neck and placed her limp body on the stretcher. She was put in the ambulance and rushed to Hamilton General Hospital, a five-minute drive away. Shortly after she arrived, the woman went into cardiac arrest. Doctors were unable to revive her.

At 9:53 p.m., three hours after the first 911 call, the woman was pronounced dead.

Staff searched her clothing but couldn't find any ID. She was a patient without a name. Then an observant nurse recognized her as the homeless woman who was written up in the *Hamilton Spectator*. Had the nurse not been there that night, at that exact time, the woman may well have died unknown and nameless.

HER NAME WAS Margaret Louise Jacobson. She was fifty-one years old, although the coroner's report from the autopsy conducted the next day would reveal that her body resembled someone much older. One year on the streets is like a lifetime anywhere else. Margaret was five feet four inches tall, fifty-three kilograms or 116 pounds and was described as "seriously malnourished." She had no teeth in her upper jaw and was missing many in her lower. There was bruising on her head and a cut on her left eyebrow. The skin on her face was described as leathery and pitted, and the cancer that had started in her right breast years earlier had spread so extensively through her upper body that the skin under her arms stuck to her ribs.

The autopsy stated that Margaret went into cardiac arrest shortly after arriving at the hospital and that she died from a ruptured dissecting aneurysm, the same condition that killed one of her brothers. Death was ruled as natural causes.

WHEN POLICE RETURNED to the sub shop and told Claudette the news, she broke down and cried. She was wrought with guilt for referring to Margaret as a "bum." She'd seen the legions of homeless people on the streets and knew they were this city's forgotten souls. She agonized about what she could have done differently and became so distraught that she missed time from work as she tried to process it all.

"I just felt so helpless," Claudette told me for the *Spectator* story. "I just kept telling her help was on the way. But nobody came."

HOPING FOR CLOSURE, Claudette ordered a copy of the 911 transcript. Maybe it would tell her something she didn't know. Maybe she hadn't called as many times as she thought. Police turned down her request on the basis that it was a breach of confidentiality, but Claudette appealed the decision to the Freedom of Information's provincial office and the denial was overturned. The transcript showed Claudette what she already knew – that she had called 911 a total of five times, and that it had taken police more than an hour to get there, even after the call had been elevated to an emergency.

The Hamilton-Wentworth Regional Police department's response was that the calls were initially classified as low priority, or a number three, because they were reports of an "unwanted person" – also referred to as nuisance calls. And while the policy stated that a number three low-priority call must be answered within one hour, according to police, those calls are "susceptible to being bumped" by another. Even though the call had been upgraded, police still concluded they had followed protocol.

Claudette could see from Margaret's sick, worn-out appearance that she'd been severely overlooked and neglected during her life. Sadly, the same thing had happened with her death.

IT'S NOT KNOWN how many homeless people died the same year as Margaret. Like most municipalities, Hamilton doesn't track homeless deaths. They didn't track them the year Margaret died and they still don't track them today. That's been a hindrance to social service agencies who, without data on seasonal, geographic trends and causes of death, don't know the full scope of the homelessness crisis and what services are needed. It means the full picture is missing and that many homeless people are disappearing like ghosts.

In death, as in life, they are invisible.

CHAPTER TWO
"She Does What She Has To"

1993
Hamilton

Margaret Jacobson had a story to tell and she shared it with me when I met her two years before that fateful night at the sub shop. I'd been writing about homelessness for years from the comfort of my desk at the *Hamilton Spectator* newsroom where I covered the social issues beat. But my stories were full of statistics and studies – they had no face. I needed to find out who homeless people were, so I talked my editor into letting me spend the night at a shelter. I chose the Wesley Centre's drop-in shelter, which was run by Wesley Urban Ministries, because it was a magnet for the hard-core homeless people who had been on the streets the longest.

They were the sickest of the sick among the homeless population, who often lived under the shadow of addiction and mental illness. They slept in doorways and cardboard boxes, in cemeteries and under bridges. Back then, the Wesley was the only shelter that would take someone who had been drinking while other shelters had zero tolerance for drugs or alcohol. There was also no curfew, so people were free to come and go. As long as there was no violence, anyone was welcome. Most folks just wanted to sleep. For many, their goal was just to make it through the night.

I ARRIVED AT the shelter around eleven on a freezing cold night in January. The shelter was in a basement and, although it had only been open an hour, was already full and choked with cigarette smoke. There were no beds or comfy chairs – just rickety wooden benches and tables. Neon lights glared and the musty basement smell mingled with the aroma of cigarette smoke. It's the smell of quiet desperation. The buzz of voices was occasionally punctuated by an angry outburst from one of the clientele. Staff tried to calm them and also offer a harsh warning that next time they'd be made to leave. No one wants to eject a homeless person on a brutally cold night like tonight. And no one here wants to be outside.

For homeless people, who had fought freezing temperatures and hunger pangs all day, the Wesley was a refuge. The soup was homemade and it was a place to grab a hot shower. The upside of no beds meant they were safe from the diseases, overcrowding and outbreaks that plagued many shelters. Instead of sleeping lying down, however, they had to grab a few winks sitting upright on the hard benches.

I interviewed several people and was looking around the room for others when I spotted a woman sitting at one of the benches smoking a cigarette. My stomach clenched when I saw how worn down she was. Her skin was grey and leathery, her hair as matted as a bird's nest and she was rail thin. I'd been a reporter at the *Spec* for nine years and had interviewed many people in desperate situations. I would later visit India and Thailand on journalism fellowships and visit some of the worst slums in the world while investigating child prostitution and mass poverty. In all of my travels, I would never see anyone like the woman on the other side of the room.

Many years of neglect and pain were etched into her tired face – many more than she had lived, I guessed. It somehow made it so much worse that she was a woman. Hunched over and frail, she looked like an inmate from a Victorian workhouse. But this was Canada, land of opportunity, where the social safety net is supposed to prevent vulnerable people from falling through the cracks. What had happened to her? How could she have ended up in this horrific state?

She had staked out her territory on one of the benches and was sitting alone. I watched as she tapped her cigarette into the dented aluminum ashtray then put it to her cracked lips and took a long drag. A wiry-looking fellow with crazed hair wandered too close to her and she barked at him in a gravelly voice, in case he had any ideas of stealing her cigarettes. Her only protection against the brutal cold was a short brown coat and thin pants. Under the table, I could see she was wearing four-inch heels. I had to talk to her and find out her story.

I guessed she was in her seventies and was shocked to learn from a staffer that she was forty-nine. She was only nine years older than me, yet our lives couldn't have been more different. I had lived a privileged upbringing with an executive father who took us on great family vacations. The closest I'd come to being homeless was when I was a teenager and hitchhiked out west one summer, sleeping in nice hostels along the way. It was an act of rebellion by a middle-class kid who knew she had a home to come back to. I'd never had to worry about my next meal or where I would sleep each night. In contrast, as I would soon learn, this woman had no home and no family. She literally had the clothes on her back. And her precious cigarettes.

While we could not have been more different, I felt a connection with her and knew that I could reach her. I had spent most of my journalism career interviewing people who were challenging to talk to; people who had been in jail or were victims of violence or had suffered great loss. In the newsroom, where black humour reigns, my many interviews with the down-and-out had earned me the nickname Mistress of Misery. Over the course of those interviews, I'd learned the importance of using a gentle touch to make people feel comfortable enough to talk. It's why social service agencies had grown to trust me, and why Wesley staff had approved my visit.

Still, this woman looked to be beyond reach. Forging a connection with her would be a great challenge.

I asked a staffer about her and was told her name was Margaret. I asked if she thought Margaret would speak to me. She cautioned me against it and said they didn't know much about her, but that, judging by her wild behaviour, they thought she had been diagnosed with schizophrenia. Margaret had been on the streets for about ten years and was a regular here, the staffer told me. She warned me Margaret could be violent and that she had a particular habit of smashing people in the face with their hard plastic coffee mugs. She'd been thrown out more than a few times for it.

"You never know what you're going to get," she said.

The staffer offered a few more details. "She's been known to flash the men if she wants a cigarette," she said, looking resigned. "She does what she has to do to get by."

I stared at Margaret, sitting alone on the bench, and curiosity overrode my fear. I walked over. Close up, the neon lights revealed skin as withered and pitted as a dried orange peel. Her hair hadn't seen a brush for years. She looked like she was a few steps away from death's door. A cigarette dangled from her hand and smoke curled around dirt-encrusted fingers so yellowed with nicotine they looked to have been dipped in paint. Beneath that craggy exterior, though, I saw something else – a flicker of warmth, intelligence. I knew she wouldn't hurt me, not unless I hurt her first.

Being a reporter means maintaining an emotional distance from your interview subjects, but with Margaret it was heart over head and my heart broke for the woman before me. I approached my interview the same way I always did – whether a CEO or an inmate, everyone deserves the same level of respect. I asked her to tell me her story.

"Hɪ, Mᴀʀɢᴀʀᴇᴛ," I said, standing across from her.

She took a long drag of her cigarette. Her hand drooped in front of her face and her cigarette dangled from her fingers. I tried again.

"My name is Denise. I'm a reporter at the local newspaper."

There's no response so I kept talking. I explained that I'm writing a story on people who come to the drop-in and asked if it's okay if I talk to her. I had no idea if she even knew I was standing there. I asked her again and she finally glanced over, although not directly at me, then pulled her ashtray toward her in case I had any plans to steal it.

"I don't care," she mumbled.

I'd made a connection. Granted not much of one, but I took what I could get. I stepped cautiously over the bench, making sure not to sit directly across from her.

"So," I said casually, "someone told me your name is Margaret."

No answer.

"How long have you been coming here?"

Silence.

"I come here a lot," she said finally. "I don't like the shelters."

Then Margaret surprised me by reaching inside her tattered coat and pulling out a crumpled-up photo that looked like it was ripped out of a calendar. She handed it to me. It was a photo of a beautiful sandy white beach with turquoise blue water and swaying palm trees, like an ad for an inviting resort.

I asked her how long she'd lived in Hamilton. Then the woman I'd been warned about did something that surprised everyone. She sat up, as if she'd gotten her second wind, and started talking about her childhood, how she played the piano, had worked as a typist and been in a hospital. My pen could barely keep up. She never looked at me as she talked but instead gazed off into the distance, always with a cigarette locked between her fingers.

"How long were you in the hospital?" I asked.

Silence again. I tried prompting her with more questions. Smoke drifted my way from her cigarette and I stifled a cough.

"A long time," she muttered. "My nerves were too bad."

I would later learn that this comment – "My nerves were too bad" – was her go-to explanation for her mental illness, the way she explained away the many years spent in the hospital. Margaret took another drag from her cigarette then told me about her stints in jail, her boyfriend Bob and why she prefers the streets to staying in shelters.

"I don't like keeping a room," she said nonchalantly.

I don't know if Margaret could play the piano or if she had a boyfriend named Bob but it was clear that she was glad to have someone to talk to. Over the next forty-five minutes, she talked about her life, sometimes waving her hands in the air while other times resting her head on her hand as if it weighed too much. Her battered face reflected the thousands of nights she'd spent on the streets. Three hundred and sixty-five days in one year times ten years: 3,650 nights. It sometimes hurt to look at her because of the mountain of pain and sadness etched into her face. Too much for one person.

Suddenly, there was yelling. Across the room, a rumpled man with wild hair began shouting and waving his arms as if being attacked by a swarm of bugs. "Get off me!" he shouted.

I learned later that his nickname was Billy the Kid – his real name was Herbie Lafleur. He'd told staff and other clients that his brother was professional hockey player Guy Lafleur. No one knew if that was true. Staff rushed over to him and hushed words were exchanged. He was allowed to stay but with a warning. By now the shelter was a cloud of cigarette smoke.

I watched as Margaret tucked a strand of matted hair behind a wrinkled ear then crossed one birdlike leg over the other, swinging it back and forth. There was something sweet and childlike about her – the upright way she sat, the swinging leg. It made me wonder if she'd lived well once, if she was loved as a child. Was I getting a glimpse of her as the person she was before she became homeless?

Then Margaret told me she had a child. A boy. She'd named him Jeffrey, she told me in her gravelly voice. He was born while she was a patient at the hospital, she said, but didn't offer details on when or where it happened.

"They made me give him up," she said, then muttered something about not being allowed to hold him. She told me she was hopeful that she would meet him someday. He would be twenty now, she told me before retreating into silence.

My head was spinning with questions, but Margaret was short on answers. Was it possible she'd had a baby while in a psychiatric hospital? Was she forced to give him up? Margaret mentioned a few times that she'd been in the hospital, and in hope of getting my questions answered about what happened to her, I asked her if it would be okay if I accessed her files. It was the only way I could get to the bottom of her story.

"Yes," she told me. She was okay with it. I told her I wasn't sure how I would go about doing it but that I would let her know. She sat up straight.

"I know five Denises," she said with a grin that revealed several missing teeth. One was the cook at another shelter and another was a guard at the Barton Street jail.

Why was she in jail, I asked.

Without missing a beat, she said, "I wanted a place to stay."

"Do you like Hamilton?"

"I call it the Valley of the Dolls because you look up and see the mountain," she said, waving her hand over her head.

She was more animated now and seemed to be enjoying herself. Then Margaret turned the questions on me. How long had I been a reporter? Did I have any children? Where did I live? I smiled and told her I'd been a reporter for about ten years, and that my son, Ryan, was thirteen. She responded to each of my answers with a cheery "That's nice."

Then there was silence. It turned out Margaret had finished talking. I had more questions, but she was staring into space and I could no longer reach her. The dark look in her eyes told me she had forgotten I was there. It was just Margaret and her cigarette. I needed to interview more people so I wandered around the smoke-filled basement. I talked to a scared-looking teenage couple peeking out from behind a sleeping bag, a young woman who was sitting alone, a fellow with long stringy brown hair and some Wesley staffers.

Night after night the staff at the Wesley do what they can to help the crowd of homeless people who wander in to escape the cold. They offer them a cup of compassion to go with the hot soup, hoping against hope that it will get them through another night. They recognize that they may be the only human contact that some of these people have all day.

Still, there are some basic rules that have to be followed and violence can't be tolerated. After another outburst, Billy the Kid was shown the door. Everyone stared in silence as he was escorted out. They didn't want to be next.

AT 4:00 A.M. I decided to call it a night. My eyes were stinging from the smoke, my clothes and hair reeked and I felt like I'd sucked in a roomful of second-hand smoke. I wondered how staff coped with this onslaught of smoke every evening. I couldn't wait to get home and crawl under my goose down comforter and lay my head on my soft pillow. What I had taken for granted all my life now felt like a luxury.

As I headed for the door, I was startled by someone yelling my name. I looked over. Margaret was standing up at her bench and enthusiastically waving both her scrawny arms above her head and smiling a toothless grin.

"Bye, Denise!" she yelled, as if we're best friends who had just had lunch.

I waved back. It was nice to see her so happy.

"Are you going already?" she yelled.

I told her I was finished for tonight but that I hoped to see her again soon.

"Okay, bye-bye then," she said, plunking back down on the hard bench.

I passed the staffer who'd warned me about Margaret. "Looks like you made a connection," she said, with a look of surprise.

The heavy metal door to the shelter shut behind me with a thud and a cold smack of night air hit my face. I pulled my coat tight around me and headed for my car, oblivious to how this unplanned meeting with a homeless woman named Margaret would change my life.

CHAPTER THREE

Psychiatric *Titanic*

1993
Hamilton

To the world, Margaret was a mystery, a tragically lonely figure who shuffled about the streets by day and slept in the city's alcoves and alleyways at night. Although she'd been visiting the Wesley for ten years, she had never opened up to anyone about who she was or how she came to be homeless. While she had relayed all number of details to me, I had no idea how much of it was true. She'd told me as much as she was able to, then shut down. My only avenue for finding out her story was through her hospital medical records.

I called the Hamilton Psychiatric Hospital (HPH) and was told that if Margaret signed a Freedom of Information request form, I could see her files. Although this was a major breakthrough, I wasn't sure how to reconnect with Margaret as she could disappear for months, either because she was crashing on a friend's couch or because she'd gone to another shelter. I decided to call the Wesley and explain about the release form then asked if someone could give her the form if she came by. It was a big "if," so I wasn't holding my breath. Less than two weeks later, however, I got a call saying Margaret had been by and signed the form.

The door had been opened.

AT THE HAMILTON Psychiatric Hospital, I was led into a small cubicle where two thick brown leather binders sat on a desk. Each binder bulged with papers and I wondered if they'd mistakenly given me files for several patients, with Margaret's buried among them. I opened the cover of the first binder and stared down at a postage-stamp-sized black-and-white photo of a teen-age girl. I leaned forward and squinted at it. Her long hair was dishevelled, like she had just gotten out of bed, and she was smiling timidly but looked apprehensive. Or maybe it was a look of resignation. The name under the photo read "Jacobson, Margaret." The date was 1962. I flipped through the pages and scrambled to find her birthdate – 1944. The photo was taken on Margaret's first admission to the Ontario Hospital. She was only eighteen.

The teen in the photo bore zero resemblance to the worn-out woman I'd met, which only heightened my curiosity. How had she gone from a sweet, timid-looking teenager to one of the city's hard-core homeless people? I flipped through the pages and saw hundreds of doctors' reports, lab tests, prescription orders, approval forms for electroconvulsive therapy, admission records, x-rays, menstrual charts, notes from social workers and dental records. Some were typed, others were handwritten.

I looked at the final date in the second binder and realized that these two binders contained Margaret's complete medical files from when she was first hospitalized in 1961 to her last discharge from the hospital in 1985. There were a staggering 869 pages, and the hundreds of reports, test results and doctors' notes documented her twenty-four years of hospitalization. They also revealed the army of people who'd been involved in her care – doctors, nurses, social workers, medical specialists and boarding home operators. Some pages overflowed with the cocktail of drugs she'd been prescribed, including antipsychotics, sleeping pills, pills for anxiety and pills to counter the side effects of those drugs.

In the midst of these reports and medical notes were handwritten letters from her family. Together the reports and letters held the clues to what had happened to Margaret. But it was the notes detailing her readmissions to the hospital that were the most heartbreaking. Several times they brought me to tears and I had to stop reading. The problem wasn't that Margaret had been forgotten inside of these hospital walls. Indeed, she'd been seen by a long list of medical professionals and had been enrolled in several hospital employment training programs, including typing classes. But was the care she'd received what she had needed? If so, how had she gone from being a patient in a psychiatric hospital to living on the streets?

ABOUT A MONTH after meeting Margaret, I tried to find her again as I had more questions. Wesley staff told me she was still coming to the drop-in regularly, so I took a chance and headed out around ten thirty one night. After forty-five minutes spent shivering in the snow in the parking lot across the street from the centre, I started to wonder whether she would show. It was almost midnight and I was ready to give up when I saw her strutting toward me with Bob, the boyfriend she'd told me about. Her hair was cut short, and when I complimented her on it, she told me she had gone to a salon at a large mall downtown. It had cost her sixty dollars.

Spending sixty dollars of her welfare money on a haircut may have seemed irrational to some but it made me smile. It showed that she still cared about her appearance and having her hair done would have given her a much-needed boost.

I tried to picture the hairstylist at the upscale salon washing her matted hair then cutting through the dirt and twigs that were likely buried in her roots. I wondered if they knew that their simple act had no doubt given Margaret a bit of her dignity back. I wanted to plant a kiss on their forehead for seeing past the street person and treating Margaret like a regular customer.

As I sat across from Margaret, I realized how much I'd been thinking about her since we'd met. I'd worried about how she was doing and where she was sleeping at night. I was saddened by her tragic life, but I also admired her tenacity and her ability to keep going. She had already begun to burrow her way into my heart.

A few months later, I met up with her again at the Good Shepherd Centres' ladies' drop-in. I was pleasantly surprised when she remembered my name then she told me again about the "Denises" she had known.

"How are you doing, Margaret?" I asked.

"Fine," she answered, not making eye contact.

But "fine" didn't match how she looked. She was even more worn down and, with her coat off, I could see was positively skeletal. Still, Margaret never showed weakness. She acted in her usual cheery way as she went about filling up her coffee cup and putting sandwiches on her plate. She sat down on a couch and crossed her legs as she had done when I met her, then she ate her food. In the same nonchalant way that one might talk about their day, Margaret explained how she had been spending some nights on the streets and also staying with friends. She liked moving around, she said, which meant circulating through her favourite hangouts, the Wesley drop-in, friends' places, the streets.

The next day, as I sat at my desk looking over my notes and her files, I thought about my meetings and conversations with Margaret. I was beginning to form a composite sketch of who she was and starting to understand how she had gone from a healthy little girl to a "bag lady." The unprecedented access I'd been granted to Margaret's files became my starting point for piecing together her incredible life story. Although I was initially only allowed to make notes of her files, later a family member provided me with the entire 869 pages as they wanted her story told.

Other members of Margaret's family helped fill in the details of her childhood and adolescence, and also sent me her teenage diary, an adoption record and a coroner's report along with photos from her childhood and teen years. I discovered that the Pentecostal Assemblies of Canada had a church newsletter, which became an invaluable resource for documenting the years the Jacobson family spent as missionaries.

Combined with interviews with Margaret's friends, shelter staff and hospital workers who shared details about her years in the hospital and on the streets, I was able to unlock the secrets of her life. The question I sought to answer – how had the teenage girl who had once written in her diary that she loved to listen to the rain outside her bedroom window, who was an A student who showed such promise at school and had played the piano at Sunday school become one of Hamilton's homeless? – was found inside this treasure trove of reports and letters.

Looking at photos of Margaret from when she was young, I realized how torturous her descent into homelessness had been. In one photo from her brother Jim, Margaret looked to be around sixteen and was wearing a pretty white dress with cap sleeves that was belted at the waist and accented her small frame. Her hair was cut into a short bob and she was wearing a small white hat, which was perfect for the daugher of two missionaries. She had white flats and was standing in a ballet-like pose with one foot positioned in front of the other as she smiled sweetly for the camera. There was something so pure and innocent about her that made the loss of what her life could have been even more tragic.

E. Fuller Torrey wrote about deinstitutionalization in his 1997 book *Out of the Shadows: Confronting America's Mental Illness Crisis* and described it as "a psychiatric '*Titanic*'" in which former patients were left devoid of dignity and with nowhere to go. "The least restrictive setting frequently turns out to be a cardboard box, a jail cell or a terror-filled existence plagued by both real and imaginary enemies."

Deinstitutionalization was Margaret's psychiatric *Titanic*. The Margaret she had become had endured horrors few of us could imagine, yet she had kept going. Even with all of her emotional scars, physical pains and the traumas she had suffered, she had found a way to survive. Right to the end, Margaret had exhibited a remarkable level of courage and resilience. She was a homeless worn-down bag lady on the outside, but inside she was a survivor.

This was the other side of Margaret I was coming to know, the one who

had surmounted struggles and barriers that would have levelled most people, and who never lost her fierce determination to survive. Something else
unexpected happened while I was writing about Margaret: the more I found
out about this anonymous woman of the streets, the more I grew to love her.

Part One

The Childhood Years

1944–1961

Margaret with her brothers David (left) and John (right). Courtesy of Jacobson family.

Abe and Verna with baby Margaret. Courtesy of Jacobson family.

CHAPTER FOUR

"Quiet, Hard-Working Girl"

1944–1960
British West Indies

Margaret Louise Jacobson was born April 5, 1944, the first child of Veronica and Abraham Jacobson, who were Pentecostal missionaries from Canada living in Barbados. Margaret's birth was slow, Veronica would later tell doctors, but there was nothing problematic to foreshadow what was to come.

Abe and Verna, as they were called, had arrived in Barbados in the spring of 1943, newly ordained by the Pentecostal Assemblies of Canada and enthusiastic about spreading the Gospel. Although they'd only been married three months and faced the constant threat of typhoid fever and the looming danger of German U-boats, which regularly sank boats off the coast of Florida, they were undeterred in their faith-based mission.

Abraham Thorgny Jacobson hailed from Midale, Saskatchewan, and received his secular education in Minnesota before attending Vancouver Bible School and then moving to Bannockburn, a small town in northern Ontario, where he became a pastor. That's where he met Veronica Jane Morden, a small-town farm girl from North Seguin, Ontario, who had found her calling to the church at a young age, having been "saved and filled with the Holy Ghost" when she was just a child. According to records from the

Pentecostal Assemblies of Canada, headquartered in Mississauga, Ontario, Verna had attended the Winnipeg Bible School in Manitoba and completed her theological studies at the Pentecostal Bible School in Ottawa. She was co-pastoring in Bannockburn when she crossed paths with Abe. They married the same day that Verna graduated from the Ontario Pentecostal Bible School in Toronto.

Physically, the two were a bit of a mismatch. Where Abe stood six feet one inch tall and had angular Swedish features, Verna was five foot nothing with a round, cherubic face. Their bond was their commitment to serve the church and they both threw themselves into their work with a passion.

When Margaret was born less than a year after they arrived Abe expressed his disappointment that his first-born wasn't a boy. Verna, by comparison, was proud of her little girl and would boast about how precocious she was, telling people that she'd started walking at only seven months. Less than a year later, Abe would get his wish when their second child, John Morden, was born. While Verna devoted herself to raising her children and seemed happy, she later confided to doctors that life as a missionary could be oppressive and that their family was expected to be role models for the community. She compared it to "living inside a glass house," where they were always on display.

By contrast, Abe enjoyed his work and was thriving as head of the Bible school. He even introduced his students to carpentry so they could make souvenirs and trinkets to raise money for the school. There were frequent problems, though, as Abe could be demanding and authoritative with his students and members of the congregation. If they didn't live up to his expectations, he wouldn't hesitate to let them know. According to a church report, Abe's tendency to openly express his frustration to his students didn't always sit well with people: ". . . any misdemeanour that challenged [his] perceptions were dealt with harshly."

The demanding behaviour extended to Abe's parenting style. His son, David, who is now sixty-seven and lives in Beijing, remembers him as a "chauvinist and perfectionist father" who expected his children to be perfect role models.

"He set impossibly high expectations for his children," wrote David in an email, adding that he was a harsh disciplinarian if they didn't obey him.

Three years into the Jacobson's life in Barbados, they were suddenly forced to move. The church had decided to make Abe the principal of a new school in Trinidad, which meant uprooting the family and starting over again. According to the church report, moving to Trinidad was a huge disruption for the family: "The news of their sudden departure proved a distress to the Barbados District, to the Bright Hill Assembly and more importantly, to the Jacobson family themselves. Mrs. Jacobson found the relocating of the family to be quite a traumatic experience. The furniture was hurriedly packed and shipped to their new home in Trinidad. The family arrived in Port-of-Spain in the month of September."

Once they arrived in Trinidad, the Jacobsons had one month to set up the training institute. Despite the heavy workload, Abe and Verna rose to the challenge and opened the school on time.

Verna (third from left) and Margaret (at head of table) at a birthday party. Courtesy of Jacobson family.

On March 24, 1947, the Jacobsons added another member to their family with the birth of their third child, another son they named James. Although the family had been through much upheaval, photos show Margaret and her brothers smiling as they played in a small swimming pool and at a birthday party. In one photo, Margaret looked to be around six years old and was wearing a smock dress. Her angelic blonde hair was curled into tight ringlets with perfect bangs.

In 1949, the Jacobsons returned to Canada for their first leave of absence, which lasted for one year. While there is no record of where they lived, it was likely somewhere around Southern Ontario, where they had family. On July 15, 1952, the Jacobsons had their fourth child, David Maurice. Margaret was now eight years old and was attending an all-girls religious school where she was a top student. She also belonged to a young people's Christian group called Christ's Ambassadors and was fully engulfed in the ways of the Lord. An autograph book that was given to her by her parents in 1954 is filled with passages from the Bible, which were written by family and friends. Margaret added her own artistic touch to the book by cutting out small drawings of flowers and kittens and pasting them to several pages. The writing often reflected the strong role religion played in Margaret's life:

> Dear Margaret,
> Some say give you silver,
> Some say give you gold,
> But I say give you Jesus
> To save your little soul.
> From, Arlene

AFTER EIGHT YEARS, the family had settled into their new life when the assembly ordered another move. They would be going to Antigua, where Abe and Verna would take on positions at St. John's Pentecostal Church.

Sickness was an ever-present threat on the island, and not long after moving to Antigua, Abe and Verna contracted typhoid fever, possibly through contaminated food or water. The recovery was long and painful, and Abe was so ill that he had to recruit another minister to give pastoral care to the congregation. It was possibly due to their illness that the Jacobsons took another leave to Canada, this time for two years. On January 1, 1958, they returned to Antigua. David recalled that John, at some later point, was sent to a boarding school in Moose Jaw, Saskatchewan. The decision may have been related to the fact that John was entering his teen years and was experiencing issues common for expat kids. It may have been related to John's behavioural problems, which had begun to surface. It would be the first of many separations between John and his parents that would eventually end badly.

According to the church report, when Abe and Verna returned to Antigua, they stepped back into their roles with an "evangelical fervour." Abe developed a construction program that resulted in a number of churches being built. His demanding personality continued to be a problem, however, and he would reprimand church members and place them on probation if he deemed their behaviour unacceptable.

Verna had her moments, as well, and once took great exception when the congregation compared her to the previous pastor's wife, who would accompany her husband on the piano at services. Verna didn't play the piano. At a church meeting, she abruptly stood up and said, "Mrs. Piper is Mrs. Piper. I am Mrs. Jacobson. All audible comparisons shall cease."

Under Abe and Verna's guidance and hard work, the church in Antigua grew and the Vacation Bible School they had created attracted hundreds of children and young people from across St. John's. In 1960, Abe and Verna hosted the General Conference, which Verna helped organize. Male delegates were accommodated in the main building, while women were put up in the homes of church members. When they needed extra beds, Verna borrowed canvas cots from the local prison.

Margaret's days were tightly scripted around her many church responsibilities, which she followed like a dutiful daughter. Like her father, she was showing an interest in becoming a teacher, as shown in this excerpt from a letter she wrote to a friend:

Greetings to you in the precious name of Jesus. How are you? I am fine. I received your letter yesterday. Thank you for that lovely picture that you sent to me. I think when I get big I will be a teacher. How are you getting on at Normal School?

I hope you are fine. As you wanted to know how many grades there are in my school, I will tell you. There are seven grades. I am sorry that there are no more grades. I am in grade five (B) and I am going to set an exhibition in the early part of the year. Send my love to all at home. How is your father and mother. I hope fine. Have you heard from grandma Jacobson yet? I must close now,

Love, Margaret.

MARGARET HAD INHERITED her father's musical talents and at church services she played the piano and an accordion that she'd bought with a fifty-dollar donation sent to her by a Pentecostal girls' group in Calgary, Alberta. She combined the donation with money she'd saved from picking berries during a trip to British Columbia, plus seventeen dollars her parents had given her as a Christmas gift. Her thank-you letter to the girls' group was published in their newsletter along with a photo of Margaret, looking off to the side, her hair cut into a tidy bob with short bangs.

I am sure it was a sacrifice for many of you. God was good and we bought the accordion from a Christian dealer who gave a big discount on it. Now I will be able to play it for open-air meetings, and for the work in the West Indies.

This year as we begin it, our family hopes to do better than ever before, and with God's help we know that we can. In closing, I again thank all of you for everything. May God bless you and use you in His service.

JOHN HAD REJOINED the family; however, he continued to draw his father's anger. Abe was furious when he discovered John had been hanging out with a boy who had once been seen smoking and punished him by making him sit on the back bench during church services for one month. Verna went along with her husband's parenting and also helped with his pastoring duties in the church, which included filling in for him on the pulpit. She accomplished all this while overseeing the renovation of the main floor of their missionary house to include a comfortable lounge to accommodate family and friends. Church was the driving force in Verna's life and when she wasn't working with the Women's Missionary Council, she was teaching the young men's Sunday school class. She was delighted when two of her pupils decided to enter the ministry full time.

A SHORT STORY written by Margaret as part of a creative writing course during her last year of high school provided insight into her parents' personalities. She called the story "Two Contrasted People: Mr. and Mrs. X," and described Mr. X as being "six feet, one inches tall with high cheekbones and blue eyes that sometimes turned to steel gray (the colour of his hair now) when he is out," while Mrs. X was described as being "five feet and quite plump with a cheery face.

"They are so unalike as any two people can be. Perhaps that's why they were attracted to each other in the first place. When Mrs. X saw Mr. X, she thought him dignified, quiet and genteel. Mr. X thought her a very nice person: friendly, good-humoured and sympathetic."

While both Mr. and Mrs. X liked classical music, Mrs. X preferred polkas, wrote Margaret. "That must be the Swiss in her."

Mr. X had "perfectionist ways" and was "a person who got that hard streak from his Swedish forefathers. No matter what he does it has to be done perfectly."

Mr. X "hated small talk, while" Mrs. X was "talkative, quick witted and on the go."

Mrs. X. always found interesting things to say and was a gracious hostess; however:

Mr. X. would rather sit in his big chair studying French or think about and sometimes discuss some deep Theological subject. Half the time, he hears not what is said around him. Mrs. X, however, listens to her children and helps the younger ones with a difficult piece of homework sometimes.

One can see, then, how different two people can be. The study of them I find most interesting.

MARGARET'S TEACHER GAVE her a B plus and noted that her writing was "clear and precise." It seemed that the girl who had expressed an interest in becoming a teacher was well on her way to realizing her dream. Despite her many church duties and chores at home, Margaret still did well in school and graduated from high school with As and Bs, while scoring high marks for her piano and accordion play-

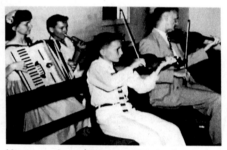

Margaret playing the accordion in church. Her brother John is beside her, and Jim and Abe are in the first row. Courtesy of Jacobson family.

ing. Because she was so reliable, teachers elected her to a position of authority in the school – a prefect. One teacher wrote on her report card that she was a "quiet, hard-working girl, with a great ambition to succeed."

Margaret's grades, combined with her musical talents and teaching abilities, foretold a promising future. Her mother, who had proudly boasted about her precocious daughter when Margaret was a baby, was pleased that she was showing such potential. There was no question: Margaret's future was bright.

CHAPTER FIVE

"I Haven't Been Very Well"

O God help me. I pray thee tonight I need thee badly.
– Margaret, in her diary

1960
Antigua

The Jacobson household would have been a busy one, with four children between the ages of eight and fifteen. Abe and Verna kept them on a tight schedule of prayer meetings, church services, Bible school and choir practices. And because Margaret was the oldest, she was expected to do the most. A diary that Margaret wrote in the year she turned sixteen showed that, for all of the pressures she was under as the oldest child of missionary parents, she still had a fun side.

She filled the pages with her reflections and thoughts and descriptions of the simple moments in her life. She may have had a strict religious up-bringing, but her writing showed that she was also a regular teenage girl. In perfect cursive, she wrote about how she loved to go to the beach and try new hairstyles, and how she worried about her appearance. On the first page, she declared: "I have named this diary 'Natalie Rose' just for the fun of it."

She was inspired to come up with the name, she said, after reading *The Diary of a Young Girl*, as Anne Frank had named her diary Kitty, most likely after a fictional character. Like Anne, Margaret would sometimes start her page with "Dear Natalie Rose," or simply "D.N.R." While Anne and Margaret faced vastly different life situations, their similarities were in the free-spirited sweetness of their writings and the rare glimpses their diaries offered into their inner lives. While Anne Frank's diary captured the bittersweet reflections of a thirteen-year-old trying to make sense of her world, Margaret's writing showed a girl who had accepted her parents' religious beliefs but still longed to be a regular girl.

She wrote about hanging out with her brothers, how much she liked playing jacks and how she baked a cake with almond icing. She wrote about her

Margaret's drawing of a prom dress. Courtesy of Jacobson family.

love of drawing and how she was thrilled to get pastels for Christmas, which she used to paint pictures of young women in beautiful gowns. Perhaps they were ones she herself longed to wear. In one of her drawings, a young woman is wearing a gown decorated with a cascade of flowers down one side. On the bottom, Margaret wrote, "For Graduation." In another drawing of a pretty gown, she wrote, "Dressed for the prom." She also wrote about things she disliked, her many chores and working with "bratty" boys in her Sunday school class.

While her diary captured much about her daily life, Margaret never wrote about the darkness that had begun to seep into her world. This was the year that she started to experience the symptoms of mental illness that would later lead her to being hospitalized. Those details were gleaned from her medical files and they documented the struggles of a young girl on the brink of serious mental illness.

CHURCH WAS A constant theme throughout her diary and she wrote about baptisms, communions, Bible school and prayer services that she attended.

Now that she was older, Margaret's involvement in the church was intensifying and she was participating more in services by reading prayers while her brother Jim read the Bible. She also taught the children's class at Vacation Bible School and helped with Sunday school classes. When her students acted up, she wrote, "Such badly behaved boys!"

Margaret once used the strap on them.

"Dad told me not to use the strap on my boys so I didn't. Will try to keep them quiet by other methods with God's help."

Where her diary shone and where Margaret's artistic side came through was when she wrote her observations, like "the morning dawned with rainy skies," or when she "watched a bride step into her taxi to take her to the base." She wrote about waking up and listening "to the birds in the trees and shrubbery out in our garden outside my window."

There were insights into her perfectionist personality, like when she chastised herself for waking up late: "Today I jumped out of bed at a monstrous time of 9:30 or so."

Then there were the many visitors who came to their home from Canada. "January 2nd – Miss Lamont came new year's day and stayed till today. Just as she was leaving she told John that she'd send him a subscription to *Life* magazine. She had previous given me five dollars. She also left me a manicure set – my first! She stayed in my room during her stay here in St. John's, Antigua, like every other visitor does."

One day, she wrote that a famous politician paid a visit to the island. "Would you believe it – Sir Winston Churchill visited Antigua! Mom and I . . . walked down at the wharf. Mom took her binoculars and camera."

Like many teenage girls, Margaret became more conscious of her appearance. "I am cleaning my teeth with salt and soda to make them whiter."

She gave herself a Toni perm and wrote about trying a new hairdo: "June 7 – I went to school early this morning on my own two legs. I wore my french roll for a change – it's real 'kool'! Patti also had her hair in a 'French' roll."

And she fretted about her weight: "Ate a big breakfast then went to weigh myself because I was worried about my weight. However I see that I weigh a bare 115 pounds. Tomorrow I begin my diet."

Given her attention to her appearance, Margaret would have been devastated when she developed severe and painful acne, something that would plague her well into her adult years. Her face and chest were covered in large, red welts that she described as ". . . a field of pimples and scars and blackheads!!! I have cut down on sweets. I have washed and washed and washed my face. Finally, or I should say along with this, I have prayed for miraculous absolute healing. I believe I will receive it from the Lord. The Doctor told me to try the hot and cold method. It helps take away grease for which I am very thankful. So much for that!"

On top of that, she also had to deal with difficult menstrual periods, which were so heavy the doctor put her on thyroid medication to try and regulate them. There were other hints throughout her diary that she was experiencing health problems, like frequent mentions of being so tired that she couldn't complete her homework or do her chores.

> August 26 – I went to the Doctor at 8:30 a.m. and I didn't get back till 12 noon. After that I slept.

> November 20 – O it's so late tonight (nearly 10:30) and I'm so tired!

In February, her hospital medical files noted there had been three deaths in the family – her grandmother, grandfather and an aunt on Verna's side had all died within a short time. Perhaps that and especially the death of a friend, noted below, were the traumas that led to what happened on February 5, as documented by her mother in Margaret's diary. "On this day Margaret did not come home from school for lunch – Miss Stewart found her in classroom trying to concentrate. She is sick. (Mother)"

Her medical files provided a more detailed description of what happened that day and described how Margaret had been found crying in a classroom. Earlier she had complained of not being able to concentrate on her ancient history lesson, and told her teacher she had been experiencing overwhelming feelings of guilt and painful headaches. The only hint in her diary that something was awry was that her perfect cursive writing became uneven, and some entries look hurriedly erased and scribbled over while other pages were left blank.

Margaret responded to the problem by doing what she'd been taught to do all her life – she looked to the Lord for help: "I feel that I've had Jesus since I was born – at least we were all born with sin, according to the Bible. However when I was a babe in my mother's arms – eight weeks to be exact – I was dedicated to the Lord. I yielded myself on and off in my childhood."

Excerpt from Margaret's diary. Courtesy of Jacobson family.

On February 10, her writing again hinted that something in her life was amiss: "Tonight it's beautiful. Wonderful fresh air is coming in my window. The moon has come up and has now gone over the house. Be ye therefore perfect even as your father which is in heaven is perfect. O God help me. I pray thee tonight I need thee badly – please help me O Jesus."

Margaret worked hard to correct her behaviour by repeatedly turning to the Lord: "What I need to do is fully yield myself to Christ."

Reaching out to the Lord wasn't helping, however, and her medical files showed that Margaret was becoming more withdrawn and staying in her room for hours. Although she had always been an introvert, according to her mother her behaviour had become even more extreme. Verna told doctors that she felt Margaret was becoming "secretive." Then came more devastating news – a close friend of Margaret's had collapsed while playing tennis and died in the hospital. Margaret's behaviour worsened. She would pace around the house, crying, then hide in her room and suddenly burst out and start yelling at her brothers, even throwing things at them. One day, Margaret told her mother that she'd heard her boyfriend calling to her from an airplane.

The orderly Jacobson home, which had been a formal place of prayer and religious study, was suddenly thrown into disarray. Margaret's parents were ill-prepared to know what to do. It was 1960 and mental health facilities on the small, isolated island would have been minimal. Mental illness was more often hidden than talked about at that time. Although antipsychotics had been introduced in the United Stated in the 1950s and were being used to control the symptoms of schizophrenia and bipolar disorders, specialty psychiatric care, including medications, would not have been available in Antigua.

Besides, her doctor still hadn't diagnosed her. That may explain why Margaret's doctor chose such a radical approach to treating her. Despite not having a diagnosis and Margaret only being fifteen years old, her doctor ordered several rounds of electroconvulsive therapy treatments (ECT), also referred to as shock treatments. Considered a tool for treating major depressive illnesses, ECT involves passing electricity through the brain to induce seizures. It was first used in 1938 to treat severe depressive episodes and was believed to have been successful because it caused changes in brain chemistry.

Back when Margaret received it, the voltage levels that were administered were much higher and less measured, and could be strong enough to burn the skin around the temples where the electrodes were placed. High dosages were also shown to cause brain damage and memory loss. While shock treatments were typically given with general anaesthetics or muscle relaxants to prevent bone fractures and dislocations, there is no record of these being used in conjunction with Margaret's treatments. She had such a negative reaction that her repulsion to them would stay with her forever.

Over the next twenty-two days, Margaret's diary pages were left blank. Although she was experiencing a nightmare beyond anything she or her family could have imagined, she kept all of it to herself with not a word written about any of it for more than three weeks. Her next entry was on March 4 and was written in her usual positive tone, only noting that she had been away from school: "God has given me a wonderful mother. Tonight she promised to let me go back to school again as from Monday. Be ye therefore perfect even as your father which is in heaven is perfect."

Immediately underneath Margaret's words, however, was an angry note written by her mother, who was obviously reading Margaret's diary:

> I did not!!!
> Signed, Mother V J J
> After **EASTER** – I said.

The exclamation marks and underlined words reflected Verna's anger as she and Abe both believed that Margaret was causing her own illness by refusing to give herself to the Lord. Margaret responded as she had been trained to all her life, by turning to the Lord. The next several pages are filled with her pleas to the Lord, as she desperately prayed for redemption and tried to behave according to her parents' wishes.

> March 6 – Believe in the Lord Jesus Christ and thou shall be saved, thou and thy house. Except ye become as little children, ye cannot enter the kingdom of heaven (God)

> March 7th – Mom says she wonders why I had to get sick. I think it is God's way of showing me that I need to rely on him more fully. Right now April Love (by Pat Boone), one of my favourites, is being played over the radio. They're praying for my healing over at the church which I am very thankful for indeed. It is wonderful to have members as well as neighbours pray for one's healing – I haven't been very well.

Margaret's extended family sent cheery get well cards and letters reinforcing her parents' message, including one card from her grandmother that was decorated with drawings of small children wearing flowery hats. Her grandmother wrote:

Keep looking to Jesus. He says "I will never leave thee nor forsake thee."
Love from Grandma.

MARGARET TRIED WRITING cheery reminders to herself, telling herself to keep smiling and to always be truthful, kind and courteous. On April 5, the day she turned sixteen, there was no hint in her diary of any problems in her life. It was as if she'd never had shock treatments or been ill. Perhaps Margaret believed that by denying what was happening, it would all go away. "Today is my birthday. I am sixteen years old – sweet sixteen – never been kissed – except by dad and my uncles. I remember when I was in Canada all the hugging or I should say – embracing and kissing we did coming and going."

Margaret wrote about how she and her brother John listened to the radio so long that they burned the tube out. They also had a visit from neighbours. "Jill and Patti came over. I was kissed at the door by both and then handed a present from each. Jill gave me a sweet half slip, while Patti gave me a beautiful box of pure Irish linen hankies. They're both so nice and full of fun."

BY EARLY APRIL, Margaret's symptoms had subsided and life had returned to normal in the Jacobson household. Margaret was back at school and church, and on April 9 she wrote about how she admired her father's sermons as she reflected on his Easter service: "Some say Christ fainted on the cross only, and was taken down, put in the tomb and the next morning revived. Others say that the disciples only thought they saw him – that it was an [sic] hallucination because they wanted to see Christ so badly."

Easter was a busy time for the family, and Margaret played the accordion during services, took care of visitors and went to an Easter bonnet parade. On April 22, her parents celebrated their wedding anniversary by going for a drive to a nearby hotel called the Half Moon Bay. They'd just left when a visitor came to their home and told Margaret a church member had died of a hemorrhage during childbirth and that her baby had been born dead.

Margaret made only casual reference to the disturbing news in her diary but it may have been what triggered her next episode. According to her medical files, her behavioural problems resurfaced. Her perfect cursive came to an abrupt halt and her daily entries were reduced to a few words.

May 25 – I was sick today, at least I didn't feel very well.

May 26 – Sick

May 27 – Not very well.

According to Margaret's medical files, she was picking fights with her brothers and using foul language. Once, she ran out of her bedroom and exposed herself to them, and another time, she ran away from home for an entire day. David was only seven years old at the time but still remembers his sister's outbursts.

"I was shielded from most of her issues but one incident that stuck with me was her crying about why God didn't make it so that people didn't have to go to the bathroom," David wrote in an email.

Verna wanted her daughter back, the perfect daughter who had dutifully helped out with chores and taught Sunday school. She would later tell doctors that prior to Margaret becoming ill, "she was a very responsible member of the family. You could always count on Margaret."

By mid-June, Verna got her wish when Margaret stabilized enough that she was able to go back to school, where she was learning shorthand. It's possible she was on some sort of medication, although what kind is not known. David remembers that his older brother Jim had been assigned the task of crossing town to pick some up, which he despised doing. Margaret was still hard on herself and wrote about her disappointment with getting a low mark. "June 17 – Had test in school this morning. We had four sentences to transpose from shorthand into long hand and vice versa. I got a half mark more than I got last week. My total mark this week – 11 1/2 out of 20. Terrible! Hope to do better."

From June 24 to August 7, the pages were again left blank. Her medical files showed that it was during this period that more ECT treatments were administered. This time, her mother helped administer them by holding her down, which suggests that Margaret had fought back. Verna later told doctors, "We personally helped him give some electric shocks. These frightened her so and also turned her against us."

The treatments appeared to have worked, and by early August Margaret was back in church and teaching Vacation Bible School. Her diary entries continued on as if nothing had happened, with no reference to the ECT or being ill. On one page, she made reference to Che Guevara being on the cover of *Time* magazine, and in a later entry she wrote about listening to the radio about Nixon.

On August 9 there was a party for her father's forty-ninth birthday. Not even birthdays got in the way of the family's church duties, and after dinner they returned to church for another service where her mother gave her father a kiss on the platform.

A few days later, Margaret mentioned a "real strong" injection she was given by the doctor. "I felt very dizzy after and I also felt like vomiting. – what sensations!"

Given her intense reaction, it may have been something to control the symptoms of her mental illness. It appeared to have worked as Verna allowed her to go back to school. It was short lived, however, and a few days later Margaret was sent home from school after she burst out crying in class. Her teacher reported that she was "overly excited." A few days later, Margaret told her mother she was in love with one of the teachers and that he loved her, too. Her parents feared she was being promiscuous and told doctors they thought Margaret had a venereal disease as she would be a "pick up" for any man. Where these sudden worries about Margaret's sexualized behaviour came from is unknown, but they would persist for years.

Doctors had still not diagnosed Margaret, but one doctor told Verna he thought Margaret might have had an acute mental breakdown brought on by the series of deaths. Meanwhile, Margaret continued writing in her diary with a lighthearted tone that disguised the chaos of her life.

Oct. 3 – I have skipped writing in this diary for nearly three weeks. That's ghastly!! Anyhow, tonight, I felt that the right thing for any girl who wishes to be noble, is to write in the diary she bought for herself!

Oct. 7 – Truly it is wonderful to be a Christian! I love Jesus very much. I am hoping, trusting and praying that He will use me as He will.

Margaret ended her diary much as she began it – with a teenage girl's observations of daily life: her dad sleeping in because he stayed up too late; the maid yelling at her for spilling water; going to typing class, of which she wrote, "I still think it's rather fun."

The last entry is on November 23: "Tonight the moon is crescent shaped – very Romantic aren't I!!"

At the back in the Notes section, she filled several pages with Biblical passages and inspirational quotes:

Let not your heart be troubled, neither let it be afraid;
Calmness is the seal of strength;
Scale the heights you see.

The last line on the back cover reads: "Lord, this is my prayer, that Thou will give me a Christian spirit of Love. – MLJ."

BACK HOME, MARGARET's illness worsened. She began flirting with her brothers Jim and David, then thirteen and eight. She would run out of her bedroom naked and stand in front of them. The doctor wrote: "She seemed to develop a strong sexual attraction toward her brother, then the master [teacher] and then towards her father and was rather passionate in her way of dealing with him. She seemed to concentrate on sex quite considerably during this time. She was misinterpreting the voices she heard in her environment, felt that someone had a definite influence."

For the Jacobsons, who had long prided themselves on being the perfect role models for the community, Margaret's sexualized behaviour would have been horrific and, for Margaret, their limited world view regarding her illness would have disastrous consequences. Back then, even the doctor may not have understood that this behaviour was in fact a symptom of her illness. Her doctor prescribed an antipsychotic medication called Largactil, which was used to treat disorders such as schizophrenia, but there were only minimal improvements.

The doctor then had to deliver the bombshell news that would change Abe and Verna's life forever – their daughter needed a level of specialized care that was beyond what they were able to provide on the small island of Antigua.

THERE IS NO explanation in Margaret's medical files or her diary or the Jacobson's church report for what Abe and Verna did next, but, given the timing, it was likely related to Margaret's illness. After devoting seventeen years of their lives to establishing the Kingdom of God in the Caribbean, they suddenly abandoned their missionary work and left the island of Antigua. The only explanation Abe and Verna offered to church members was "they felt the leading of the Lord to terminate their ministry in the West Indies."

The Jacobsons had been pioneers in building churches, recruiting students and leading services for the Pentecostal Assemblies of the West Indies, and they were proud of their achievements. The islands had become their home. Now they were leaving it all behind. In one of his last sermons, as recorded in the *Pentecostal Herald* newsletter, Abe told his congregation, "Lord speed the day when Antigua shall experience a Christ glorifying, devil defying, hell shaking, church filling revival and spiritual awakening."

Several years later, Abe would reflect on his work in the Caribbean and admit that he had put the interest of the Lord's work first, and had neglected his children and been "too severe in the discipline he imposed on them."

CHAPTER SIX
"Pains of Hell"

She believes that her mother is unwilling to see her grow up and has always been jealous of her.
– Doctor's note in Margaret's file

1961

Galt (now Cambridge) and Hamilton

On January 13, 1961, the Jacobsons left the Caribbean islands that had been their home for almost two decades and moved to a quiet suburb in the town of Galt, in Southern Ontario. Galt would later become part of the City of Cambridge and was a ninety-minute drive northwest of Hamilton. They likely chose that location as Verna's sister lived there and perhaps helped them settle in. Another sister lived in the neighbouring city of Kitchener and an uncle was close by.

It didn't take long for Verna to find a job and she soon began work as a counsellor at the Ontario Training School in Galt, a provincially run reform school for delinquent girls aged twelve to eighteen.

Abe remained passionate about working again as a missionary and set his sights on restarting his career by applying for a new position with the Pentecostal Assemblies of Canada (PAOC). His vision was to take the gospel to the French-speaking Caribbean and open a Bible school in Martinique.

First, though, he wanted to upgrade his French and so he scouted around for courses. The Jacobsons were no doubt hoping the move would help their daughter, and that the less rigid schedule and having extended family nearby would make a difference. Instead, Margaret became more erratic and rebellious, and was angrily acting out toward her parents, even telling her mother to "shut up."

On March 18, 1961, Abe and Verna took their daughter to the Homewood Sanitarium of Guelph, now known as the Homewood Health Centre, obviously concerned about her behavioural problems. The doctor noted in Margaret's files, "Her mother and father seem decent people, but overly religious and probably overly strict." Margaret then told the doctor that she felt "locked up" and said her parents were too restrictive, then described her mother as a "jailer." The doctor wrote, "She is antagonistic toward her mother and to her father but mostly towards her mother. She feels that she has not been treated as a grown-up but has always been discriminated against in the family as her brothers have always been favoured and that she has been subjected to a great deal of restrictions that she did not think were warranted."

Margaret's problems must have been severe as she was admitted immediately. Soon after, doctors began the process of determining a diagnosis. Much has changed since then in the treatment of mental illness; however, making a diagnosis still relies on tracking behavioural patterns, monitoring how a person processes information and how they respond to their environment. Back then, there weren't as many medications available as now and there was less importance placed on talk therapy. In short, there were fewer options. Margaret was placed on an antipsychotic medication and, within a short time, her behaviour began to stabilize. One month later, she was discharged. There was no mention of a diagnosis.

IT WAS EARLY April and the beginning of spring, and with that came new hope. Margaret was only seventeen and most of her years leading up to this point had been good; she'd been an excellent student and high achiever as well as a talented musician who played the piano and led Sunday school classes. Staff knew what she was capable of and were hopeful that with the right treatments she could get back on track. A hospital social worker encouraged Margaret to enroll in a local business college to improve her typing so she could get a job. The worker told Verna that by having an employable skill, Margaret might someday live on her own. That must have filled Verna's heart with hope. Upon discharge, Margaret was obviously feeling confident about her future as she told doctors her goal was to finish college and get her Bachelor of Arts degree then go into teaching.

On April 18, 1961, Margaret left Homewood and enrolled in seven courses at a local business college, which was almost a full load. Verna was concerned it would be too demanding and urged her daughter to cut back. When she refused, according to Margaret's hospital files, Verna contacted the principal at the college, but nothing was done. Margaret threw herself into her studies and stayed up late every night trying to finish her assignments. Less than one month later, she began to feel overwhelmed and eventually stopped going to all classes. As her condition worsened, she went for days without eating or sleeping. Then the violence started. She began throwing objects around the house and having screaming fits. One night she stayed out until 5:00 a.m. When she got home, she told her mother she'd been walking all night. The next night, she ran out of the house. One of her brothers, fed up with her behaviour, locked the door behind her. Her medical file read: "Her mother made no attempt to find her but she was returned to the house by the Family Services Bureau after being found in the park."

Margaret's aunt, Marion Bergquist, who was Abe's sister, lived in Regina, Saskatchewan, and wrote to ask how she was doing. Years later, when everyone had fallen away and Margaret had no one left, Marion would continue to care about her like she was her own daughter. Marion wrote:

Dearest Margaret:
"As thy day so shall thy strength be."

That's what God has promised. Don't know if I've written to you since I got your very interesting letter from Homewood. I think you type very well indeed. How I wish I'd mastered a typewriter when I was young.

It never occurred to me then how very useful it might be. In those days it was considered not really polite to type personal mail. Letters of that kind should be completely long hand. Times change, don't they. And I never dreamed I'd have my own people scattered far and wide over the face of the earth.

Now if I had <u>plenty</u> of money – what do we call plenty? – I'd board a plane at various times and sail through the air to see all my dear ones here and there. I'm so glad you have a lovely place to stay at and that you are so much better. Don't feel discouraged if you don't land a job soon. There is a lot of unemployment this year. Guess we really have to put <u>wait</u> into practice."

Aunt Marion

VERNA WAS STILL locked into the belief that her daughter's illness was related to her lack of faith, and so she contacted a minister to come to their home and talk to Margaret. The doctor chose a more medical-based option and put Margaret back on Largactil. It's not clear why she had stopped taking it. The drug helped stabilize her; however, a few weeks later, her outbursts returned, and this time they were both more severe and more frequent. Margaret would binge eat by stuffing herself full of food then make herself vomit. She lost more than twenty-five pounds in a few months. Her doctor noted: "She seemed to be overly religious when she was sick."

David was nine and doesn't remember a lot from those years, but he does recall one episode in which he walked into the bathroom and Margaret was sitting there completely naked. "I ran away from her as she called after me to 'not be scared.' Perhaps this fit in with some of those episodes of my parents saying she exposed herself to my brothers," wrote David in an email.

By mid-October, Margaret's condition had deteriorated to the point that doctors readmitted her to Homewood. She was put in a semi-private room on ward B2. The nurses there described her as "withdrawn, asocial, seclusive and under-productive." For the first time since becoming ill, doctors rendered a diagnosis. They concluded that Margaret had had an acute mental breakdown in the British West Indies that was characterized by hallucinations, bizarre behaviour and excitement. The diagnosis was schizophrenia, a complex biochemical brain disorder recognized as a disease. It can affect a person's ability to determine what is real, and is often characterized by delusions and withdrawal from reality.

Some people with schizophrenia claim to hear people talking to them, as Margaret did when she told her mother she heard her boyfriend call her from a plane. Others become withdrawn and fall into disturbed thinking. Schizophrenia can be one of the most challenging mental illnesses to treat and some patients fail to respond to medication or therapy. Margaret's brother David believes his sister was likely genetically predisposed to it, and that her breakdown was a result of that fact combined with the immense pressures she'd been put under as a child.

"Margaret grew up with an intensely fundamentalist [Christian] couple. She was also a white girl living in a black society where she attended an Anglican grammar school, where they still caned misbehaving children," wrote David in an email.

The nature versus nurture argument around mental illness is a long and complicated one stemming from the question of whether illness is brought on by hereditary factors, trauma or severe stress. One of the most fascinating cases in this regard involved the Genain (pseudonym) sisters, identical quadruplets who were born in the States in 1930. All four were diagnosed with schizophrenia by the time they were twenty-three, leading psychiatrists and researchers to believe this confirmed the genetic connection to mental illness. However, the more they learned about the girls' upbringing – one riddled with horrific abuse from the time they were infants – the more it became clear that their environment had played a strong part as well.

In Robert Kolker's book *Hidden Valley Road: Inside the Mind of an American Family*, he tells the story of the Galvin family of Colorado who had twelve children, six of who were diagnosed with schizophrenia. They were one of the first families to be studied by the National Institute of Mental Health, and, like the Genains, the Galvin family was found to also have been filled with a shocking level of violence and abuse. Both stories raise questions about the root of mental illness and point to the lasting impact it has not only on those who are diagnosed but on the people around them.

OVER THE NEXT month, under 24-7 medical supervision, Margaret's behaviour began to improve. Where previously she had been hostile and angry, nurses now described her as "pleasant, fairly active and fairly cheer-ful." Margaret was obviously feeling better and told doctors she was eager to get out of the hospital and wanted to work. On November 15 of that year, doctors obliged. A short while after leaving the hospital, she got a factory job, likely with help from hospital staff. However, two months later she quit and told her mother it was because she couldn't stand the "petty jealousies among the other girls."

She then got a job as a maid in a nursing home, which only lasted a few weeks before she quit because she was bored. Her next job was as a domes-tic, helping out a woman who, according to the files, was "receiving shock treatments." She quit that job as well and, true to fashion, downplayed any problems by saying the work was too much for her. Later, Verna told doctors that her daughter lost her job as a domestic because she was "carrying on" with the woman's husband. Her behaviour suggested that Margaret had gone off her medications, but there is nothing in her medical files about this.

MEANWHILE, ABE HAD moved to Missouri. Although French courses would have been available in Ontario, he instead enrolled full time at a college in Missouri. Rumours of problems in the Jacobson's marriage had persisted when they'd lived in the Caribbean, which may have played into his decision to move far away. Or perhaps Margaret's erratic behaviour factored into it. This was supposed to be his first step toward moving back into missionary work; however, he would soon receive news that would change this.

The mission board, which commissions new missionaries, turned down his request to receive an appointment because he had exceeded the age limit of fifty. He had turned fifty-one only a few months earlier and had just barely missed the deadline. This devastating news meant that Abe would never return to the work that he loved. According to the church report: "The decision grieved him immensely. Tired, worn and somewhat disillusioned over the rejection of his offer for missionary assignment in the French West Indies, Abraham spent the rest of his life teaching in the educational establishments of the USA."

Margaret's behaviour was worsening, and with Abe gone, Verna was left to cope with her daughter on her own. Margaret wasn't eating properly, was still losing weight and had started to act violently, to the point where she would break furniture and smash windows. Doctors later learned that she had again gone off her medication.

One night in September 1962, the family heard a peculiar scratching noise from behind Margaret's door. They opened it and found her lying on the floor. She had slashed both of her wrists. Blood covered the floor and was splattered across the wall. Verna called an ambulance. David was eight at the time and still remembers the image of the blood splatters.

"I was chagrined because an ambulance had to come pick her up and I didn't know what to tell my school classmates, should they have seen it come to our house," David wrote in an email.

Margaret was rushed to the emergency department of South Waterloo Hospital where she downplayed the incident by telling doctors a friend she'd met at Homewood had attempted suicide and that she "wanted to see what it was like." She never intended to kill herself, she told them, because if she had, she would have had to endure the "pains of hell." She said that she had stopped cutting herself because of the pain and told doctors, "My father always said that I was afraid of pain."

Verna came up with another possible reason for her daughter's problems.

She asked doctors if Margaret's acne might be to blame as she'd recently been diagnosed with cystic acne and her cheeks had become inflamed with a mass of angry red welts. The unsightly and painful acne is typically caused by a hormonal imbalance and, in Margaret's case, the scarring was severe. Verna told doctors, "She loves beauty and therefore hates herself because she has an allergic skin problem."

But Margaret's problems proved to be far more complex and serious than anyone could have imagined. After several more weeks of hospitalization, doctors delivered the news to Verna, which was similar to what they'd heard in the Caribbean: her daughter needed more extensive and specialized psychiatric care than they were able to provide. She needed to be in a long-term psychiatric hospital. The closest one was the Ontario Hospital in Hamilton, Ontario, which was about an hour's drive from Guelph. It would later be renamed the Hamilton Psychiatric Hospital.

There are no notes on how Verna received the news, but she obviously agreed with doctors as she signed the paperwork to have Margaret transferred. Two weeks later, in a move that would mark the beginning of Margaret's long and painful journey through the psychiatric hospital system, she was admitted to the Ontario Hospital.

Part Two

THE HOSPITAL YEARS

1962–1984

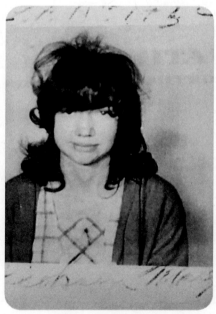

Margaret's first hospital admission photo. She was eighteen. Taken at Hamilton Psychiatric Hospital. Courtesy of St. Joseph's Healthcare Hamilton.

CHAPTER SEVEN
Revolving Door

1962–1968
Hamilton

On October 9, 1962, Margaret was admitted to the Ontario Hospital and became patient number 31932. She was eighteen. At an age when most teenage girls are finishing high school and dreaming about their futures, Margaret's new identity was as a psychiatric patient and her new home was a sterile hospital ward. A black-and-white photo taken on admission shows her with tousled hair, as if she'd just gotten out of bed. It looks like the before shot of a tragedy.

Her admission record described her as five feet six inches tall and 115 pounds. The clothing she brought with her included three bloomers, two coats, one dressing gown, two gloves, two handkerchiefs, two nightdresses, two skirts, two shoes, one half-slip, one pair of stockings, three sweater coats, three brassieres, one girdle and three pairs of slacks. Her new home in the G wing was a crowded ward reserved for patients who lived in the Hamilton area, most of whom had been diagnosed with schizophrenia. An IQ test placed Margaret at 88, which was considered to be in the "dull to normal" range of intelligence.

At the time, the Ontario Hospital was the largest mental institution of its kind between Toronto and London, Ontario, with more than 1,750 patients.

According to former staff, medications were used liberally and most patients were passive, although it was still a chaotic environment. Although Margaret had at an earlier point flippantly told doctors she'd slashed her wrists just to try it, perhaps she now understood the torturous turn her life had taken and revised her story. This time she confessed to them that she had done it because she felt life wasn't worth living and thought she should never have been born.

These comments, along with what doctors did next, pointed to the likelihood that Margaret had fallen into a deep state of depression. Two days after being admitted, doctors ordered several rounds of electroshock treatments. Many psychiatric hospitals had at that time moved away from ECT due to concerns it was being used to subdue patients; however, it was still being administered for serious depression and its use reflected the severity of her problems. Verna signed the forms. But Margaret had ample reason to be depressed. She was eighteen and had been pulled away from her family and was living in a hospital with strangers. She'd left behind her piano and her pastels and any dreams she'd had of becoming a teacher. And though her family was only an hour's drive away, Verna and her brothers rarely visited. Not surprisingly, Margaret told doctors she felt completely rejected by them. Her brother David, who was ten at the time, only vaguely remembered his mother going to Hamilton.

"Margaret was pretty much left in the hands of Hamilton friends or the hospital," wrote David in an email.

Perhaps as an act of rebellion, Margaret took to walking the hospital hallways wearing only a skimpy nightgown and acting, according to nurses, in a "sultry and seductive way." Perhaps this was a result of her declining mental health. Or maybe she knew this type of behaviour would anger her overly religious family more than anything.

WHEN THE ONTARIO Hospital first opened in 1876, it was known as the Hamilton Asylum for the Insane and was located on a large 529-acre farm. It was only accessible by dirt road and was its own city within a city with cattle, chickens and pigs, as well as fruit, vegetables, a bakery, a butcher's shop, a greenhouse, a root cellar, a milk-processing house, a tailor's shop, a sewing room, an upholstery shop, a fire hall, skating and curling rinks, a bowling green, tennis courts and a chapel. It was originally intended for "inebriates"; however, the need for beds for the "mentally disturbed" was much higher, and so the number of patients with mental illnesses grew. In the first year, there were around two hundred patients, and by 1889 that number had grown to 832. By the next year, there were more than nine hundred.

Farming was an important component of patient therapy and many patients worked in the fields and with the animals, alongside some of the 119 hospital employees. Some patients even helped with road maintenance and masonry, and inside the hospital, others sewed and did laundry. In 1907, the asylum established a training school for psychiatric nursing, which graduated more than 240 nurses before closing in 1956. At that time, all but eighty-six acres had been auctioned off for residential and community college development.

When Margaret arrived in 1960, the farming activities had long ceased, and patients were largely kept indoors and occupied with board games, TV and arts and crafts such as pottery. Occupational therapy programs were set up, including rooms with typewriters to teach typing to the female patients. According to a 1963 document produced by the Canadian Mental Health Association (CMHA) called *More for the Mind*, many psychiatric hospitals during the 1960s were located in oversized buildings that were deemed obsolete and inadequate even by minimum health standards. Although inadequate, they were a far cry better than the earliest psychiatric hospitals or insane asylums.

The first separate private asylums recorded in England were the Hospital for Lunatics at Newcastle upon Tyne (1765), Manchester Lunatic Hospital (1766), York Lunatic Asylum (1777) and Leicester Lunatic Asylum (1794). In the United States, one of the first institutions for the mentally ill opened in 1773 in Williamsburg, Virginia, and was called the Public Hospital for Persons of Insane and Disordered Minds. In Canada, the first recorded asylum opened in 1836 and was built in a former pesthouse in a quarantine-like facility in Saint John, New Brunswick. According to *More for the Mind*, the building had originally been built to care for immigrants with cholera. In 1848, a new facility called the Provincial Hospital for the Insane was opened.

Many of the early asylums were overcrowded and filthy, and patients were sometimes chained inside small cells where they slept on straw and were fed starvation rations. The prevailing attitude was that the "madman" was a wild animal that needed to be weakened through barbaric treatments, wrote Robert Whitaker in *Mad in America*: "A near starvation diet was another recommendation for robbing the madman of his strength. The various depleting remedies – bleedings, purgings, emetics and nausea-inducing agents, were also said to be therapeutic because they inflicted considerable pain and thus the madman's mind become focused on this sensation rather than on his usual raving thoughts."

It was under these conditions that a young widow named Hannah Mills was admitted to the Lunatic Asylum in York, England. It was 1790 and she had been diagnosed with melancholy, which was likely clinical depression. When she died only a few months later, it sent shockwaves through the Quaker community and prompted an English businessman and Quaker named William Tuke to investigate. He uncovered the appalling conditions and vowed to make changes, and over the next few years, Tuke and other Quakers worked on developing a more humane and compassionate approach to treating the mentally ill.

In 1796, they opened the York Retreat, an institution in a country house in northern England that housed about thirty patients. Rather than starving and purging their patients, Retreat patients were given chores to do and told to follow a set of rules that gave them a sense of control and made them feel productive. Patients who behaved well were rewarded for their behaviour while those who behaved poorly were put into restraints, although only minimally. The Retreat became known worldwide for its progressive practices, and Tuke's pioneering approach to treating patients came to be known as the "moral treatment" of care.

Coincidentally, in France in 1793, a French physician named Philippe Pinel was working toward a similar approach. Pinel had been appointed to oversee two asylums in Paris and, like Tuke, became concerned about the way patients were being treated. He leaned toward a more compassionate approach that was tailored to each individual's need. As Whitaker wrote, "He believed that many of his patients had retreated into delusions or become overwhelmed with depression because of the shocks of life – disappointed love, business failures, the blows of poverty."

Pinel believed that patients should be given a nurturing environment where staff could talk them through their difficulties and they could heal. Whitaker wrote in *Mad in America*: "Moral treatment worked as a medical remedy precisely because it restored, or otherwise soothed, the irritated nerves. The pastoral environment, the recreational activities, and the warm bath were all medical tonics for the nervous system."

Over the next few years, this new and radically different approach, introduced by Tuke and Pinel, spread throughout other institutions in Europe and the West. As Whitaker wrote, "Pinel and the York Quakers had presented European society (and by extension American society) with a new way to think about the mad. No longer were they to be viewed as animals, as creatures apart. They were, instead to be seen as beings within the human family – distressed people to be sure, but 'brethren.'"

In the States, the first humanitarian-focused asylum opened in Philadelphia in 1817 and many others followed. The requirement for each asylum was that they had to be governed by a superintendent who was humane, gentle and compassionate. Patients were encouraged to garden, read and play games, and the location needed to be in the country where, as Whitaker wrote, "the grounds graced by flowerbeds and gardens, where the mentally ill could take their fill of fresh air and find solace in tending to plants."

Although many asylums were modelled after this more compassionate approach, over the next few decades, they came undone. Their undoing was due to both financial problems and the huge growth in patient populations. As Sana Loue wrote in *Therapeutic Farms: Recovery from Mental Illness*, asylums became filled with the "marginal elements of the population who could not or would not conform or could not subsist in an industrial, largely laissez-faire society, one that was increasingly utilized by families to care for those members who had become too burdensome to bear."

The larger patient populations made it impossible to provide the individualized type of care that was a critical component of the Retreat. As Torrey wrote in *Out of the Shadows*, "The era of moral treatment was rapidly forgotten as public psychiatric hospitals in the United States became overwhelmed with patients."

Torrey cited the Pilgrim State Hospital in New York as an example of what institutions looked like during this period. It housed more than fourteen thousand patients, which, as Torrey wrote, ". . . were virtual cities unto themselves. Hospitals that had originally been built as humane asylums had become on the best of days merely human warehouses. On the difficult days, they became much worse than that."

This was also the case in Canada, where patient numbers inside asylums were growing. According to the CMHA report, following the passing of the British North America Act in 1867, which resulted in the creation of the Dominion of Canada, care of the mentally ill became recognized as a provincial responsibility. The running of asylums consumed a significant percentage of each province's budget and the number of people needing care began to increase. As those numbers grew, the small family-like asylums disappeared and were replaced with larger institutions. The increased growth in asylums continued across Europe and North America during the mid to late 1900s, and with it came a gradual move toward clinical care and away from the "moral treatment" of patients. The fiscal responsibility for the institutions also shifted from local authorities to state governments, and more emphasis was placed on the protection of the public as opposed to the care of the patients.

All of these factors came together to create the perfect storm of horrific conditions inside asylums. By the early 1900s, wrote Loue, patients were being kept in caged beds or locked inside cupboards, with frequent reports of violence. In 1946, those brutal conditions were exposed in an in-depth article published in *Life* magazine called "Bedlam 1946: Most U.S. Mental Hospitals are a Shame and a Disgrace." Writer Albert Q. Maisel focused on conditions inside Pennsylvania's Byberry and Ohio's Cleveland State hospitals. He wrote:

> Through public neglect and legislative penny-pinching, state after state has allowed its institutions for the care and cure of the mentally sick to degenerate into little more than concentration camps on the Belsen pattern. . . .
>
> Thousands spend their days – often for weeks at a stretch – locked in devices euphemistically called "restraints": thick leather handcuffs, great canvas camisoles, "muffs," "mitts," wristlets, locks and straps and restraining sheets. Hundreds are confined in "lodges" – bare, bedless rooms reeking with filth and feces – by day lit only through half-inch holes in steel-plated windows, by night merely black tombs in which the cries of the insane echo unheard from the peeling plaster of the walls.

The article showed how psychiatric institutions had once again become cruel places of torture badly in need of reform. But while the article was a wake-up call for action, before change could take place an even darker period in the history of psychiatric care would arrive. Doctors were beginning to experiment with radical psychiatric medicine and such invasive therapies as insulin shock treatments and lobotomies. According to Harvey G. Simmons's book *Unbalanced: Mental Health Policy in Ontario, 1930–1989*, psychiatric hospitals began using insulin shock or insulin coma therapy on patients in order to induce temporary comas. Electroconvulsive therapy was being used without anaesthesia and lobotomies were being performed on patients without their consent.

Lobotomies involve the surgical removal of a part of the brain, which some doctors believed could stabilize a person's behaviour. The practice continued despite the fact that patients were basically being used as case studies. Many were left permanently disabled and some died. The person most responsible for popularizing lobotomies in the US was a controversial American neurologist and psychiatrist named Dr. Walter Freeman who, throughout the 1940s and 1950s, is said to have performed more than three thousand lobotomies along with his associate, Dr. James Watts. The majority were performed on women.

The most high-profile of those cases was Rosemary Kennedy, older sister of President John F. Kennedy. In Kate Clifford Larson's book, *Rosemary: The Hidden Kennedy Daughter*, the author writes that at McLean Hospital in Belmont, Massachusetts, between 1938 and 1954, women made up 82 percent of the total number of lobotomy patients. Rosemary was strikingly beautiful and today would likely be diagnosed as intellectually disabled. Larson wrote that the powerful Kennedy household was headed up by Joe Kennedy, the ambitious father, and Rosemary's spirited and flirtatious behaviour was considered a "menacing disgrace to the Kennedys' political, financial and social aspirations."

In November 1941, when Rosemary was twenty-three years old, her father secretly arranged for Dr. Freeman and Dr. Watts to perform a lobotomy on her. According to Larson, Joe was told that the surgery would "calm Rosemary's agitated depression. She would become docile, less moody." Instead, the surgery went terribly wrong and Rosemary was left almost completely disabled, unable to walk or talk, with the mental level of a toddler. Larson wrote, "The operation destroyed a crucial part of Rosemary's brain and erased years of emotional, physical and intellectual development, leaving her completely incapable of taking care of herself."

Rosemary would spend the rest of her life in institutions and died in 2005 at the age of eighty-six. In the fifty-three years she was institutionalized, her family rarely visited.

It's not known how many lobotomies were performed in Canada, nor are the outcomes of those operations known, but, as Larson wrote, there were statistically few positive results and many patients became worse, acting more belligerent, more forgetful and less able to engage via social interactions. Some experienced epileptic-type seizures, catatonia, incontinence and the inability to walk or talk.

THE 1960S WERE a time of major social change and gave birth to an anti-psychiatry movement that sought to discredit the mental health system. The movement got a huge boost from the 1962 book *One Flew Over the Cuckoo's Nest* by Ken Kesey, which portrayed psychiatric hospitals as places where heartless medical staff unwillingly subjected patients to lobotomies. This image was perpetuated in the 1975 movie, in which the character of Nurse Ratched, played by actress Louise Fletcher, was a psychopath while the patient Randle Patrick McMurphy, played by actor Jack Nicholson, was a free-spirited and likeable rebel who represented freedom. After Nurse Ratched ordered a lobotomy be performed on McMurphy, he was transformed into a lifeless robot. Many believe the movie had a lasting impact on the field of psychiatry and helped sway public opinion against psychiatric hospitals, which helped pave the way for their closures.

The 1982 movie *Frances* was based on the turbulent life of actress Frances Farmer, who spent more than five years in a mental institution and was said to suffer from depression. There was no mention in Farmer's autobiography of her having a lobotomy; however, the film included a dramatic scene in which a doctor hammers an ice pick–like instrument through Farmer's eye socket, which is how Dr. Freeman performed the surgery. It was unforgettably horrific and, like *Cuckoo's Nest*, helped change public opinion on psychiatric hospitals.

In 1949, psychiatric facilities across Canada were upgraded as a result of mental health grants that were given to the provinces from the Federal Government. Despite the number of beds at mental hospitals across Canada being increased to nearly eighteen thousand, overcrowding remained a big problem and the bed count couldn't keep up with the demand. While much had happened in the history of psychiatric care up to this point, the breakthrough that would change everything arrived in the 1950s with developments in psychopharmacology.

The introduction of antipsychotic and tranquilizing drugs, including lithium carbonate, revolutionized the treatment of bipolar disorder, as did the first antipsychotic drug, chlorpromazine, or Thorazine, which came to Canada in 1954. Chlorpromazine would become widely used in psychiatric hospitals, eventually replacing the use of shock treatments for depression and lobotomies for schizophrenia, mania and psychotic disorders.

The new drugs transformed not only patient care but also the psychiatric system, as they allowed more patients to live outside of the hospital.

MARGARET WAS PUT on two antipsychotic drugs, Stelazine and Largactil, along with chloral hydrate syrup, a sedative that caused drowsiness. Along with trouble sleeping, a psychological test showed she was also having problems concentrating, that her thinking was scattered and that she had "impaired intellectual functioning," which was typical of "schizophrenic disturbance." Her doctor wrote:

> She ascribes to a heightened sensitivity that allowed the thoughts of others to impinge on her consciousness. She freely expresses her hostile and negative feelings towards her family and various acquaintances. A few people seem to have earned her respect and admiration, mainly those with whom she has had more formal relationships, such as teachers. Her attitude toward negroes and coloureds, to whom she has been exposed most of her life in the West Indian Islands, borders on the paranoid.
>
> This patient's symptoms indicate a schizophrenic disorder of long standing.

Slowly Margaret's behaviour changed and, with consistent medical care, she improved. Six months after taking her first IQ test on March 25, 1963, in which she scored 88, another test was administered. Her new score was 104, which put her in the average intelligence range. This was a huge step forward and showed that the right medications and a regular schedule of care could dramatically improve her mental state. Her doctor noted: "The improvement in the quality of her thinking is perhaps more impressive than the actual change in score. She no longer shows any of the confusion, over inclusiveness or contamination of responses noted earlier."

Now that she was doing better, Margaret was able to enroll in typing and shorthand courses at the hospital. However, she was still having behavioural problems, and a nurse described her as "unsociable" and wrote in her files that she had a tendency to flirt with male patients, even having sex with some. Whether this was consensual is not known as the wards were coed, and male and female patients were allowed to openly mingle. On May 27, 1963, she was given the first of many pregnancy tests. It came back negative.

Margaret was still showing signs that she was depressed and would wear old, shabby clothes and deliberately neglect herself in order to, according to one nurse, "conform to the 'witch-like' person she perceives herself to be." Doctors thought it might help if they could cure her cystic acne and ordered a special acne cream, but the scarring and lesions on her face, chest and back were too extensive. One doctor wrote, "I doubt that treatment will be of much value in this case."

Over time, Margaret settled into a routine and began taking better care of herself. She bathed more regularly and began attending typing and house-keeping classes daily. Staff felt she had improved enough that she could handle a part-time job outside of the hospital and found her one at a local dry cleaner. While Margaret was initially excited about having a job, she quit after only a few weeks and told her boss she was having trouble concentrat-ing because the job was "too monotonous."

A short while later, in late April, she decided she would stop going to typing school and told staff that the work was too easy for her. She was now spending most of her days watching TV on the ward and smoking for hours. The lack of motivation that Margaret exhibited is a key symptom of schizophrenia and depression, and Margaret was also likely missing her family, who she only heard from through cards sent on her birthday and at Christmas.

Verna would have known little about her daughter's real life as the cards were her main form of communication. Abe's cards always included quotes from scriptures, which he used to chastise Margaret. In April 1963, when Margaret turned nineteen, her father sent a colourful birthday card decorated with a pop-up umbrella. The card's message read:

There isn't any day at all, at any time of year,
that's any nicer to recall than just your birthday dear.
There isn't anything that brings more pleasure all year through
than wishing all of life's good things, especially for you!

On the back of the card, however, was Abe's message to his daughter:

Dear Margaret,

The words of this card pretty well express my wishes for you. We do wish you well. As you may have heard me preach many times, God wants you to have pleasures made perfect and made permanent. But the pleasure of the scarlet road or the way of the world leads to no pleasure that is worth a straw. At His hand are pleasure forever more. God alone can satisfy. Jesus loved righteousness and . . . was anointed with the oil of gladness above all others.

I believe the Lord has something real good in store for you. He can deliver you from all carnal desires so that they won't bind you. Paul said: "Oh wretched man that I am, who shall deliver me. I thank God thru Jesus Christ!"

How well I remember the day you came into our home. That was a happy day for your mother and me, even if I had been sort of expecting a boy! You have been a blessing. What a help you were before you got sick both to the home and church. Your piano playing and teaching were so much appreciated.

Isn't it a fright how fast time has sped by. You have grown so quickly just think you are now 19. I can hardly believe it. I am praying that you will find work and your proper place in life. "No good thing will He withhold from them that wall uprightly.

Love to you – Congratulations on your 19th.

Dad

P.S. Wish I had something to enclose . . . a nice hanky or something . . . but at the moment . . . !? Sorry.

While her brother David wasn't aware of the letters his father sent to Margaret, he said they fit with his character.

"It surprises me not that he would say this," wrote David. "Dad thought Jesus could fix everything. Not that I believe he thought Margaret had one, but in Antigua I believe he was once called on to cast out a demon from a girl there."

Before receiving the card from her father, Margaret had rejoined the typing program. Shortly after his card arrived, however, her attendance began to slide and she started arriving late for class. When she did show up, she would get anxious over small things. Her anxiety level was high enough that staff began to limit her activities. Her doctor wrote in her files: "The less stress and pressure in her work situation, the better her chances will be to carry out her duties efficiently."

Whether Abe's letter to his daughter was the stress factor is not known.

IN THE SUMMER of 1964, a few months after Margaret's twentieth birthday, her family made a decision that would change her life forever. Verna decided to move to the States with David and Jim. Abe had earned his degree at Evangel College (a private Christian university now called Evangel University) in Springfield, Missouri, and had secured a teaching job at a secondary school in Janesville, Wisconsin. David was only twelve at the time and wasn't privy to the reasons behind this decision, but he believes the move was painful for

Verna as she had begun to establish herself in her career.

When Abe returned to Galt to help the family with the move, David recalls "great bouts of loud crying in Mom's arguments with my Dad." While his mother always "fell in line with the 'father-knows-best' creed," she didn't always like it.

"It was undoubtedly hard for her to give up what she was seeing as her own life and possible career," wrote David in an email.

David wrote that he didn't know how they felt about leaving Margaret in Canada. "They also abandoned John at the exact same time, at least according to John's comment when I saw him in 2004. As a matter of perspective, you might say that these two kids, Margaret and John, were not in step with the 'way of the Lord.'"

While the decision affected Verna, it was Margaret who would feel the biggest impact. It meant that at the age of twenty, she would be alone in the hospital without anyone to help her navigate the psychiatric system. No one would be there to advocate on her behalf if she became seriously ill, and there would be no one to call if she felt alone or afraid. Persons afflicted with schizophrenia can have disorganized thinking or delusions, but they are still capable of experiencing emotions – including rejection.

John had long ago dropped out of boarding school, and for a few years he had worked in a lumber camp in Ontario. According to the medical files, John, who had just turned nineteen, decided not to go with his parents and instead moved to Vancouver to join the hippie movement and study Zen Buddhism. John would later confide to David that this wasn't true, that this was something his parents told people while in fact he had wanted to go but wasn't allowed.

"This was axed by one of our parents. He didn't know who nixed the idea but he suspected it was my mother," wrote David.

During John's adolescence, he had shown growing signs of rebelliousness. Given how Abe and Verna had responded to Margaret, it was possible they did not like the prospect of having another problem child. John would later completely disconnect from his family, changing his name from John Morden Jacobson to Lucian "Luke" Arthur Mahon. Over the course of the next several years, John would end up living his own sad life on the streets.

IT HAD BEEN two years since Margaret's admission to the Ontario Hospital, and although it must have been difficult knowing that her family had left her behind, she was benefiting from having consistent care in a supervised environment. She had settled into hospital life and was behaving more rationally. The downside was that she was beginning to experience one of the dreaded side effects of antipsychotic medications: leg tremors or involuntary muscle spasms. Tremors typically affect the legs and can result in people unconsciously rocking from foot to foot, or shuffling or swinging their legs while they're sitting. These tremors can be so extreme that many people go off their medication. To counter the tremors, doctors added Cogentin, typically prescribed for Parkinson's disease, to Margaret's list of medications.

JANUARY 8, 1964, was a significant date in Margaret's psychiatric care – she was discharged from the hospital and placed in a boarding home, only six months after her family had moved to the States. It would be the first of many moves that would continue despite poor outcomes and that would, over the long term, have a devastating effect on her mental and physical health.

Margaret had become part of "one of the largest social experiments in American history," one that was doomed to fail.

THE STARS WERE aligned for deinstitutionalization to unfold, beginning with the introduction of antipsychotic medications – like chlorpromazine – which freed people from the troubling symptoms of their mental illness. The bed closures that began in the 1950s swept across Canada with such fervour that eventually 80 percent of beds were lost. The plan had been an easy sell as copious studies showed that community programs were the most effective ways of treating people with mental illnesses and, compared to hospital environments, they were less restrictive. People could rebuild their lives and become more productive.

Mental health programs were to be set up in the community and funded with the money saved from bed closures. By the 1960s, the deinstitutionalization movement was moving full steam ahead, and while there were great variations in how the individual provinces proceeded (Alberta dropped from 4.1 beds per 1,000 people in 1965 – the highest per population in the country – to 0.7 beds per 1,000 by 1980), the impact was the same. There were fewer beds inside psychiatric hospitals, although psychiatric beds were being developed in general hospitals in an early attempt to integrate mental health and physical health care.

According to the research paper "Forty Years of Deinstitutionalization of Psychiatric Beds in Canada: An Empirical Assessment," the number of beds in psychiatric hospitals between 1975 and 1981 dropped from 53,801 to 20,301, a decrease of more than 62 percent. Although the number of psychiatric beds in general hospitals increased, it was a far cry from what was needed. The end result was that between 1963 and 1977, the psychiatric bed capacity in Canada went from 3.7 per 1,000 general population to 1.0 beds per 1,000 (according to a 2015 article by Steve Lurie and David Goldbloom called "More for the Mind and Its Legacy").

By 1977, the number of patients in psychiatric institutional care had dropped from 79,707 to 24,362, a threefold decrease. The report concluded that the shift toward a community-focused mental health system, however, was "still an elusive goal," in essence because supports for people who had been moved into communities were not being set up. At the same time as the beds were being reduced, a new short stay policy was started, which meant that patients admitted to psychiatric units in general hospitals were staying for much less time. Between 1985 and 1999, the average number of days of care decreased by 41.6 percent. Prior to 1960, admissions into Ontario psychiatric hospitals far outnumbered discharges because people were staying in for extended periods. According to the 2006 report *The Human Face of*

Mental Health and Mental Illness in Canada by the Public Health Agency of Canada, between 1960 and 1976, the number of beds in Canadian psychiatric hospitals dropped from 47,633 to 15,011.

As a result of patients being moved out so quickly, by 1976 the number of admissions matched the number of discharges. The short stay policy meant that patients were not only being discharged sooner, they were also being admitted less often. Part of that was made possible because of medications that were now available; however, some patients still needed longer stays. As a result, patients were experiencing multiple admissions largely because they were being discharged before they were ready.

With so many bed closures, it was now possible to close entire hospitals, and in Ontario the 1970s saw the closure of the Goderich Psychiatric Hospital, Lakeshore Psychiatric Hospital in Toronto and Dr. MacKinnon Phillips Hospital in Owen Sound. One of the biggest was the Lakeshore Psychiatric Hospital, which had opened in 1898 under the name Mimico Lunatic Asylum and at its peak in 1950 had housed more than fourteen hundred patients. When it closed in 1979, there were only 280. The bulk of Lakeshore beds were transferred to the Queen Street Mental Health Centre, which is now the Centre for Addiction and Mental Health. Other patients were set up in the community and registered as outpatients.

How patients fared once they were discharged is anyone's guess as there was a shocking lack of follow-up. The US seems to have done a slightly better job at this – an American study by mental health researcher John R. Belcher that looked at 132 patients who had been discharged from Ohio's Columbus State Hospital in 1985 showed that 32 percent had been arrested and jailed within six months of their release, and 36 percent had become homeless. It shouldn't have surprised anyone that more people who were suddenly homeless also had a mental illness. There have been numerous stories about psychiatric hospitals in the US renting buses and loading them with patients, some still in their hospital gowns, then driving them downtown or to another city and releasing them. While this may sound like an outrageous urban legend, in fact there were enough reports on these incidents that someone coined the phrase *Greyhound therapy.*

In 2018, the *Sacramento Bee* newspaper reported that psychiatric patients at a Las Vegas psychiatric hospital were given one-way Greyhound bus tickets to cities across the country without their consent. Some patients filed a class action lawsuit against the psychiatric hospital as well as an adult mental health service, which oversees the hospital, and various treatment professionals. On March 21, 2018, the *Bee* reported that a Nevada court ruled in favour of a former patient and potentially hundreds more, allowing them to pursue the lawsuit for damages.

A similar lawsuit led to the closure of the Philadelphia State Hospital in 1990. After that, $200 million was transferred to the City of Philadelphia to fund community-based services. Philadelphia now spends more than $1 billion annually on community-based mental health services and is recognized as a world leader in trauma-based care and prevention.

As for how patients in Canada fared under deinstitutionalization, little is known as the reports are scarce. Helen Kell, who worked at the HPH when Margaret was there and watched patients being shipped out, said that once patients left the hospital, many were simply forgotten. In 1980, McMaster University's Dr. Nancy Herman followed 285 patients after they had been discharged from a psychiatric hospital as part of her doctoral thesis on how well patients transitioned into communities. Between 1980 and 1985, Dr. Herman visited the former patients daily in boarding houses, doughnut shops and malls, and found that only about one-quarter of them successfully made the transition to the outside world while the rest struggled. According to a May 13, 2000, story in the *Hamilton Spectator*, Dr. Herman discovered "[former patients] eating rancid sardines in substandard boarding homes, using any tactic they could to hide their condition from the world and coping with uninterested psychiatrists who went through the motions of weekly meetings with patients." One person was found living in a large cardboard box that had once housed a TV.

Her analysis of deinstitutionalization?

"I think we have failed miserably."

MARGARET, ALONG WITH thousands of other patients, was caught in the revolving door that came about as a result of deinstitutionalization. Even though it was clear she wasn't benefiting from being moved into boarding homes, the practice continued. One of the main problems with boarding homes, which were largely located in older homes in the downtown core, was that operators were poorly trained. The shortage of social and outreach workers meant that former patients relied heavily on operators who knew nothing about caring for persons with mental illness. It meant that they went from receiving 24-7 care to suddenly being left on their own. In a short period of time, they would stop eating properly and stop taking their medications, and their mental and physical health would deteriorate.

In 1962, the year of Margaret's first admission, there were 11,907 psychiatric beds in the province of Ontario. By 1980, that number had dropped to 4,948. What happened to all of those patients isn't known, but it's likely their fates were similar to Margaret's who, over the next fifteen years, lived in nine different boarding houses. That's the official count – the actual number may be much higher. As she told one nurse, she lived in several boarding homes in a matter of months. Those weren't recorded in her files.

PAT SAUNDERS HAD a front-row seat to what deinstitutionalization looked like because she saw it from the inside. She was a social worker at the HPH from 1973 to 1995, one whose sole job was to find housing and supports for patients who were being discharged into the community. In the years that she worked in the psychiatric care system, about a quarter of her time was spent at the HPH while the rest was at various mental health clinics. Over her twenty-three-year career, during which she worked with hundreds of patients, she said it was clear that the motivation behind the plan wasn't to improve patient care; it was to save money. Hospital beds cost a lot more than boarding home beds, which were unlicensed and unregulated. She recalled that hospital beds cost around $500 a day while boarding home beds cost less than $100.

Trying to find a decent boarding home that had a good reputation was her biggest struggle, and more often than not she had no choice but to settle for homes that were less than adequate. The quality of the care depended more on the personality of the operator than the physical building, she said, and often the operators were in it for the money.

"A big part of [a patient's] recovery was based on their ability to stay on their medication, but there had to be some supports in the boarding homes to make sure they did that. The problem was the boarding house operators were untrained. When I asked them about [dispensing medication], some of them would balk and say, 'I'm not a psychiatrist.' They were business people and they were people who saw an opportunity to make a living," said Saunders. She added that whatever there was in the hospital in the way of supports also needed to be in the community, but it wasn't.

"That was upsetting to me. I was always trying to work on setting something up in the community but there were only bits and pieces here and there. Some [homes] were better than others but you were always fighting against a big system and the overall trend that was happening."

Because of the shortage of well-run boarding homes, Saunders was forced to place patients in homes that were rundown and poorly operated. "They were often crowded and dirty. And they got away with it because there was so little monitoring."

She was also responsible for finding community supports for patients, which was a constant source of frustration. She knew first-hand how inadequate the services were and feared for the safety of patients once they left the hospital. "Our goal and what we were told to do was to get everyone out," said Saunders. "There was little consideration of how well the patient coped or whether they were able to live independently."

While patients were supposed to be followed up by social workers after leaving the hospital, Saunders rarely saw any of them and wondered if they visited at all. She said some patients were transferred to the HPH from surrounding hospitals, only to be moved into the community. "They came in the front door and got discharged out the back door."

During the period that Saunders worked at the HPH, the catchment area was massive, reaching from Halton to Brantford to Niagara, known as the Golden Horseshoe. The hospital building had separate wings labelled A to H, each extending out like the arms of an octopus from one central area where the nurses' station was located. Patients were placed in wings according to where they lived, with male and female patients in the same ward but separate rooms.

Her first job at the HPH was in ward G1, which was for patients from Wentworth, including Ancaster, Stoney Creek and Flamborough. Most patients had been diagnosed with schizophrenia, said Saunders, and many had severe psychiatric problems. It upset her seeing patients like Margaret discharged when they needed hospital-level care.

"Some disappeared after they left the hospital and were never seen again There was one particular boarding home where I was always hoping for a vacancy because I was always comfortable about placing people there. But most weren't like that."

Some owners would kick residents out during the day and lock their front doors until 5:00 p.m., forcing people to roam the streets all day. The lucky ones, said Saunders, were those who were transferred to the general hospital psychiatric units, although even there they were only allowed to stay for short periods.

During her last few months on the job, she placed a fellow in a boarding home and, as a treat, started taking him out for lunch. Andy had been diagnosed with schizophrenia at the age of seventeen and was thirty-four when he was placed in the home. Even though she retired more than twenty years earlier, Saunders still takes Andy out for lunch regularly, though rather than meeting monthly they get together on significant days, like his birthday,

Christmas, Easter and Thanksgiving. Lunch is always at Pizza Pizza and he always orders the same thing – an extra-large pizza and a bucket of chicken wings. He eats three slices of pizza and a few wings then takes the rest home for the other residents.

"He's a hit at his home when he comes back," says Saunders, smiling. She also buys him a case of diet pop, a bag of goodies and, on his birthday, he gets a seventy-five-dollar Tim Hortons coffee card. "I know if I didn't provide for him, he'd have to go without. It gives him some quality of life," she said.

Andy is one of the lucky ones. His boarding house is well run and he receives ongoing support from Saunders and from his family. This isn't the case with most of the patients Saunders saw who left the hospital. For them, there was no happy ending.

"They'd come back in such rundown condition because once they left the hospital, they were forgotten."

THERE WERE NO notes for Margaret's first year in the rooming house describing how well she did. That suggests she wasn't being monitored. It's likely that she had to rely solely on the boarding home operator for help. There was a short note stating that she was moved to a different home after about a year but no details were offered as to what prompted the move. What happened next showed things didn't go well. On July 30, 1965, Margaret was found sitting on the floor in her room surrounded by ripped-up newspapers. The room was described as being in "shambles," and according to her files, Margaret was filthy and dishevelled, and covered in abrasions and bruises. There were no notes detailing what had caused the bruises, but as a young mentally ill woman all on her own, Margaret would have been highly vulnerable to physical and sexual assaults.

Her files stated she had likely been sitting there on her own for more than a week, and that she hadn't eaten for several days and was severely depressed and ill. It was the other tenants who brought her plight to the attention of the boarding home owner, not the social worker who was supposed to be watching out for her or the operator who ran the home. Perhaps it was because Margaret's mental state was so frayed that she refused to go back to the hospital. A nurse was sent to get her, but, according to the files, "the girl disappeared at the suggestion of going to the hospital."

She was picked up the next morning by a motorist who brought her downtown then called the police. When Margaret saw the police, she bolted again and wasn't captured until much later, when she was taken back to the hospital. Doctors wrote of Margaret's state: "Patient is filthy, dirty and very untidy. Will only answer part of questions asked. Handcuffed – very violent toward police."

In 1964, Ontario passed the Homes for Special Care Act, which introduced regulations to boarding homes. Hamilton Psychiatric Hospital staff were supposed to monitor conditions and patients inside of the homes, as each provincial psychiatric hospital was responsible for the homes in their catchment area. There was also an Approved Home program with legislation dating from 1934.

ONCE MARGARET WAS back at the hospital, a nurse contacted Verna in Wisconsin and told her what had happened. She then asked Verna what she wanted them to do with Margaret. It's not clear what options were presented to Verna, but it's likely she could have taken Margaret home. Instead, Verna told the nurse to return Margaret to the hospital. Margaret's new patient number was 36835. Verna later wrote a letter to the hospital asking doctors if Margaret's acne may be part of the reason she was so promiscuous. Or maybe, wrote Verna, she hoped for a show of affection through sex. In the letter, Verna described her daughter as "idealistic, musical, and artistic." She wrote, "I understand that she is a very sick girl. She surely has great ability and potential but evidently not the nervous stamina to live in society. Do you feel there is a chance of our girlie being rehabilitated?"

With Margaret back at the HPH, a flurry of admission tests were conducted. A black-and-white photo taken at her readmission shows her looking thin and washed out. Her face was blotchy, possibly due to her acne, and although she was only twenty-one years old, she looked much older and hardened. Back on the ward, nurses noticed that Margaret would stare vacantly into space for long periods in total silence. Her legs shook constantly; she was unable to focus on anything and had problems answering questions.

Her doctor diagnosed her as having "persecutory delusions," which are common among people with paranoid schizophrenia, fostering the belief that others are out to harm or kill them. Given Margaret's horrific living situation, perhaps they weren't delusions at all but a reflection of what had happened to her.

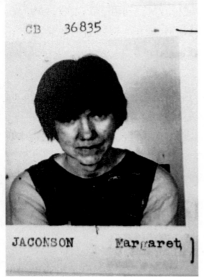

CB 36835

JACOBSON Margaret

Hospital admission photo of Margaret at twenty-one. Taken at Hamilton Psychiatric Hospital. Courtesy of St. Joseph's Healthcare Hamilton.

After a few weeks back in the hospital, Margaret's health began to improve. It was clear from the outcome that she couldn't cope outside of a hospital environment with 24-7 care. She had become used to a highly structured environment where she received her medications on a strict schedule, and where she always had a bed and meals provided. A nurse wrote in the files that Margaret was "pleasant and cooperative, although withdrawn."

Margaret was not one to make her needs known, but after her ordeal she opened up to a nurse and told her she feared leaving the hospital again. The nurse wrote that "it appears that she feels quite protected and safe in this hospital setting."

But as Margaret settled into hospital life, a troubling pattern began to emerge. Even though this first attempt to move her out had been so disastrous, the hospital set her up for another discharge. It was, as Pat Saunders said, all part of the revolving door.

With each discharge, Margaret's health diminished further. By the time she was twenty-one, she looked decades older than her age.

THERE ARE SEVERAL troubling references scattered throughout Margaret's files referring to her being "promiscuous" with male patients. But it's questionable whether Margaret knew what she was doing or whether the sex was even consensual. If it was, Margaret may have exchanged sex for money to buy cigarettes. Years later, Margaret would tell a friend that she was once pushed into a washroom by a male patient at the hospital and almost raped. Meanwhile, her family remained largely absent from her life. Aside from the occasional note, she rarely heard from them. On December 15, 1965, one doctor wrote in her files: "Her parents are continuing to take very little interest in this patient. They have failed to come and see the examiner throughout Margaret's hospitalization."

Margaret was upset about her family's absence and told her doctor she felt rejected by them. Still, she never shared these feelings with her family and continued putting on a brave face in her letters home, like the one she wrote on September 23, 1966:

Hi mom and dad,

I guess you thought that I was never going to write! It's just that I never seem to feel like writing – no good energy, I guess! I think I spent most of my energy on smoking! Thanks for your parcel mom. I've seen Gwen again and gave her a pair. Those bare heels are quite the rage. I was hoping to buy a pair for myself and was thrilled when you sent me just what I wanted.

So are you coming to see me in October? That's nice. And how about bringing a picture of John when you come. I guess he was quite thrilled to get married at long last! Maybe I'll be the old maid in the family. You never can quite tell, can you!

I hope you won't have to move too much more. Well, bye for now. Gese [*sic*]. I hate writing – not you.

Marg.

But just as Margaret was writing to her family, hoping for a visit, they were moving farther away. In 1967, they relocated to New Orleans, Louisiana, where Abe had taken a new teaching job. He would teach at a grade school there for about three years. In January 1967, Margaret had a move of her own. She was discharged from the hospital ward and sent to a residential unit that was connected to the hospital. Patients there had more independence and the move was an indication that the hospital felt Margaret was doing better. After a few weeks, they signed her up for a typing program and had her doing needlework. Margaret again reminded staff that she couldn't manage things outside of the hospital walls. Her doctor wrote: "She thinks that life outside of the hospital would be a bit too difficult for her right now unless she were in a protecting setting, much like the hospital."

Meanwhile, Margaret kept writing to her family. She sent another letter in October 1967:

Dear mom and dad,

The weather is getting colder here. This morning I went to a rock garden and a tree garden – there's a special name for it which I can't remember. Tonight, right now I am watching the Dean Martin show – it's our late night and we stay up till eleven. Christmas doesn't seem too far away now. The "year" sure went fast, didn't it! I am still typing in Auchmar but haven't found a job as yet. Somewhere it may turn up.

I'm not going to push things. I want to feel that I'm ready when I do go! How do you like your work dad? I hope mom can get some work, too. That ashma [sic] is a nuisance?

I still use your purse Mom, it is so handy! Aunty Georgina wants me for Xmas. Her girls are so cute!

Well, there isn't too much to say. Gwen doesn't come for me so I guess she's mad at me – she's living shacked up from the last time I was there. Keep smiling! Sorry about not writing but you know me. I hate writing letters! Now I must go to bed. Tomorrow is fish day and I hate it. Well, bye for now!

Margaret

A FEW WEEKS later, her letter was returned unopened. Margaret wasn't deterred and sent them another letter in which she offered more encouraging news: "I feel that I have gotten a lot better in the last few weeks. I'll give Gwen those chocolates when she comes up. Four presents were a very big surprise! I hope you guys have a nice Christmas, too. Maybe about this time next year I will be out of the hospital!"

ALTHOUGH HER LETTERS were upbeat, the notes written in her files told another story. Margaret was showing up to the typing program so filthy that on one occasion staff had to send her back to the ward to take a bath. The quality of her work had declined and she was chronically late. On July 23, 1968, a social worker wrote: "I told her that I had seen her recent work assessment sheets and they were not particularly good. She remarked that she had been in the hospital for years and didn't care much about the tasks she was given to do. I explained to her that from now on we wanted to see her at her best."

Margaret told the social worker she didn't like the lack of independence and was miffed that she couldn't even come to the worker's office without a nursing assistant. It then came out that during a recent "privilege" in which Margaret had been allowed to go downtown, she had gotten drunk with a friend. The social worker told Margaret this kind of behaviour would not be tolerated: "She agreed but added that she had only done it because of the frustration felt at being in the hospital."

ON AUGUST 21, 1968, doctors added antibiotics to her list of medications and also gave her a special soap and anti-inflammatory cream for her acne. Both had little effect. Meanwhile, her attendance at the training program continued to slide and, over the next year, her work habits became so sloppy that it was clear to staff she needed more supervision. On February 4, 1969, Margaret was admitted back to the hospital. It was her fifth admission to a psychiatric hospital in eight years, counting Homewood. Her new patient number was 43460. A nurse wrote: "It was felt that she did not benefit from

the general atmosphere of Ward 21 – she is younger than most of the patients there. Recently, attempts have been made to encourage her to look
outwards from the hospital but efforts have met considerable resistance from
the patient whose behaviour is unsatisfactory even in respect of most basic
self care, e.g. does not wash, bathe regularly."

Margaret wasn't a bad patient. She never refused to take her medication,
willingly participated in training programs and never complained about
being moved into boarding homes. While her hygiene habits were poor and
she was often late for appointments, this hardly put her in the category of
being a bad patient.

She responded well to round-the-clock supervision where her meals,
shelter and medication were looked after. More often than not, Margaret's
main complaint was that she was bored – she was smart, and it's possible that
the type of programs being offered to her were below her intelligence level.
The solution doctors came up with to keep Margaret on track was to have her
sign a form in which she promised to conform to the rules and regulations of
the hospital and co-operate with medical staff.

CHAPTER EIGHT
"I Still Want Margaret"

1969
Regina

Although Margaret rarely heard from her parents, aside from the occasional card, there was one relative who never stopped caring about her. In the eight years since Margaret had been admitted to the hospital, her aunt, Marion Bergquist, had been in constant touch with doctors, checking to see how her niece was doing and asking whether she could take her to her home in Regina, Saskatchewan, about 2,600 kilometres away from Hamilton. She told doctors she was worried about her niece's well-being and said that she had wanted to visit but couldn't because of the distance. Marion had known Margaret since she was a child. When Margaret was ten, Marion had written her a sweet poem in her autograph book:

> To Margaret,
> A glad "hello" and a hearty grip
> Are the first beginnings of commradship [*sic*],
> We learn by the smile and the shake of the hand
> To know each other and understand
> And I hope someday you'll find in me
> The kind of friend I wish to be,
> Love, Auntie Marion

Marion had contacted Abe and Verna several times over the years to check on Margaret, but she'd never heard anything back and was concerned that her niece had been abandoned by the family. As she wrote to doctors: "Frankly we [relatives] have been very much in the dark as to her condition for her parents were always vague in their statements and we didn't like to press them."

On February 25, 1969, Marion wrote to doctors at the Ontario Hospital that she was coming to Montreal and would like to drop by on her way back and visit Margaret. She also asked if she could bring Margaret home for the summer, as there would be lots for her to do and several relatives nearby. Much to Marion's delight, doctors approved both requests. On March 7, 1969, Marion arrived at the hospital and took her niece shopping for a dress to replace what she described as the "very unflattering" clothing she was wearing. Marion had already bought Margaret a train ticket. However, Margaret had other ideas, as shown in the letter Marion later wrote to doctors: "As you know, I was not able to persuade my niece to come with me home to Regina. She kept saying she would rather try to get a job in Hamilton and come later to visit us on a holiday. Since I could in no way guarantee her a job here at this time of year, for jobs are very scarce here, I could not use that as an inducement."

On March 21, Margaret's social worker wrote: "I explained [to Marion] that probably Marg would find it difficult to accept the fact that someone wanted her and would provide a home for her."

AFTER SPENDING THE day with her niece, Marion was even more determined to bring Margaret home and surround her with a loving family. She wrote to the hospital again and peppered the doctor with questions about Margaret's diagnosis, explaining that her family was composed of Christians who went to church regularly and didn't drink. In one letter, she wrote that she felt Abe and Verna were likely embarrassed by their daughter:

It would have been awkward if their daughter's conduct was the opposite of what they believed and taught to be right. I know how kids can rebel and do crazy things and put you on the spot but still that's no reason to get them put away somewhere. There must have been more than that. As I said to you, my sister-in-law was always a great one to know everything medically and to diagnose the family illnesses as just a little worse than they were. So maybe she was honest when I asked her a couple of years ago . . . if she never got Margaret home for a visit and she answered that since Margaret was on drugs she wouldn't dare to take the responsibility. Or maybe she was hiding the fact that she didn't want her, or else, that Margaret didn't want them.

On April 1, 1969, Marion wrote another pleading letter to Margaret's doctors: "I still want Margaret. We will treat her like our own daughter."

Doctors did not know whether Marion was capable of providing the care Margaret needed, but they felt they had run out of other options after failed moves to the residential unit and two boarding homes. On April 9, Marion got the news she'd been waiting for – she could take Margaret home. Margaret was now twenty-five and had been in an institution since she was seventeen. Was she ready for family life? Was she stable enough to handle life outside of the hospital without 24-7 supervision? The staff psychiatrist offered Marion some cautionary words:

Dear Mrs. Bergquist,

I feel that of all the possibilities that are available, Margaret's being discharged to your care is the most promising. The domestic set up which you have described in your letters would provide the sort of stimulation that is needed at present.

Margaret, as you know, has been troubled by psychiatric illness since 1961. It is not uncommon for such illnesses to cause a person to be very disturbed for a short period – imagining things, hearing things, behaving uncharacteristically, etc. – following which these acute signs of illnesses subside, leaving the patient not obviously disturbed, but not quite the same person as he or she was before the illness started.

This is the way Margaret's illness has manifested itself. At present, there is little in her appearance, conversation, etc. that is particularly odd. The main problem is stimulating her enough to get her interested in such important matters as a job, a place to live, getting out of the hospital, etc. and it is in these areas that an interested relative or friend is so helpful. We feel that Margaret would be quite content to stay in the hospital for the rest of her life, but that this would be most unfortunate for a woman of her age.

I am not able to give you a complete assurance that Margaret is "mentally sound" in the sense that she will not at some time in the future become more obviously disturbed. It is not possible to forecast such developments accurately in the individual case. However, if she did become unwell again, psychiatric help would be easily available.

She is at present on relatively small dose of tranquilizers which we would recommend should be continued. If she were to go to live with you, the family doctor who would be looking after her could obtain summaries of her case from our hospital files.

It seems likely that the main problem you will encounter is that you would require to maintain a certain amount of pressure on Margaret to keep going to work, maintain her personal hygiene, and that sort of thing.

I hope you will find this note useful. As far as we are concerned, Margaret can be discharged from hospital any time.

BEFORE BEING DISCHARGED, Margaret underwent a round of tests, including a pregnancy test, because of ongoing concerns about her so-called promiscuity. It came back negative. Had Margaret been living in Alberta or BC at the time, she might have been subjected to another practice – forced sterilization. Known as the eugenics movement, it was considered one of the lowest points in the history of psychiatric care and saw the forced sterilization of countless psychiatric patients. The logic was that sterilization would prevent the transmission of undesirable traits to offspring, protecting the gene pool. It resulted in countries around the world enacting laws for compulsory sterilization of the so-called "feeble minded."

In Alberta, that law came into effect in 1928 with the passing of the Sexual Sterilization Act by the Legislative Assembly of Alberta. Three years later,

British Columbia followed suit with a similar act, which wasn't thrown out until 1972. In that period, it is believed that more than three thousand people were forcibly sterilized, many of them female psychiatric patients who had not given their consent.

While the practice was reported to have stopped in the '70s, stories continue to surface to this day, including one in 2018 where Indigenous women stated they had been forcibly sterilized in Saskatchewan in 2017. At least two were alleged to have occurred in Manitoba hospitals. As Karen Stote wrote in her book, *An Act of Genocide: Colonialism and the Sterilization of Aboriginal Women*, the eugenics movement that occurred within the Indigenous population in Canada was part of the overall plan to eliminate the country's so-called "Indian problem": "It is now clear that the federal agency responsible for the health of Native Americans abused its power to administer policy upon Indian women and used sterilization as a population control measure in the face of the high birth rate of Indian children and the perceived inability of Indian women to use other forms of birth control."

MARION WAS THRILLED to have her niece finally home and living with her. Family was important to her, and she felt strongly that with lots of love and home-cooked meals, she could make Margaret well again. The hospital gave Marion a one-month supply of the antipsychotic drug Stelazine, along with prescriptions for Margaret's other medications plus face cream for her acne. For the first few weeks, Margaret was so grateful to her aunt that she would follow her around the house and shower Marion with thank yous. While her behaviour seemed odd to Marion, she was pleased to see her niece so happy.

Marion found Margaret a part-time job as a cleaner in a nursing home, and after picking her up from work, Marion would often take her shopping. They also went on family outings to the library and church. Throughout, Marion kept in touch with doctors back in Hamilton and told them her daughters had taken Margaret to a beauty parlour, given her some of their clothes and showed her how to set her hair. The picture Marion painted was one of family harmony; however, problems started to surface a few weeks into Margaret's new job when she was fired for not doing her work properly. It didn't faze Margaret – she told Marion it was too much for her to handle anyway. But with Margaret home full time, things slowly began to unravel.

She would stay in her room most of the day and smoke while listening to her transistor radio. Marion was worried about the health impact on Margaret and her own family, but all of her attempts to get her to smoke less failed. Determined to find her another job, Marion visited employment agencies and stores where she helped Margaret fill out job applications. When no job materialized, she tried to teach Margaret how to iron and clean the bathroom; however, she soon found Margaret wasn't able to follow instructions.

Marion wrote to doctors: "She seems not to have enough muscle to do such work with speed and vigor or it may be lack of interest and ambition."

Despite Marion's home-cooked meals, in the first two months Margaret's weight dropped from 120 pounds to 112. Marion attributed it to the fact that she forbade Margaret from having chocolate or Coke because of her acne. As Marion wrote to doctors, "she would buy [C]oke at any chance she got." Marion was running out of ideas as to how to motivate her niece and wondered if the sedatives that doctors had prescribed for Margaret's anxiety might be to blame.

Marion had once taken tranquilizers herself and remembered how tired and lethargic they made her. Based on this, she made the decision to stop giving them to Margaret. Within a few days, Margaret began to complain about feeling jittery and told her aunt she wasn't sleeping well. She began smoking obsessively and refused to bathe. Then Margaret told Marion she wanted to stop taking her antipsychotic medication. Whenever Marion tried giving them to her, she would spit them out. From Margaret's behaviour, it appears she had stopped taking the pills altogether but didn't tell her aunt.

At church, Margaret sat by herself and chewed her gum loudly then, after the service, refused to stand beside Marion, instead hovering behind her as if a stranger. During family walks, Margaret would walk behind the family or in front of them, and during one outing, she carried her purse in her mouth with her hands by her side. When Marion took Margaret to a movie, she would sit in a separate row. Marion struggled to understand her niece and wrote to Margaret's doctors: "It was not as if she hated me. She just seemed to like being alone."

Margaret's acne was still severe. Marion took a trip to a dermatologist, who recommended that Margaret wash with a special lotion and use beauty grains three times a day. The workload of caring for Margaret was starting to wear on Marion. She wrote to the doctors, "Of course her keeping it up depended entirely on my vigilance."

Perhaps needing a break, Marion arranged for Margaret to stay with an uncle on a farm for a few weeks. When Margaret returned, she was even worse. She would obsess over little things and repeatedly wash her hair, and explained to Marion that she was trying to get rid of her terrible headaches. Once, Marion walked in on Margaret while she was washing her face using only one hand. "I said, 'Why don't you use both hands?' She said, 'I have to hold this piece of grass' and she showed me a tiny piece of grass between her pointer and thumb."

One night during dinner when they had company over, Margaret began gulping her milk and refilling her glass only to drain it again. After a few times, she tipped her head back with the glass hanging from her mouth while laughing loudly.

She was like "a little child doing a trick," Marion wrote to doctors.

Time slowly revealed the severity of Margaret's illness and Marion began to question whether she had done the right thing in taking her in. In a lengthy letter to the hospital, she confessed to doctors that she had underestimated the work involved in caring for Margaret and recited the long list of problems that had started from day one: excessive smoking, bizarre behaviour, weight loss and concerns about her family's safety due to the smoking. Marion had once walked in on Margaret as she tossed a burned match into her dresser drawer and closed it. Marion wrote, "We have asked, coaxed, scolded and commanded and she has refused to quit."

Marion's hope that love and kindness could cure her niece was beginning to fade. She was coming to the same painful realization that so many families come to: that caring for a relative who has a mental illness can be an all-consuming round-the-clock job. Meanwhile, as Marion struggled to figure out what to do, Margaret seemed oblivious to any problems, as shown in a letter she wrote to her parents:

Dear mom and dad,

Today is another windy and cold day here in Regina. I can't seem to get warm. I think it is warmer in Hamilton. I had a housekeeping job at a nursing home for eight days but it didn't pan out. I am too weak for that sort of job, I think. My pay was $59.30. So you can see that it required a lot of work.

I went to CMP [possibly Canada Manpower Employment] to find out if I could take a course this fall but haven't found out for sure whether there is one for me. I don't want to take too much math course or bookkeeping if I can help it. Maybe just a short math course along with typing, dictating machine, etc.

I don't know what I'll do for the summer but have prayed for a steady job. I wish I could settle down. It seems I never get there. I am going to see a dermatologist on June 4. My face is still quite a mess. Aunt Marion makes quite a lot of desserts and I keep buying [C]okes but I'll have to stop sometime.

The flowers, especially the lilacs are coming out in the backyard and I have some in my room. I just wish it would warm up. I got a letter from Uncle Maurice and he sent me a dollar. We also went to Midale and I had a ride on one of the two horses and fell off. I scraped my back a little.

The job I just had seemed to require more muscle than I have – pushing a dust mop and wet mop in a very little time. I hate this kind of thing anyway.

Also, a lot of dusting and washing sinks, mirrors, toilets, etc. I don't seem to have the strength. I like typing but I don't know how my stamina would hold out. Anyway, maybe if I picked up speed, I would be all right. It's nice to be away from the hospital but I don't like to be a burden on the Bergquists either. I think most of the kids Barbara and Peggy and Brian are coming home for some time in the summer or fall. I should write to Sarah and the hospital but wish I had something substantial to say concerning working.

Well goodbye.

love Margaret

The tone of Margaret's letter was in dramatic contrast to those that Marion had written to her doctors. As the days and weeks passed, the harsh realities of caring for her niece became increasingly heartbreaking and Marion realized she had to send her back. In July 1969, Marion wrote: "This hurts me so much and it seems such a defeat. You can't imagine how discouraged I have gotten. Especially when she told someone she would really rather be back in your hospital."

On August 4, 1969, three months after taking Margaret into her home, Marion sent a final letter to the hospital:

You must have been amazed or amused at my naivete last March when I was so sure I could help her, so firm in my belief that she was never going back there again. My ignorance of her case and history, plus my deep belief that people are sometimes left in institutions because no one cares enough to help them, my memory of her as a bright, lively child, my feeling of love and pity for her when I saw her in Hamilton that night with her old and unhappy face, plus all the years of wondering what was happening to her.

Perhaps when Margaret has left here she will remember that there were many happy things and that I tried to show my love to her. I have tried my hardest to be loving and patient. It could be that she loves me, even though she doesn't show it.

Signed, Marion Bergquist

But Marion's naïveté could hardly be blamed. She should have been provided with medical supports, and access to a social worker and mental health clinic. A specialist could have educated her about the importance of Margaret staying on her medication, and Margaret could have gone to various day programs. Instead, the strain of trying to help her mentally ill niece was too much and Marion was forced to send Margaret back.

When Marion broke the news to Margaret, she was so devastated she began to shake, then she burst out crying.

On August 10, 1969, four months after Margaret moved in with her new family, Marion put her niece on a train and sent her back to the hospital.

CHAPTER NINE

"It Was a Numbers Thing"

1969–1971
Hamilton

A black-and-white photo taken of Margaret when she was readmitted to the hospital, which had been renamed Hamilton Psychiatric Hospital, showed the toll the years had taken. The date was August 15, 1969. This was her sixth admission in eight years. She was only twenty-five, but her withered face and scraggly hair made her appear years older. Her eyes were dark and hooded, her hair was unkempt and her skin was badly scarred. She weighed 110 pounds and was wearing a patterned dress, perhaps one her aunt had picked out for her – a reminder of kinder times. She stared into the camera with a shy, resigned smile, her head tilted slightly downward. Given how upset she'd been when her aunt had told her she was going back to

Hospital admission photo of Margaret at twenty-five. Taken at Hamilton Psychiatric Hospital. Courtesy of St. Joseph's Healthcare Hamilton.

the hospital, even a hint of a smile seemed out of place.

Under the best of circumstances, Margaret would not have been considered very attractive with her flattened nose and badly scarred skin. But the years of heavy smoking, strong medications and rough living had shaped her into a stereotypical bag lady. Her patient number remained the same: 43460. As with the other admissions, a flurry of tests were ordered: blood tests, x-rays, dental exams and a physical exam, adding to her growing medical file. The pages were filled with lab results, doctors' notes, ward admission records, treatment records listing drug orders, results from gynecological exams and pregnancy tests, as well as a monthly menstrual chart. Some notes were typed while others were scrawled in almost illegible handwriting. The different names on the reports may speak to the high staff turnover, a common problem in psychiatric hospitals.

Nurses in the hospital immediately noticed Margaret's bizarre behaviour. She paced back and forth in her room like a caged animal, then wandered into the ward where she lay on a couch and stared at the ceiling while laughing loudly. Other times, she would sit on the couch and thrash her arms and legs about as if she were fighting some invisible foe. She walked around for one whole day with all of the fingers on her right hand crossed. Another time staff caught her burning a hole into her housecoat with her cigarette. Margaret had slipped into her own world.

Mostly though, she would sleep, spending hours in bed like an exhausted traveller trying to recover from a perilous journey. Did she wonder what she'd done for her aunt to have sent her back? She'd tried to be good but the illness that had infected her mind had taken control. A form in her file dated August 20 showed how far down she had slipped – it was a consent form for several rounds of shock treatments. Margaret had signed it, although given her fragile mental state and her negative reactions to shock treatments in the past, it's questionable whether she was fully aware of what it meant, especially given the intensity and duration of the treatments this time – eight rounds to be administered from August 21 to September 11, with the number of shocks increasing with each session, from one shock on the first day to eight on the final.

According to her Electroshock Treatment Record, each session was set at two hundred voltages and the number of grand mal seizures she experienced increased each time in accordance with the number of shocks. On the final treatment date, she experienced eleven seizures. Before each session, Margaret was given sodium pentothal, a short-acting barbiturate and general anaesthetic that was used to prevent bone fractures that could occur due to the sheer force of the treatments.

Pages from Margaret's medical files. Courtesy of St. Joseph's Healthcare Hamilton.

SYLVIA PLATH WROTE in her semi-autobiographical novel *The Bell Jar* about the painful experience of undergoing shock treatments:

> I shut my eyes.
> There was a brief silence, like an indrawn breath.
> Then something bent down, and took hold of me and shook me like the end of the world. Whee-ee-ee-ee-ee, it shrilled, through an air crackling with blue light and with each flash a great jolt drubbed me till I thought my bones would break and the sap fly out of me like a split plant.
> I wondered what terrible thing it was that I had done.

Plath herself had undergone electroshock treatments so the description is said to have come from her own experience. A later round of the treatments was said to have been more positive as it was administered with a muscle relaxant and Plath only required two sessions.

FOUR DAYS AFTER Margaret's first treatment, before the full impact hit her, she wrote a cheery letter to her parents. Margaret's family was now living in the small town of Wiggins, Mississippi, where Abe had taken a job as pastor in a church.

August 25, 1969
Dear Mom and Dad,

Believe it nor not, I am back in the Ontario Hospital here in Hamilton. I came back three Sunday's ago. I boarded the train in Regina at 2 a.m. on the Friday morning and arrived in Toronto at 6.15 p.m. on the following Sunday. My nerves were kind of bad and Aunt Marion and I both felt that I should come back to Ontario. I really like it better here anyway by far.

She wrote once and said that you had sent me some money but she sent it to Jimmy. I don't mind this but I could sure use a little cash here for cigarettes, etc. Do you know that I had one shock treatment since I've been here. I don't think I'll have any more.

I was getting up one night and going to the bathroom too many times – I had drunk a lot of water previously. So I had a needle and the next day I practically fainted from it – it was so strong. Then the doctors thought I should have a treatment. With the Pentothal I felt nothing but I sure had one heck of a headache for about three days afterward. Even with aspirins it wouldn't go away.

Well, how are things going with you. Here the weather is very hot still. Don't forget to send me a little bit of money for cigarettes, I hope you can afford it.

Lots of love, Margaret

Lethargy is a common side effect of shock treatments, as are headaches, nausea, disorientation and short-term memory problems, and soon enough, Margaret began to experience all of them. She would escape to her bed during the day and sleep for hours, and at night she was often restless and agitated. Her hygiene was a recurring problem and staff wrote repeatedly about how she was often dirty and dishevelled. Margaret was put back on the antipsychotic drug Largactil, and Cogentin was added to the list to control her leg tremors, this time to be given by injection every ten days. After a few months of round-the-clock monitoring, Margaret slowly began to improve.

On November 24, 1969, her doctor wrote: "Margaret is probably at the best level anyone in this hospital has ever seen her. She is much more active than before, is performing much better than had been expected at typing and at last seems to be showing some response to encouragement about looking after her personal hygiene."

This was good news but it also meant that she would soon be considered for another move. The staff ignored her repeated pleas to stay at the hospital, as she told them she couldn't manage on her own. On January 26, 1970, Margaret was once again discharged to live in a boarding house, this one at 74 Emerald Street South, a few blocks from downtown. She asked to be enrolled in a day program at the hospital, which included a twenty-four-week refresher typing course at the adult education centre, and was told to come to the hospital every two weeks for her Moditen injection.

ANOTHER AVENUE OF community support was the Homes for Special Care (HSC), which matched psychiatric patients with families in the community. Hamilton Psychiatric Hospital staff were to monitor the homes, and operators could call the hospital if they felt a resident needed to be readmitted. Some residents of the homes could attend local community programs, like the Hope Centre program operated by the Canadian Mental Health Association Durham for residents in Bowmanville Homes for Special Care.

However, when HSC were set up, most families received little or no training in treating psychiatric patients, and for some patients it was largely a roll of the dice in terms of whether the arrangement worked out. The same problem existed in boarding homes, which were the standard place for housing former psychiatric patients. Because of the lack of follow-up, it's not known how successful the HSC homes were in helping patients.

The full impact of how the new plan impacted patients was never documented. What's known is that, for Margaret, the outcome was a disaster.

MARION CONTINUED WRITING to doctors at HPH, asking about her niece's condition. In a letter dated March 6, 1970, a doctor informed her that Margaret had shown "marked improvement" and that she had been moved into another boarding home. He added that the refresher course in shorthand and typing could even lead to her getting a job. Marion wrote back on April 4, 1970, thanking doctors for the update, but said that having lived with Margaret and witnessing first-hand how sick she was, she questioned whether Margaret still needed 24-7 care.

The doctor reassured her that Margaret was doing well and said that she was sharing a room in the boarding home with a friend she'd met at the hospital. He also stated that a social worker was working with her. Marion responded with gratitude: "I was so thankful to hear of that improvement in her condition and to know we had some part in it. For my part, I give credit to yourself, social workers, and others. Perhaps most of all to God for answering our prayers. We had prayed so continuously and earnestly. My experience with God is that He does answer prayers though it is not always as soon as we wish."

Margaret continued going to the hospital to participate in workshops and, for a while, the reports showed she was doing well. Her evaluation worksheet (May 22, 1970) had checks beside statements on punctuality, accepting direction, adapting to job changes and remembering the work routine. Her total score was twenty-nine out of forty. On July 17, she scored thirty out of forty. The higher score was earned because she was able to "learn and remember detailed work routine."

IN MAY 1970, Margaret received word from her family that they were coming for a visit. Abe and Verna had recently become grandparents – perhaps that made them think about the daughter they'd left behind. Margaret's brother Jim, who had married the year before, had recently become a dad. Their first child was a boy named Ben. The plan was for Abe and Verna, along with Margaret's youngest brother, David, to drive first to Vancouver to visit

John, who they hadn't seen in six years, then make the trip to Hamilton to see Margaret. David recalled the Vancouver visit and said they saw John for "about one minute before he [John] took his leave."

With John rejecting further contact with his parents, Abe and Verna continued on to Hamilton. David, now sixty-seven, has lived in Beijing since 1986 with his wife, Yang Zhi. He originally taught at a university in northeast China then took a job as editor with the Chinese Academy of Social Sciences before he and Zhi set up a media monitoring firm in Beijing. They sold it ten years ago and retired. David lost touch with John after he moved to China but later learned that he had worked as a mailman for a while and had struggled with spiralling bouts of depression, ending up on social assistance.

John and Margaret had been close as children, and when Margaret was ten, she pasted a small black-and-white photo of John in her autograph book. The photo shows John with tidy blond hair and a closed smile wearing a white T-shirt and shorts. His hands are tucked into his pockets. John's words to his sister showed their closeness:

Margaret (left) hugging John. Courtesy of Jacobson family.

To My Sister Margaret
I love you!
I love you!
I hope you love me to!
If you do not love me,
I'll still keep on loving you!
Your loving Brother John

AFTER ABE AND Verna left Vancouver, they drove to Regina to visit the Bergquists. Marion was disappointed when she later found out that Abe and Verna had been critical of her, as shown in a letter Marion wrote to Margaret's doctors:

At another relative's they visited near here they said Margaret had been worse after her stay with us. There were also some sharp criticisms of me by letter. So much for gratitude. Maybe she was worse, but was that an overall picture, or a passing phase? Brought about by the cessation of tranquilizers (about which I wrote you at the time), by boredom with or discouragement with no job. Perhaps coming here gave a sure sign of new hope or will to fight. You, at least, were kind enough to credit us with having been a help. I know that I expect her to be completely well some day and hope it is soon.

Marion continued writing to Margaret's doctor expressing her concerns, like the time she'd written to Margaret "two or three times but have received no reply. I know she hates to write letters, and I thought if I could get her phone number I could then phone her and learn something first hand about her."

The doctor didn't offer much help. "I think it is better that you should get the information which you want from Margaret herself . . . I would say that we feel that she is making satisfactory progress, and I would repeat that I am convinced that the efforts made by yourself and your family contributed a great deal to this happening."

MUCH LIKE THEIR visit to see John, Abe and Verna's visit to Hamilton didn't go as expected. Margaret was now twenty-six and living in a boarding home and, according to David, who was eighteen at the time, she was in rough shape. "Her fingers were yellow from roll-your-owns. About the only thing that stuck in my mind was my father asking her why couldn't she stop smoking. I remember thinking, 'this is all you have to say to Margaret after all these years?'"

David said his father's chastising attitude toward Margaret was typical of how he had treated Margaret and all of his children throughout their childhoods. He describes his father as a "demanding and authoritarian father," as well as a "perfectionist and Jesus freak," and remembers him being cold and negative. David considers himself lucky as the youngest child because by the time he was born, his father "left me mostly to my mother to raise."

After he left home, David "investigated and abandoned his spiritual roots," and today describes himself as an apatheist, someone who is apathetic about the existence of God.

HELEN KELL REMEMBERS her first meeting with Margaret well because of Margaret's shockingly ragged appearance. Kell had begun working at the HPH in the 1970s and had close contact with many patients, but she remembers Margaret the most. She had never intended to work at a psychiatric hospital and, at the time, was a stay-at-home mom with three young children. She had tagged along with a friend who wanted to apply for a job at the HPH and who'd asked Kell to come for support. On impulse, Kell's friend started telling her she should apply, too, and, on impulse, Kell agreed. "I never thought I'd get it. I was twenty-one and the only job I'd had was a hairstylist."

She had never worked in a hospital, let alone a psychiatric hospital, and so she was shocked when she got a call saying she was hired to help with the patients. "I was as green as grass," said Kell, who is now in her seventies. "I didn't even know what a patient looked like or what a psychiatric patient was and here I was."

Although it was many years ago, Kell could still remember her first day on the job. The ward was loud and chaotic, and within minutes she was seriously questioning why she had accepted the position. "One patient told me she was too scared to come out of her room and I could relate. If you woke up and found out that's where you were, oh my god, you'd want to get out."

One day she was on the receiving end of an ashtray thrown at her by a patient – it broke her nose. Some of the male patients would expose themselves to her as she walked down the hallway. "The first time it happened I was so shocked I ran the other way. Then staff told me that's the reaction they wanted, so after that I would just ignore them."

One patient was a burn victim who had been placed there because there was no room in the local nursing homes. "I always felt sorry for her because if you weren't crazy when you went in, you were crazy when you left."

On her first day, Kell was instructed to help feed breakfast to the patients.

She walked into a room and was shocked to see more than sixty patients sitting there, packed in like sardines. "I almost fell over," said Kell. "Fortunately, most of the patients were so pumped full of all these drugs they were like zombies."

A staffer taught her how to feed them assembly line–style, four at once, spooning out food to one person at a time. After breakfast, she was taken to a closet-sized room and told that was where she would cut hair. It didn't take her long to notice the sickly condition of the patients who were brought to her. When she asked what had happened to them, she was told they had just come back from a boarding home. "They were completely rundown and their hair would be filthy and matted. Sometimes it was so filled with head lice, I could see them crawling everywhere."

She remembered Margaret showing up filthy from head to toe, her head filled with lice and fingernails caked with dirt. Though she was badly in need of a cleanup, Kell said she only came when forced by a nurse. "Margaret was very ill and she was always very angry. She would lash out. You would try to be nice but she would lash out right at you. She would almost hiss at you when she was mad. She wasn't a nice person but I think it was because she was so badly hurt that she didn't want to let anyone in."

Kell recalled one time when Margaret's fingernails were more than two inches long and so filthy that they looked black. If staff hadn't forced her to come, said Kell, ". . . she would have stayed in bed all day. Her hair was always a matted mess."

During her first years there, many of the patients did assigned chores, including making beds, doing laundry and emptying bedpans. Some male patients even painted the walls while others did heavier work like carrying medical equipment. The practice was so common among higher-functioning patients that some were paid. While it was only twenty-five cents an hour, it was enough for them to buy cigarettes.

"They didn't have a lot of staff, so they would say to a patient, 'go get the pee bucket,' or the patients would go to different units that were short staffed and help them make beds," said Kell. She initially felt that the patients were being taken advantage of – until she noticed how happy they were. Kell said it was unfortunate that the practice was stopped a few years later after employees complained that patients were taking away their jobs. "The patients looked forward to it. Some didn't think it was proper but the patients liked it. They felt productive, and patients respected the staff and did as they were told."

Of all the patients Kell treated, the ones who were the most ill were those who had just returned from having electroshock treatments. She remembers how staff often lined them up on Friday mornings – "probably to rest them up for the weekend."

"When they came back from their treatments it was like there was nobody there."

As the years passed, Kell saw the impact of the revolving door on the patients and said that most would come back from their boarding home stays sicker than ever. "It was nothing to see them back again, and when they came back they were just as sick. I used to say to some of the families, I see them at their worst and then I see them when they're better, and then you know they're going to come back just like they were before or even ten times worse."

One fellow she remembered was found sleeping in a cemetery. He'd been discharged several months earlier and the hospital had lost track of him. Someone found him in the cemetery and alerted the hospital, who contacted his family and asked if they would take him in.

"The family didn't want anything to do with him anymore," said Kell, adding that this was a common response. "If you didn't have people who really cared for you, you didn't have a prayer, you really didn't."

Patients were supposed to have regular check-ins with a social worker, to make sure they were taking their medication and to see if they needed help.

But Kell, like Saunders, saw so many patients come back sick that "I often wondered if many of the [social workers] really showed up."

Some female patients would come back to the hospital with only the clothes on their backs. Some had been in jail or out on the streets. Others had sold their clothing to buy cigarettes or food. Because they had so little, Kell set up a clothing donation room and would pick up donated items from friends, family and staff. She told the female patients they could come to the room anytime and take what they needed. She also noticed how many of the women had poor hygiene habits and started classes to teach them how to wash their hair, brush their teeth and clean their fingernails.

ALTHOUGH KELL RETIRED more than ten years ago, she still thinks about the sad lack of services for patients. When she recalls all of the patients who were moved out and how poorly they fared, she is incredulous that such moves were allowed to continue. She said she tried to help them by setting up various groups, including one in which she taught life skills, such as how to take a bus or go to the laundromat – even how to read grocery store flyers. Several times, she took patients to grocery stores to teach them how to shop. She knew it was never enough.

Although Margaret would have benefited from Kell's groups, she refused to participate. All she wanted was to sit on the couch or lean against a wall and smoke. "If Margaret didn't want to do something, she wouldn't do it. You couldn't make her. There was nothing you could do. Some of the people didn't want to take a bath but you could sit and yack with them and they'd change their minds. You couldn't do that with Margaret. She was a very, very angry, sick girl."

The lasting image Kell has of Margaret is of her standing hunched over in the hallway with a bag underneath her arm. "She would prop herself up against a wall and sneer at people as they walked by. She seemed so angry all the time."

Among the hundreds of patients that Kell worked with, there were few success stories. She pointed, as an example, to a female patient who was discharged from the hospital to live on her own. It fell on Kell to find her an apartment and set things up. Kell bought her a TV, microwave, towels and soap, and when the hospital budget didn't cover everything, she asked her friends to donate gift cards to buy more. "I got her all set up with everything she needed but she had a really hard time. She'd call me at home, because I didn't live far, and she'd say, 'Helen I can't do it,' and I'd say, 'You're fine, yes, you can. You can do this.'"

The calls went on for months, on evenings and over the weekends. Each time Kell would try and boost the woman with encouraging words. Sometimes, on weekends and on her days off, she would drive over to the woman's apartment to check on her and help in any way she could. After several months, the phone calls started coming less frequently and the woman started to sound more relaxed. Kell breathed a sigh of relief.

Then the woman met a fellow who lived in the same building. He was an alcoholic.

"He made her feel important and she fell for it," said Kell, shaking her head in frustration. "He started getting her to buy his alcohol for him then, before you know it, they were drinking together."

Then the woman went off her medication. "Once she went off her meds, she lost her apartment and everything fell apart."

A month later, the woman had to be readmitted to the HPH. She was only in the apartment for five months, but to Kell, it "felt like an eternity" because of all the work. A few months after being in the HPH, the woman was discharged into a boarding home where there were more supports. As far as Kell knows, the woman still lives there today.

"Honest to God, I worked so hard for that girl. It broke my heart to see it all fall apart," said Kell.

BECAUSE KELL'S JOB took her inside boarding homes, she understood Margaret's anger. She saw the horrific conditions and knew that many operators, because they were paid per resident, would try and squeeze in as many people as possible.

"I mean, some of those boarding homes were disgusting," said Kell, shaking her head. "There was one on East Avenue, when you walked in, they had the parlour, and eight beds in a line. They had a toilet under the stairs and a young girl cooking the meals and cats running around. The woman who was running it worked as a nurse and worked all night and slept all day and had this eighteen-year-old girl looking after all these people."

Kell worked at the HPH for thirty-nine years and, having seen the appalling conditions inside many boarding homes, wasn't surprised when patients would return to the hospital looking filthy and malnourished.

"It was awful how they treated them. They'd feed them in the morning and send them out with a peanut butter sandwich and tell them not to come back until five o'clock, so they wandered the streets all day. They ended up down at Jackson Square [a major downtown mall in Hamilton] and you'd see them down there begging all day."

She remembered one operator who served residents cold cereal and water for breakfast, and day-old food for dinner. Because they would squeeze in as many beds as possible, the patients had zero privacy.

"They were supposed to have social workers come and check on them but I often wondered if they really showed up."

Kell recalled only one or two patients who did well after leaving the hospital, while most were like Margaret, caught up in the never-ending revolving door of being moved out, coming back in sick, then being moved out again. Over time, they would inevitably get sicker and sicker. "It was a numbers thing. Get them in, get them out, get them in, get them out."

DURING HER MANY years at the hospital, Kell said her favourite job was sorting through the archives. Though her office was in a dungeon-like basement, it got her away from the chaos on the wards. Her job was to sort through the suitcases that patients brought with them when they were admitted and take notes of what was inside. After she'd written everything down, she was told to throw out the contents and the suitcases. It frustrated her because many of them contained personal letters.

"It was like everything was discarded there without much notice, whether it was the suitcases or the patients," said Kell.

IN AUGUST 1970, Scott (a pseudonym) came into Margaret's life. He was her new hospital social worker, and his approach to Margaret's care would have a major impact on her health, both in the short and long term. A social worker is an important part of a psychiatric patient's health care team as they're expected to keep up-to-date notes on the patient's condition and determine their needs. They're a critical component of a patient's overall care as the notes are shared with doctors and nurses.

While living in her boarding home Margaret was beginning to experience problems. According to the landlady where she was living, Margaret was sleeping in her clothes, constantly borrowing money from people and had stolen a fifty-seven-cent ring from Kresge's, a downtown department store.

In Scott's first report dated August 31, 1970, he described the litany of problems Margaret was having, including that her workshop teacher had said Margaret had been extremely "restless" lately and had wanted to leave. She had persuaded her against it.

Scott met with Margaret to get to the bottom of things, and she told him that she didn't like having to come all the way up to the hospital to work and that she would prefer to work at the Amity or March of Dimes downtown. She also requested a medication change and said that the present one wasn't helping her. When Scott questioned her about sleeping in her clothes, Margaret told him she didn't have enough money to buy a dressing gown. Scott wrote in his files that it was "probably because she was little lazy." As for the theft of the ring, Scott wrote: "Margaret said that she had impulsively stolen the ring from Kresge's, that she was looking at them on the counter, touching them, and suddenly realized she had left the store with the cheap ring in her possession. She felt that she would not do such a thing again and that she would definitely not plan ahead to steal something."

Margaret told Scott many of the problems she was having were due to her lack of money. A few times she'd been forced to move out of her boarding home and into a cheaper one as she couldn't afford the rent. She was likely on some form of welfare assistance, although it's not known how much she would have received. Normally, if a person on assistance wasn't able to make ends meet, the social worker could help either by setting up a trusteeship to assist them in managing their money or teach them ways to budget.

A few months after her first meeting with Scott, Margaret was again forced to move into a cheaper boarding home, this one on Stinson Street, a few blocks away. The rent was eight dollars a week. Even at this low amount, Margaret was worried that she wouldn't have enough money and told Scott that with the winter coming, she was scared the boarding home operator might kick her out during the day, as some operators had done in the past.

Instead of helping her by finding more supports, Scott chastised her for being irresponsible with her money. It would be the first of many conflicts that reflected Scott's attitude toward Margaret.

CHAPTER TEN

"Why Do You Think God Wants to Punish You?"

1971
Hamilton

Margaret missed her family. It had been nine months since her parents had visited. While it hadn't been pleasant, they were still her family and were all she had. She told a friend she was seriously considering flying to Mississippi to see them, and on February 21, 1971, she wrote a heartfelt letter to her parents asking if she could come down.

> Dear Mom and Dad,
>
> How are you? This is Sunday night and I have just read about 11 chapters in Luke. I went over to the Hancocks for dinner and they said that you had phoned Mom about my going down to your place. I don't know what exactly you said but I must tell you that if I go to the states I will not be able to collect welfare from Hamilton for it is only while you are a resident of Hamilton. My nerves have been so bad lately and I can't seem to get a hold of myself.
>
> I asked the doctors about this but he (to me) brushed it off as a light thing and would not change my medication. I really feel as if I'm in a rut going up to that hospital every day with no job to look forward to or work. Maybe there is more chance of work where you are.
>
> I am getting my welfare check on the 26th of this month which is this coming Friday. I am payed [*sic*] up till the 28th. What to do? Could you

either write or telegram whether you feel I should come or not, before the 26th or the 28th. My welfare money will almost cover my trip if I go by plane.

It is $98.00. Umm, how do you think I shall make out by plane? I hope I don't have any trouble getting across the border. I'd like to come at the end of this month. I hate the waiting.

If I get a job things will be brighter. How are you fixed for a job Mom? There are some thousands out of work here in Hamilton and my future seems so black at the moment.

I have a very bad time keeping still. I seem to wiggle all the time – such unrest!

Hoping to hear from you as soon as possible.

Love, Margaret.

Any visits home would have to wait, however. Before Margaret's letter would have arrived at her parent's home, her father wrote this letter to her:

February 23, 1971

Dearest Margaret,

I hope these few lines find you successfully weathering the snow and cold of another Canadian winter. The months of February and March and April can be trying. So often there is that promise of spring in the air, only to be submerged in a fresh blanket of snow or blown away in some icy gale.

Maurice and Alice have been with us over two Sundays. They just left a few hours ago and are now on their way for a visit with Jim, Barbara and Ben there in Springfield. Mom had thought some of taking advantage of a free ride, but thinking about getting back, and especially leaving me alone to conduct next Sunday's meetings, she decided against going. I appreciate her thoughtfulness.

We had hoped that it might be possible for you to come down and spend some time here. However, Margaret, it seems that the time is not "ripe" just yet. When you come, dear, we want to be able to introduce you to our people as True Christian.

Really, we do not know why you do not come back to the Lord, Margaret. He is so wonderful, so gracious, so loving. It is the devil that has you bound and has made you a slave to your lust and to your own will. God has not given to us the spirit of an unsound mind.

As Paul says in Timothy 1:7, "For God hath not given us the spirit of fear, but of power and of love, and of a sound mind."

As long as you are not willing to surrender yourself to Him, you will continue to be fooled and deceived. I know you love to read your Bible. But just reading it is not enough. "Be ye doers of the word, and not hearers only deceiving your own selves." says James (Jas. 1:22)

Margaret, why don't you ask your pastor and the people at the church where the Hancock's attend to pray with you and for you.

"Why should ye be stricken any more? Ye will revolt more and more: the whole head is sick and the whole heart faint . . ." (Isaiah 1:5) "Wash you, make you clean, put away the evil of your doings from before mine eyes; cease to do evil: learn to do well . . . if ye be willing and obedient ye shall eat the good of the land: but if ye refuse and rebel ye shall be devoured . . ."

"Though your sins be as scarlet they shall be as white as snow; though they be red like crimson, they shall be as well." (Read 1. 1:16 . . .)

God has raised up some wonderful friends for you Margaret. I'm sure George and Doris Hancock would want what is best for you. Does it seem to you that God has robbed them of any worthwhile thing in Life? Why do you think God wants to punish you, to make you miserable or to hinder you in any way?

The Lord can give you victory over lust, over sex, over your carnal appetites. It is unwillingness to be delivered from the bondage of Satan that is the trouble. God waits to save you.

We love you Margaret. We want you to come down and visit. You could be such a help to people. If you came here, even for a few weeks, you could be such a help. But not if you come as a sinner.

You're still our daughter, we still love you. But, oh how we long to see you living with the joy of the Lord in you. We are always praying for this.

Love, Dad

Margaret had been a dutiful daughter. As a child, she had tried her best to please her father by being a good student, teaching Sunday school class and playing piano in church. She was deeply invested in winning Abe's approval, and because he had always been so disapproving of her, she likely longed for his love and acceptance. There is no way of knowing how Margaret reacted to being described as a sinner and accused of taking the scarlet road, but it must have hurt her on some level. How must she have felt to read her father's words – that he felt so ashamed of her that he didn't want to introduce her to their "people"? In the days following receipt of his letter, there was a marked improvement in Margaret's behaviour. Perhaps she was trying to live up to his expectations. Whatever the reason, both her attendance in the typing program and the quality of her work improved. In an evaluation report from a few days after Abe's letter would have arrived, staff wrote: "Margaret is progressing very well. She is keen and applies herself very well."

ON MARCH 12, she had one of her highest ever work performance scores – thirty-five out of forty; however, things soon began to slide, and a report on her clinical record dated April 15, 1971, noted that her attendance was faltering and her hygiene habits had become so poor that one staffer noted she smelled like she hadn't bathed for a week. Staff were "quite concerned about Margaret's appearance, she appears to only be spending money for cigarettes and soft drinks and not paying any attention to adequate food nourishment for herself."

Staff were fed up with her uncleanliness and tardiness, and warned her that she would be dismissed from the program if she didn't shape up. Margaret tried to defend herself, saying, according to Scott, "I do need clothes, I have been spending quite a bit of money on clothes and actually I have never really felt that hungry."

It's possible her appetite was suppressed due to some of the medications she was on – a common side effect. As to why her hair had been dishevelled, Margaret told Scott, "I just walked over from the candy shop and the wind was blowing quite strongly."

But it was true that Margaret wasn't looking after herself. Her appearance and how much she cared about herself had fallen a long way from when she was a teen and liked to dress up in pretty dresses and a matching hat. But as it turned out, there was a significant reason as to why Margaret was slipping.

According to her files, she had failed to show up at the hospital for her Moditen (antipsychotic medication) injections, and without her medication, she was in free fall. Although staying on her medication was critical to her mental and physical well-being, she told Scott she had decided to take it only when she felt it was necessary.

It was no surprise then that her behaviour failed to improve, however staff likely weren't informed of this. On April 21, 1971, she was dismissed from the hospital's typing program. According to her files, she even lost interest in seeing her family: "She does not express any desire now, as she did a few weeks ago, to return home to her parents."

Lack of money once again forced Margaret to move. Her poor financial situation may also have factored into why she decided to visit the hospital for the free hot lunch program. She still wasn't taking her medication consistently and likely wasn't in good shape. Scott chastised her when he found out she'd had a meal at the hospital but hadn't gone to the typing program, as that was a condition – that she attend the program in order to have a meal.

Margaret told Scott she didn't have enough money to buy food and that she was worried about getting through the rest of the month. His response was to tell her that she needed to start budgeting properly. There was still no suggestion of putting her on a budgeting program. On April 28, things took a turn for the worse when the welfare office discovered that Margaret was living with "another patient" named Ted who was also on welfare.

Margaret had met Ted at the Wesley drop-in shelter, and when she mentioned her lack of money, he'd told her she could move in with him and they'd share the rent. It seemed like the perfect solution to Margaret's money shortfall. What she didn't know was that the province's social assistance rules dictated that a woman who was collecting social assistance could not live common law with a man who was also on social assistance. Known as the "spouse-in-the-house" rule, several years later it was ruled to be discriminatory against women and was thrown out.

It's not known who told the welfare department about the living arrangement, but two staff from the welfare office, accompanied by Scott, promptly showed up at Ted's door and told Margaret she either had to move out or go off welfare. If she went off welfare, she would have to rely on Ted; if she moved out, she would be homeless. Margaret tried to explain that she'd been forced to move in with Ted because her landlord had raised her rent; however, the welfare worker told her she should have just looked for a cheaper room. Margaret tried to explain that she had no money and had run out of bus tickets.

Scott wrote: "These were the same reasons she gave for her failing to come up to the hospital for more Moditen therapy this past week. It appeared that Margaret was finding excuses for everything she had not been doing to better herself."

IT WAS NO secret that affordable housing was difficult to find in Hamilton. It had become a chronic problem in cities across the country. Margaret's challenges in finding a place she could afford had been well documented – between February 1970 and May 1971, she had lived in three different boarding homes and had made it known to Scott that she didn't have enough money to get by. Given her diminished mental state, combined with the severe shortage of affordable housing and low amount she received on social assistance, it should have been no surprise to Scott that she was struggling.

None of that appeared to matter. Scott threatened to cut off her welfare unless she moved out immediately and so Margaret had no choice but to leave. Not that living with Ted had been ideal as it later came out that he had been physically abusive toward her. But like many homeless women in desperate situations, Margaret had put up with it in order to have a roof over her head. In forcing her to move out, Margaret was now officially homeless.

She turned to Scott for help. He wrote in his report, "Several times during the interview Margaret mentioned that she wished to come into the hospital until things get settled, not to be permanently admitted, but just come in until things were better and she could find herself a room."

Instead of offering to find housing, Scott sent her off with a couple of bus tickets. "It is the feeling of this writer and the treatment team that admitting Margaret at this point would not be advisable and would really only be a detriment to her being able to function as a member of the community. We believe Margaret is capable of finding a room, of budgeting her money and of attempting to find employment for herself."

Margaret's pattern – spiralling downward once she left the hospital – had been well documented. Hospital life provided the more intensive supports that she needed. Without those supports, the outcome for her was predictable. Scott's decision to forbid her from being readmitted would have serious long-term consequences on both her health and her life.

There were no notes in Scott's files on Margaret's whereabouts over the next month. There were no shelters in Hamilton for homeless women at the time and domestic violence shelters rarely had any empty beds. Because Margaret was in such a desperate situation, she may well have engaged in survival sex to find shelter, or it's possible she went back to Ted. Numerous studies show that it's the norm for homeless women to feel pressured to perform sexual favours in exchange for shelter. In one study, respondents said landlords had propositioned and even stalked them, then forced them to engage in unwanted sex and told them they would be kicked out if they didn't comply.

At the end of May, the welfare office notified Scott that they hadn't heard back from Margaret and were cutting off her social assistance. There is no note from Scott telling them to do otherwise. With no housing and her only means of financial support now cut off, Margaret did something that could only be described as desperate. On May 28, 1971, she left Hamilton and made her way to Winnipeg. She later told police that a stranger had asked her if she wanted to hitchhike there with him, saying he "needed some company." Perhaps Margaret thought there might be more supports in Winnipeg as she hadn't had much help in Hamilton. Or maybe she was on the run from Ted.

Whatever the situation, a few days later she was found wandering the streets of Winnipeg with only the clothes on her back. When police picked her up, she had no suitcase or money. She was taken to a women's shelter. An intake worker sent a note to the HPH: "She is destitute at present, has brought no personal belongings with her and does not wish to return to Hamilton."

Although Margaret pleaded with them not to send her back and city staff who were dealing with her in Winnipeg said they were willing to keep her, the decision was made. A week later, on May 28, she was put on a bus, likely by the police, and sent back to Hamilton. When she arrived, police in Hamilton picked her up at the station and took her to a domestic violence shelter.

When shelter staff asked her why she'd gone to Winnipeg, Margaret answered in her usual casual way: "I just wanted to travel around."

CHAPTER ELEVEN
A Child Is Born

It was obvious to the worker how proud your birth mother was of you.
— Children's Aid Society adoption report

1971–1972
Hamilton

Margaret was twenty-seven and still struggling to find affordable shelter. Her stays at domestic violence shelters were being cut back due to bed shortages. Not that they were appropriate places for a homeless woman with a severe mental illness who had stopped taking her medication.

On the evening of June 13, Margaret met Scott on a downtown street. It's not clear why they met at night and not at the hospital. Scott knew that Margaret had missed her last two Moditen injections, which meant she hadn't been on any medication for a month and was likely unstable. Still, Scott wrote in his files that Margaret showed "no signs of unusual psychiatric behaviour." There were no notes about him offering her any help. Instead, he told Margaret to notify him when she got a new address.

Less than two weeks later, on June 23, Margaret showed up at the hospital in, as Scott wrote in the files, a "rather dishevelled condition." She told Scott she'd been forced to leave her rented room on Bay Street South because someone had stolen seventy dollars of her one hundred-dollar welfare allowance and she couldn't afford the rent. Staff at the domestic violence shelter had recommended she contact the Hilltop Tourist Home, which rented out rooms. When she told Scott about the possible room rental, rather than offering to make a call to them, he suggested she take the bus there to check it out. He offered Margaret one favour – she could use the shower at the hospital, but she would have to leave right after. Scott wrote: "Margaret refused and in an abrupt angry manner left the [hospital]. She does not appear to be acting or thinking realistically about her situation."

A few hours later, Scott received a call from the Hilltop saying Margaret had shown up there and requested a room, but because she didn't have any funds, they wouldn't allow her to stay. Scott should have known how inadequate the housing situation was but wrote with a sense of surprise, "Definite lack of community resources in Hamilton for emergency boarding of females – any age!"

Later that evening, the Hilltop contacted Scott and told him they would agree to take Margaret in for the night if the welfare office was contacted in the morning. Scott wrote, "Possibility of Margaret being picked up by the police and charged with vagrancy, and question of whether she should be admitted on a temporary basis are two factors for consideration at this point. Margaret becomes very dependent upon hospitalization and shows no motivation to leave if admitted."

There is an alarming absence of notes over the next several days, which suggests that Margaret was left on her own. Things obviously didn't work out at the Hilltop because, one week later, she showed up at the hospital's downtown office and told staff she'd been forced to move back in with Ted, having nowhere else to go. She also reported that Ted had taken her welfare money. Given Ted's aggressive behaviour toward Margaret in the past, this was entirely possible. Scott chose to see things differently: "The writer feels that Margaret is over-exaggerating her situation."

In the same notes, Scott wrote, "When confronted by writer [Scott] with the question of what she needed, she was unable to answer. The writer suggested, as he has done several times in the past, that to change her living situation she must make a decision to leave or to stay. She will have the resources to do so."

WITH NO REMAINING supports, Margaret was officially homeless. Two days after she met with Scott downtown, Margaret went to the hospital to see him again and told him she had nowhere to go. Scott called a women's shelter and found her a bed for one night. What happened to Margaret after that is a mystery.

Over the next three weeks, there were no notes from Scott on where she was living. There were also no notes on what, if anything, he did to help her, so it appears Margaret was left to fend for herself. Aunt Marion still hadn't given up on her niece, however. During this time, she wrote a touching letter to Margaret's doctor, expressing concern that she hadn't heard from her since November. She told the doctor she had sent three letters and a Christmas parcel to the boarding home where Margaret was supposed to be living and hadn't received any replies. "No matter what, I will never stop loving her or praying for her."

She ended the letter with a request: "If she is back in hospital might it be possible for you to ask her to write me."

Margaret's doctor wrote back with an update and explained about Margaret going to Winnipeg. "I am sorry to report that things are not going at all well at present." The doctor also told her they'd made many efforts to get Margaret involved with the hospital but that she had resisted. "Unfortunately, she has not agreed to do this. She was last seen by Scott on June 23 at which time she was short of money and had no permanent address."

DESPITE THE LACK of assistance and almost insurmountable obstacles, Margaret kept going, perhaps engaging in survival sex or sleeping on the streets, until she eventually found herself a room. On July 22, one month after returning from Winnipeg, Margaret returned to the hospital to inform

Scott that she had found a room in a boarding house and was back on welfare. Scott noted that she was clean and presentable, and allowed her to be readmitted to the hospital's therapy workshop on a typing contract. "Margaret's grooming and physical appearance have improved tremendously over the past week," he noted in his files.

It's not clear how Margaret pulled it off with so many obstacles against her, but for the first time in a long time things were going well. She had a roof over her head, a steady income and was back in the typing workshop. At the end of Scott's report, he wrote that Margaret "has expressed a concern about possibly being pregnant. The appropriate tests will be made."

On July 23, 1971, came the life-altering news. Margaret was indeed pregnant. Another test was administered on July 27 to make sure – it, too, came back positive. No one was surprised. One doctor wrote that Margaret had a "history of sexual relations with several men over the past few months, in fact, this has been going on for a much longer time." Based on the March due date, conception would have occurred sometime in early June, which is when Margaret had taken the desperate trip to Winnipeg – something she'd done after Scott had failed to help her find housing. She was also with Ted around that time, again because she had nowhere else to go.

Hospital staff talked to her about the possibility of terminating the pregnancy, but she wouldn't hear of it. In her mind, Margaret saw her pregnancy as being only good news and was overjoyed. Perhaps it was the fulfillment of a childhood dream, or maybe for the first time in her life she felt a sense of purpose. She was adamant about keeping the baby and told doctors she was capable of caring for it. On July 27, her doctor wrote:

> She obviously has not devoted much thought to the matter and is generally rather flippant and giggly about it . . . she feels that she would like to have a child but talks of a child as a new toy. She would appear to regard being pregnant as something of an increase in status. She comments that she has never had much luck with men. She is 27 years old, there is little likelihood of her meeting and marrying a respectable man with a good

income, and that perhaps she should make the best of the situation and realize her ambition of having a child, as she may not be able to do so in the future.

How many babies are born to homeless women every year? A 1998 study was conducted on this issue as part of a collaborative effort by Young Parents No Fixed Address (YPNFA), a network of agencies serving under-housed women. The group compiled data from seventeen agencies they work with and found that the number of babies born in Toronto to under-housed mothers was between 275 and 315 for each year from 2012 to 2014.

Young Parents No Fixed Address was formed in 1997 to examine the increasing numbers of young pregnant women who were being seen by agencies that dealt with homeless youth. The issue gained urgency following the infant death of Jordan Heikamp, born to a nineteen-year-old homeless woman in Toronto. The five-week-old baby starved to death while his teen-age mother, Renee Heikamp, was living in a women's shelter.

Other statistics show that some three hundred homeless women give birth in Toronto each year. Most women don't keep their babies and some are taken by child protection services.

Margaret was in need of prenatal care. She needed stable housing, nutritious food, vitamins and medical care for both her and her unborn baby. Instead of allowing her to be readmitted to the hospital where this would have been guaranteed, Margaret was sent back to her boarding home. Two weeks later, she showed up at a crisis intervention centre and told them her landlord had ordered her to move out. Although she had found another place on Margaret Street for fifteen dollars a week, she was stone broke and didn't have the money for it. The welfare office approved a fifteen-dollar advance but told her the money would have to be deducted from her next cheque, which would arrive in six days. There were no follow-up notes on how things worked out, but a few months later, Margaret reported to Scott that she was living at yet another address.

Ten days later, Margaret announced she was quitting her job at the hospital employment agency because "her pregnancy was interfering with her work." She was offered prenatal care at the hospital but there are no notes on whether she made it to any of the appointments. On Friday, November 19, Margaret told Scott she was "short on funds and couldn't make ends meet." Scott told her it was "very inappropriate" for her to come on a Friday afternoon when "arrangements with the Public Welfare would be difficult." Scott wrote, "She could not answer writer's [Scott's] questions as to why she had left it until today . . . she confessed herself that she had difficulty budgeting her domestic and financial responsibilities."

Scott told her to come back on Tuesday, four days later; however, there were no notes showing that she returned. Four days is a long time to wait when you're pregnant, homeless and broke.

MARGARET SHOWED UP at the hospital again two days before Christmas. She was six and a half months pregnant and homeless. "Again, the same problems presented itself with Miss Jacobson's mismanagement of funds and continual moving from lodging to lodging," Scott wrote in his notes.

This time, perhaps because it was close to Christmas, Scott agreed to call a landlord on Margaret's behalf who said he had a room available. The landlord wanted to meet with Margaret first before deciding if she could stay. Her welfare cheque wouldn't be arriving for at least another week so Margaret wouldn't have been able to pay her rent, and because many landlords won't commit to giving someone a room until their cheque comes in, Margaret's housing situation remained extremely precarious.

There were no notes on what happened next – whether the landlord agreed to rent the room to Margaret. Scott wrapped up his report with his familiar sentiment: "Writer feels that she is at this time manipulating the system to seek hospital admission again."

Scott was right. Margaret *was* hoping to get a bed in the hospital. And for good reason – she needed a place to stay. To say she was "manipulating the system" to get readmitted was an odd way to look at a situation that involved a mentally ill pregnant woman who was homeless in the middle of winter. It was clear to many people, even Margaret, that she needed much more care than she was receiving, and several doctors had said that the hospital was the only place where she could get that help. In short, there were more than enough reasons to admit her.

DESPITE THE CHAOS in her life, on March 5, 1972, Margaret gave birth to a healthy baby boy weighing seven pounds, seven ounces. She named him Jeffrey. When I spoke to her at the Wesley on that cold winter night in 1993, she told me Jeffrey had been taken away from her immediately after birth by the Children's Aid Society (CAS) of Hamilton and put up for adoption. The CAS adoption report, which was later given to her son, told a far different story. Her medical files from the psychiatric hospital should have been accessible to the CAS, but even without them, one look at Margaret would have revealed how seriously ill she was. By this point she was so worn down it was obvious to anyone that she was homeless.

Her medical files noted that her mental state had deteriorated to the point where she had been catatonic, that she had been so ill she would burn cigarette holes in her clothing and leave a trail of menstrual blood behind her when she walked. Instead, the CAS report described Margaret as a "single woman who enjoys playing the piano, listening to records, reading and playing cards," and that Margaret's parents were Protestant and Pennsylvania Dutch.

It stated that Margaret's mother was five feet five inches tall, quiet and hard-working, and had been employed as a cashier. The description of Abe was closer to the truth and stated that he was six feet one inch tall, of Swedish descent, with a large frame, dark hair and blue eyes. Rather than telling the real story, that the family had moved to the US and left Margaret behind, the CAS report stated that Margaret "had no contact" with her family and that she hadn't informed them of her pregnancy. The picture painted of Margaret was one of a healthy, stable woman who came from a traditional family.

In Scott's notes, he wrote that while Margaret was in the hospital, she was "smoking excessively and not caring very much for her personal hygiene." In contrast, the CAS report stated, "Following your birth, she named you Jeffrey and fed you whilst you were in hospital."

Margaret stayed in the hospital with her son for the next eight days. Although she had previously been adamant about keeping him, she abruptly changed her mind after an unexpected visit from her mother, who had likely learned of the pregnancy through Scott. Verna was said to have been shocked at the news and, according to the CAS report, had considered taking the baby to the States where a member of her family might adopt him. After much discussion with Abe, however, "she decided with great reluctance that since a family had already been found for you, that the plan in place should go ahead."

On March 13, Margaret signed the forms to give up her son, who was then placed in a foster home while awaiting his new family. There is one paragraph in the five-page CAS report that may well have reflected the truth: "It was obvious to the worker how proud your birth mother was of you and how much she enjoyed caring for you. However, she decided that the best plan was to place you for adoption, as she felt she would be unable to care for you once she left the hospital. The worker was supportive of her and her decision."

On the same day that baby Jeffrey left the hospital with his foster family, Margaret's files indicated that she was discharged. It had only been eight days since she'd given birth and her hormones would have been fluctuating wildly. Her breasts were likely engorged since she hadn't breastfed him, which can be extremely painful, and in her rundown state she was at high risk for postpartum depression.

IT HAD BEEN eleven years since Margaret first entered the psychiatric hospital system. In that time, her mental and physical health had seriously deteriorated. Her placements in boarding homes had been nothing short of disastrous and each time she had come back severely malnourished, covered in bruises and with filthy fingernails and head lice. Doctors who had treated her and seen the broken-down woman before them had written in their reports that she should never again be released. All of those warnings and notes had been overlooked.

It's highly questionable as to whether Margaret had the capacity to understand what was happening to her – without medication, people with schizophrenia can hear voices and feel overwhelmed, guilt-ridden and paranoid. It's not clear where she went after leaving the hospital, but the next day, on March 14, she met with Scott. He noted that she was late for her meeting, that she was filthy and smelled as if she hadn't bathed for a couple of days, and that her legs were twitching and shaking. These were all signs of her poor mental and physical health. It's not clear if she'd had somewhere to live at this time as such details weren't included in Scott's report.

In his two-and-a-half-page report, which read like a discharge summary, Scott wrote that Margaret had lived in numerous rooming houses since she was last at the HPH in February 1970; that she had left the hospital's rehabilitation program because she felt she wasn't getting anything out of it; that she had gone from the hospital to boarding homes several times (including living in four different homes in one three-month period); and that she had "abused" the welfare system many times and "squandered" her money on cigarettes and junk food, like potato chips and soft drinks, so often that her welfare cheques were now being sent directly to her landlord. Scott also noted her "promiscuous behaviour," writing that she had mostly male friends and liked to sleep most of the day.

According to Scott, Margaret's "main problem" was her "manipulative attempt" to be readmitted to the hospital. Why it wasn't obvious to him that Margaret may have been encountering these problems because she was mentally ill is more than a little confusing. Then, in a bizarre twist, Scott concluded his report with the comment that "Margaret wanted someone to be very domineering and over protective of her."

Scott ended with the statement that Margaret needed to "present as a clean and tidy person when she comes to the next interview." That he was more concerned about her cleanliness than her health and housing situation was perplexing. His only offer of help was to schedule a follow-up meeting one week later.

BABY JEFFREY APPEARED to be doing well, according to the CAS report, and his foster parents reported that he was feeding and sleeping well. They described him as a "very good baby." He was also gaining weight, and one month after leaving the hospital he weighed in at eight pounds, eleven ounces. According to the CAS report, which was written for Jeffrey: "You were said to be a contented and alert baby who smiled and was vocalizing. You were already sleeping through the night."

One month later, a Hamilton couple adopted Margaret's son, and on April 27, the adoption was finalized. Coincidentally, the couple already had an adopted son named Jeffery, so they renamed their new son Jeremy. According to the CAS report, "They were delighted and took you home the same day."

Although Jeffrey had been healthy at the time of adoption, he developed a severe health problem that caused him to chronically regurgitate his formula. He was eventually diagnosed with pyloric stenosis, a form of gastric outlet obstruction or blockage from the stomach to the intestines. By September, the problem had cleared up. According to the CAS report: "You were sleeping through the night and were an easy baby to care for. The worker described you as a lovely baby, a big boy who was enjoying time in your jolly jumper. She stated that you had a large face and were very fair in colouring. She also commented that the adoptive parents loved you very much."

The last sentence in the CAS report read "On November 13, 1972 your final adoption order was signed."

Many years later, Jeffrey/Jeremy would meet his birth mother, but not in the way either he or Margaret had hoped.

CHAPTER TWELVE
"Seriously Deteriorated"

1972–1983
Hamilton

D id Margaret ever wonder what she had done to deserve such a difficult life? Or did she still believe, as her father had told her, that this was her punishment for taking the "scarlet road"? Did she miss the child that had grown inside of her? There wouldn't have been time for Margaret to ponder such questions as she was again thrust into survival mode. With her body still recovering from the pregnancy and childbirth, now,

Margaret (right) at the Good Shepherd Centre drop-in. Courtesy of Bill MacKinnon.

more than any other time, she needed stable surroundings where she could regain her health and come to terms with the emotional loss of her child. Instead, she ended up in another seedy boarding home, living a crushing life that would pull her down again.

Dr. David Dawson was chief psychiatrist at the HPH from 1985 to 1995 and, while he didn't know her, he treated many patients like Margaret who'd had early onset mental illness and exhibited similar behaviours. In his experience, patients often became stuck at the age they were when their mental illness first surfaced and often failed to progress past that stage, like a form of arrested development. That would explain why Margaret related to her parents the way she did and why she still exhibited such childlike, approval-seeking behaviours toward them, said Dr. Dawson.

"[Her childhood] was the period where she learned her roles and how to engage in the world so she kept that with respect to how she interacted with her parents. She didn't go through a period of sorting that out by either rebelling or anything else," said Dr. Dawson.

This might also explain why Margaret had so much difficulty with simple tasks. According to Dr. Dawson, she would have had the mental capacity of someone much younger. Margaret's fifteen-year-old self was someone who liked to draw pretty prom dresses, whiten her teeth with baking soda and read her favourite mysteries. She had no capacity for finding housing or budgeting her funds.

"The illness came before she had any adult skills so she didn't learn about responsibility or didn't develop any actual skills, like social skills or vocational skills. She didn't have any of those," said Dr. Dawson.

NOT SURPRISINGLY, THINGS didn't work out in the boarding home. Whatever the reason, Margaret had moved into another home, which proved to be even worse. On April 18, 1972, six weeks after giving birth, she was found in a dilapidated home with a group of men described by police in her medical files as "five drunks." She was so ill that she had to be rushed by ambulance to St. Joseph's Hospital's emergency ward where doctors admitted her on an Involuntary status. That meant she couldn't leave the hospital on her own accord because she was deemed to be at high risk of serious physical impairment.

On the hospital form, she was described as "very neglected, shockingly poor hygiene, laceration over right wrist, sutured, inflamed, disoriented and considerable weight loss."

Margaret's legs were twitching so badly that her whole body shook.

According to one doctor, "It was felt that the level of her living and dignity were far below what could be considered reasonable." Her mental state had also taken such a sharp downward turn that the doctor described her as being almost catatonic: "Ignores most questions. Sounds very angry when she does speak." The concern about Margaret's condition was so great that Verna even flew up from Mississippi to see her. There are no notes on how things went.

That it had taken only six weeks for Margaret to fall into this state speaks to the horrific conditions she must have been living in. The hospital contacted Scott, who was still listed as her social worker. Although he was accustomed to seeing Margaret looking sick and dishevelled, even he was taken aback and described her in his notes as being in a "shockingly poor" state, adding that her health had "seriously deteriorated since the birth of her illegitimate child."

During the period that Scott had overseen Margaret, her health had deteriorated faster than at any other time in her life. She had been homeless several times, become pregnant, fled to Winnipeg, been in and out of several boarding homes, and now this. Doctors, nurses and medical staff had relied on Scott's notes to determine what kind of care she needed, and during that time she'd received very little. This time, however, it hadn't been up to Scott to decide whether she would be admitted and after being treated at St. Joseph's, Margaret was sent back to the HPH. She was admitted to ward H-1. Her patient number was the same: 43460.

As with all her past readmissions, a flurry of tests and treatment orders were drawn up to get her back on her medications: Moditen injections; the antipsychotic Largactil; Cogentin and Disipal, a muscle relaxant to control her tremors; Valium three times a day for anxiety; and an antibiotic, possibly for her acne. She was also given chloral hydrate to help her sleep and was placed on birth control to prevent further pregnancies.

Margaret's face was now deeply lined and disfigured with acne scars. Her hair was tangled and filthy and her legs jerked constantly. She was so severely withdrawn it was like she was in a fog. It would take several weeks before she started to come around. She signed herself up for the hospital's work program but a few days later asked if she could stop going as her nerves were too "bad."

Even the simple act of typing had become too much.

ADMITTING SOMEONE TO a psychiatric hospital against their will isn't always easy. The current process, which has changed little since Margaret was hospitalized, starts with prescribing a Form 1 – an application for a psychiatric assessment – which allows for seven days between when a doctor signs the form and when the person is taken to the hospital. Once there, a doctor can delay the patient for more than seventy-two hours, then the person must either be released, admitted as a voluntary patient or continue being held as an involuntary patient with a certificate of involuntary admission or a Form 3.

A Form 3 allows a patient to be held for another two weeks, and after that, the doctor must complete a Certificate of Renewal or Form 4, which allows the hospital to keep a patient on involuntary admission when the Form 3 expires. Throughout this entire process, however, patients can have access to a review board where they can ask to have the certificate removed. Once a request is made, an independent tribunal comprised of three people is set up: a lawyer, a psychiatrist and a layperson with relevant qualifications. Patients can either represent themselves or have someone state their case. The person who has been involuntarily committed also has the right to appeal to the hospital manager to be discharged.

Mental health acts were set up in various provinces with the goal to ensure fair and equal treatment for those who needed mental health care and were an attempt to balance patients' rights with the protection of that person; however, many family members have complained that they felt shut out of any decision making at times when their loved one may not have been in the best position to make a healthy decision.

In Ontario, there have been many revisions to mental health legislation.

In 1978, the Mental Health Act went through a landmark amendment in which there was substantial tightening of criteria for psychiatric assessments and committal, which would be permitted only on the basis that a person's mental disorder had resulted or would result in "serious bodily harm" or "imminent and serious physical impairment of the person."

This remained the criteria for involuntary hospitalization until the end of the 1990s. While it gave patients more power over their own treatment, it took away some of the rights of doctors.

In 2000, the act was changed to give police expanded powers and responsibilities. It happened after the 1995 death of Ottawa sportscaster Brian Smith, who was killed by a man suffering from paranoid schizophrenia. The act provided treatment orders that facilitated treatment for people in the community who'd had previous psychiatric admissions. The change also meant that police no longer had to observe a person's disturbed behaviour first-hand.

THE INVOLUNTARY STATUS forms that the doctors had filed to keep Margaret in the hospital longer meant she could stay for several months. Doctors had extended them as they could see she needed more time to get better. They were also worried about her getting pregnant again and talked her into getting an IUD, or intrauterine device, a long-term contraceptive device. It had to be removed a few weeks later due to heavy bleeding. Doctors tried to convince her to have a tubal ligation but Margaret refused, saying she wanted more children. On May 4, 1972, for reasons unknown, she changed her mind and signed the forms. Nine days later, she changed her mind back and said she someday wanted to get married and have children. The forms had been signed, however, and the surgery went ahead. On August 31, Margaret was transferred to the Hamilton General Hospital where a tubal sterilization was performed. She was twenty-eight.

Margaret was still so rundown that doctors renewed her Involuntary Status form two more times, on June 22 and again on July 19. There were serious concerns about her inability to function independently, as shown in her files on July 19: ". . . she lacks insight into her condition and shows very poor judgement in inter-personal relationships. She is still unable to function outside of a closely supervised setting."

More than a few doctors had written similar comments about Margaret's inability to function outside of the hospital; however, it's unlikely the renewals were even needed as Margaret herself wanted to stay. But five months after being readmitted, on September 11, all warnings were thrown aside and Margaret was again released into another boarding home.

The hospital discharge sheet used one word to describe the prognosis: "Guarded."

OVER THE NEXT two months, Margaret stuck with her routine of making biweekly visits to the hospital for her Moditen injections and also attended the hospital's rehabilitation program. But as had happened previously, her attendance began to slowly drop and by November she had quit. She then began missing her injection appointments. On November 23, when a social worker called the boarding house to find out why she hadn't shown up, Margaret told them she was tired of going all the way to the hospital. By bus, it would have been a fair distance and may well have required transferring along the way.

If mental health clinics had been set up in neighbourhoods, or had teams of nurses and social workers been making regular visits to boarding homes, as was part of the plan, Margaret would have had easier access to supports and may well have stayed on her medication. As it was, she was again going into free fall.

On December 18, Margaret arrived at the hospital, her whole body shaking due to the severity of her leg tremors. She told nurses she was feeling agitated then admitted she had recently saved up her Valium and taken eight at once because it got her "high." A doctor adjusted her medications. After three years with Scott as her social worker, Margaret now had a new worker who seemed to take a more compassionate approach to her job. When Margaret told her that she felt "very lonely" since quitting the hospital rehab program, the social worker offered to sign her up again for the program so she would have the opportunity to be around people.

Even the new worker couldn't perform miracles, however, and Margaret began showing up late at the hospital or not coming at all. When she did arrive, she was "filthy" and smelled of "strong body odour." Her files over the next few months were scattered and difficult to follow, but it appeared, for reasons unknown, Margaret had moved to another boarding home. Her visits to the hospital were still problematic and there were ongoing reports of her smelling of urine and dressing inappropriately for the weather.

During one visit, Margaret told staff she'd lived in ten rooms over the last three months.

In January 1973, a sheltered workshop program was set up by the Ontario government. It was designed to help provide jobs for people with disabilities. The end goal was to help people with disabilities feel productive and earn money by dishwashing, packaging materials into boxes and building wooden crates. The workshops would later become controversial when it was alleged that participants were being segregated; however, at the time they were considered a viable option for people like Margaret who couldn't manage in a regular workplace. Margaret's social worker felt she might benefit from the program and wrote a positive referral letter on her behalf, noting that she was living in a boarding home and coming to the hospital regularly for her injections.

She is 29 years old and has been in and out of the hospital since the age of 17, diagnosed with schizophrenia. Miss Jacobson has completed grade 12 and has had some business school training, but years ago. She has never had a job for any length of time. As a patient of this hospital she has often worked at Industrial Therapy. At present Miss Jacobson is receiving Moditen injections every two weeks. At times her hygiene is not too good, but the staff at the Moditen clinic are working on this with her.

Miss Jacobson at this time wishes to work in the community rather than in this hospital. If you check your records you will find that she was referred to you in February 1971. I do not think that she ever entered into any workshop because she deteriorated soon after.

WHILE MARGARET AWAITED word about the program, she was placed back in the hospital's Industrial Therapy program where, once again, she fell into old habits – coming in late and looking sloppy. Her new social worker seemed to understand that this was due to her illness and took her to a thrift store and bought her some clothes. She wrote in Margaret's file, "Patient is probably of above average intelligence but her abilities are limited by her illness."

WHENEVER MARGARET LEFT the hospital to try and manage life on her own, things would inevitably break down. This time was no exception. On March 22, 1973, she was kicked out of her boarding home after having a fight with her landlady and, with no other options, went to a domestic violence shelter. There were no notes detailing where she went next. There was one program, the Hamilton Program for Schizophrenia, that provided a clinic, and their services were seen as a positive example of a community-based treatment. But there are no notes in her file on whether she attended their clinic.

A few months later, Margaret arrived at the hospital complaining of extreme thirst and told her social worker that the shaking in her legs had become so extreme she couldn't participate in the hospital program. She also complained of feeling like she had "no drive," which may have been another side effect of the medication, as were the tremors and extreme thirst. All combined, it easily explained her faltering attendance.

Staff sent her away with a warning that if she didn't smarten up, she wouldn't be allowed to go into the sheltered workshop. Margaret tried hard to live up to their expectations, and one week later she showed up at the hospital looking tidy and proudly announced she'd had her hair done. A few weeks later, however, she arrived smelling of urine and wearing an old dress and worn-out boots. Poor hygiene is an extremely common behavioural problem among people with a serious mental illness and so it was no surprise that it was a chronic issue for Margaret. Sometimes, however, it was rooted in her budgeting problems, as shown in this excerpt from her files: "Her poor hygiene continued to be a problem but when a nurse told her she needed to start using deodorant, Margaret answered that she couldn't afford to buy it. Yet she spent $20 on a new silk dress, which she was wearing and which had large cigarette burns in it, and she can eat steak for $4 in restaurants. We discussed how she should budget her money better. Margaret does not appear to be motivated to change her ways, but says that she will try."

BY AUGUST, MARGARET had lived in several rundown boarding homes, with bouts of homelessness in between. As much as she had tried to change, it seemed that she faced a never-ending list of insurmountable obstacles. Once again, her evaluation reports noted a high absentee rate, and that her appearance was becoming sloppier. She told staff she was having problems concentrating. By now, there were serious questions about whether Margaret would be able to manage in the sheltered workshop.

ON NOVEMBER 3, 1973, Margaret's father died. Abe was sixty-two and had suffered from heart disease. There was no burial as he had willed his body to the Tulane University School of Medicine in New Orleans for scientific research. Although he had often been distant from his family, he had developed close relationships with members of the church, as seen in a piece written by a former member and published in a Pentecostal church report: "Abe left behind a spiritual legacy that still reverberates throughout the West Indies. I was grieved that there was no grave at which one could lay flowers; no spot on which his students could converge to reminisce; no venue at which to weep. The West Indies School of Theology stands as a monument to his main achievement. His photograph hangs predominantly in its foyer of the Administrative Complex of the PAWI in Maracas Valley, Trinidad."

The Administrative Committee of the West Indies School of Theology, in recognition of Abe's "outstanding contribution made to WIST," had named the building after him that housed the ladies' dormitory, dining hall and kitchen. "We are ever grateful to God for Rev. Jacobson's vision."

After Abe's death, Verna retired to Springfield, Missouri, where her son Jim had recently bought a house.

It's unclear how Margaret found out about her father's death. Did she mourn the loss of a man she hadn't seen in years, who had made it clear that he didn't approve of her? While there are no notes showing she talked about the loss – that wasn't Margaret's style – there were indications that the loss hit her hard. Her hygiene became even worse and her work habits diminished to the point where she was pulled from the program. As one worker wrote: "She frequently smelled of strong body odour and wore dirty unpressed and uncoordinated clothing. With respect to work habits, she frequently was absent, late for work, took extended lunch and coffee breaks and spent much time in the washroom smoking."

THE MANY YEARS of unhealthy living, chain-smoking and heavy use of medications had aggravated Margaret's acne, and on January 4, 1974, she was again hospitalized and doctors performed a full facial dermabrasion. It appeared the surgery had little effect, but that may have been partly due to the fact Margaret was not able to show up for follow-up appointments.

THROUGHOUT MARGARET'S NOW lengthy medical files there were constant references to her poor hygiene. Despite being reminded over and over to clean herself up, she simply couldn't follow through. She also had problems making it to appointments and was often late for programs. When she did arrive, as shown in her Clinical Record from the hospital's therapy program, dated February 28, 1974, staff noted her "extremely poor hygiene, smelling of body odour, high absenteeism and poor work habits." Margaret was having increasing problems managing her money and holding onto housing. These weren't life-altering behaviours and she was never violent with staff or other patients.

Did these behaviours make her a bad patient? In the twelve years since she was admitted, Margaret had never refused to take her medication and had agreed to whatever course of treatment was suggested, including shock treatments. Despite disastrous outcomes, she had gone along with each move into a boarding home. At what point should a patient's care be re-evaluated if said patient isn't responding to the type of care they're receiving? In Margaret's case, it appeared that the patient's role was to bend to the treatment plan as opposed to the treatment being tailored to the patient's needs.

Medical staff knew that Margaret was suffering from severe schizophrenia and that she was unable to follow through on even simple requests, such as keeping herself clean. It wasn't that she was purposely trying to be bad. Her mental illness made it difficult for her to function fully. Staff would have known about the absence of community supports and poorly supervised boarding homes, yet they overlooked this when they decided to discharge her from the hospital. As a result, the onus was on Margaret to make things work. As shown in this evaluation written by hospital staff after she was pulled out of the hospital's IT program, she was often treated in a punitive manner when things didn't work out: "Margaret blamed her entire situation on not having a suitable place to live. She admits to about 10 rooms in the past 3 months but I did not accept housing as a valid reason for her situation. She was given three days to improve or be faced with a suspension. Originally, she accepted this but later she apparently stormed out of the workshop and has not returned."

MARGARET WAS NOW dangling on the precipice of homelessness. It wasn't clear where she was living or how much financial support she had. Any notes in her files were overly focused on her poor attendance at workshops and lacklustre hygiene. In a report dated July 12, Margaret's psychiatrist wrote that her condition had been "relatively unchanged," and that he had only seen a "marginal" response to treatments. He appeared fed up with Margaret's behaviour and gave her an ultimatum: "If this patient does not return to the clinic within three months of our last contact, she will be technically and automatically discharged."

On December 10, 1974, that's exactly what happened. Margaret's file reads: "The patient has refused to attend the clinic . . . and all attempts at contacting the patient since then have failed. There has been no contact with the patient for 3 months hence she is technically discharged."

Not only was Margaret discharged from the hospital but no arrangements were made for follow-up care. The section in her report under follow-up simply states, "None, as the patient has refused all contact with us."

ONCE AGAIN, MARGARET was in free fall without a parachute. One month later, on January 12, 1975, police arrived at a McDonald's restaurant after staff called because they were worried about the homeless woman outside. Margaret had been sitting on the front steps for hours. It was a frigid day and she was wearing only thin clothing. With nowhere else to take her, police dropped her off at Inasmuch House, one of the city's domestic violence shelters. Margaret hadn't been on medication for weeks and was behaving oddly – staff described her as being a "disruptive influence," saying she refused to abide by the rules. They also noted she was "extremely emaciated."

Two days later, Margaret poured white dishwashing powder into her coffee and drank it before staff was able to grab it from her. An ambulance was called and she was taken to St. Joseph's Hospital. She told doctors she had mistaken the soap for sugar. She was given syrup of ipecac to make her vomit, then transferred to the HPH.

Margaret was now thirty years old. This was her eighth admission in fourteen years, including Homewood. She weighed 103 pounds. Her patient number remained the same: 43460. Her medical record stated: "The patient appears undernourished, emaciated, unkempt. Skin is in poor condition with pimples and blackheads plus infected lesions."

The hospital tested her for syphilis due to the ongoing concern about her "promiscuous" behaviour. It came back negative. A day after being admitted, a physical exam was conducted in which the doctor noted Margaret was "of leptic body frame." *Leptic* refers to someone afflicted with a condition that makes them prone to violent seizures, which suggests her leg tremors had become even more severe. "She shows inappropriate crying and laughing during the examination."

Most days Margaret refused to get out of bed, and when she did, she would wander into the common area and sit by herself, refusing to eat. A January 17, 1975, report noted that she had changed her underwear five times in one day, while another day she sat in the ward with her legs wide open while not wearing any underwear. Repeated warnings by nurses to sit properly were ignored. One nurse wrote: "Margaret does not appear to be improving. She lays in bed each morning with her nightie up around her waist, sans underwear, and must be covered up. Not one morning has she got up and dressed of her own accord. We have eventually nagged her into getting up and into the bathtub. It is useless to try and get her to sit in a lady-like position so mainly we have been trying to just keep her adequately dressed."

On January 22, another nurse wrote:

Since admission Margaret has mainly spent her time either laying on her bed or sitting in the T.V. room, smoking. Her hygiene is extremely poor. She wouldn't bathe, I don't think, unless we ran the bath water for her and more or less told her to get into the tub, nor would she wear underwear. Even at this she constantly changes her clothes and constantly takes her underwear, that is her panties off, and disposes of them.

Her eating habits are extremely poor and she must be encouraged even to get into the dining room. I have talked to her about this and she was startled to find that her weight has dropped to 101 pounds and that she has lost three pounds even in the last week.

THE NURSE MADE a note to talk to Margaret's doctor about acquiring an appetite stimulant to help her gain weight. On January 27, a note from another nurse showed there had been little improvement:

> Margaret continues to function at an extremely low level. On the weekend she started to menstruate and was told to have a bath, but otherwise wouldn't keep her sanitary pads on and her clothing and bedside area were saturated with blood. I have my doubts whether she would have done anything about it herself as it doesn't bother her and perhaps she knows it is offensive to other people, particularly staff.
>
> With encouragement and with tobacco as a reward, she bathed and washed down her bedside area this morning, however, she needs constant supervision as she rushes through everything at a high speed and leaves the place in a mess.

MARGARET WAS IN her late twenties when Pat Saunders met her.

"I remember the first time I saw her and saw the condition of her skin. It was tragic, it was so shrivelled and lined. It aged her terribly. She certainly looked like a street person," said Saunders, who worked as a social worker at the HPH. "She would interact with you or others only if she was approached, but she wouldn't do it on her own. Some patients weren't shy about asking for something, but Margaret wouldn't ask for anything unless you asked her first."

Saunders believed Margaret's rough appearance played a part in how she was treated.

> My overriding impression was that she would have been treated differently if she had been beautiful. I did see that play out over the years in the hospital. It's just a fact that we pay more attention to a beautiful person and Margaret wasn't beautiful. Women who are attractive will get more attention, and I still wonder if she was given less attention because of that.
>
> She was what I would call a tragic case.

Margaret may not have been beautiful, but Saunders said there was some-thing about her that suggested she had been a "culturally refined woman."

"She was no dummy. She was well-spoken. I thought perhaps there was something in her background, or where she was from."

Margaret was now in the "patch them up" stage, but this time it was differ-ent. Her health had dropped to such a low level that there was some question as to whether she would ever get better. Weeks passed and she was still be-having bizarrely, still being combative and rude to staff. Her behaviour could occasionally be destructive – staff caught her burning holes in the couches with cigarettes. When they told her to stop she refused. One would hope staff would understand this was part of Margaret's sickness, especially given what she'd been through; however, her doctor's comments showed that wasn't the case. He described her as being "angry and sarcastic": "This behaviour appears to be acting out rather than psychosis and she should not be able to get away with it and I will confront her about this. In other words, either she shapes up or ships out. We do not feel it is our role to get her a room and if this is what she expects she can search herself."

Perhaps Margaret was still the angry and rebellious teenager that Dr. Dawson described as being stuck in her teen years. But her behaviour may also have been symptomatic of her mental illness combined with her horrific living conditions. Schizophrenia is a serious chronic illness that impacts a person's ability to perceive reality. Although Margaret was still on antipsy-chotic medication, they don't erase all behavioural problems and she was still experiencing difficulties with her concentration and her memory.

On February 3, staff asked her if she wanted to look for a room in the community. Margaret told them that she wanted to stay in the hospital because it was too cold outside. On February 17, her Involuntary Status expired, meaning she was now on Informal Status, which meant she could leave whenever she wanted.

WOULD MARGARET HAVE responded to the model of compassionate care that had been developed by William Tuke and offered at his Retreat in York,

England, in 1796? The model relied on sympathy, respect and compassion, and patients were treated as if they were part of a large family. They were encouraged to participate in daily tasks such as churning butter, pumping water, chopping wood, sewing clothes and cleaning shoes – which were also seen as occupational therapy – as well as farm work and gardening. Later, the Retreat set up sports teams, including cricket, tennis, football, hockey and golf, and patients were also encouraged to write and read and go for walks in the tranquil surroundings.

The "moral treatment of care" that was based on humane and compassionate values played a major role in reshaping the treatment plan for people who have a mental illness. Today, it is believed that the most compassionate choice is to help people live in the community, with supports. Few cities in the world have achieved this goal as well as Trieste, in northeastern Italy, which has become famous for its network of social and housing supports.

Back in the late 1970s, Italy, and other countries across Europe, experienced the same fallout from the failures of deinstitutionalization as Canada and the US. In some ways the impact was even worse. Italy's phasing out of psychiatric hospitals began in 1978 when the country passed a mental health law that forbade the admission of new patients to large state mental hospitals. It also made involuntary commitments much more difficult, and those patients who were already in hospitals were put on short stay policies.

When community services failed to materialize as promised, Italy saw a deluge of homeless mentally ill people. One city acted quickly to manage the problem. In Trieste, which has a population of 240,000, a network of Community Mental Health Centers was set up to provide therapeutic, social and rehabilitative care on a 24-7 basis. Supported housing facilities were developed including social and work enterprises, and neighbourhood clinics provided services to patients who had housing. Home care services included social clubs, work co-ops and recreational activities.

Although the plan met with some initial resistance, it eventually took form. As reported by the BBC in 2019, Trieste soon became a model for other cities and mental health practitioners from around the world came there to learn about their approach to mental illness.

As reported by the BBC, "In 1978, Trieste led a 'revolution' in Italian mental health care by closing its asylums and ending the restraint of patients. Today the city is designated as a 'collaboration centre' by the World Health Organization in recognition of its pioneering work."

This community-based model has become a global example of what other cities can achieve. It's unfortunate one has to go halfway across the world to find it.

WITH EACH READMISSION, Margaret took longer to recover. Two and a half months after her last admission, on March 17, 1975, a nurse wrote that they were finally seeing some changes: "Margaret appears to have made some progress this month. She is not as angry or impulsive and has taken a greater interest in her personal hygiene. She is also dressing herself more appropriately. Her manner is pleasant and cooperative."

One month later, on April 15, there was more good news: "Margaret has continued to show improvement this past month. She is following her program. Margaret has expressed a desire to work in Industrial Therapy doing typing."

But recovery was never a straight line for Margaret and she could be easily derailed. When she was told there were no typing jobs available, she became visibly upset and two days later was caught shoplifting from the Woolco Department Store downtown. Things took an upward turn when she was placed in a new program in the laundry area, and there was even more positive change when she started doing pottery. On May 6, in one of the most positive comments in her medical files, a nurse wrote: "She enjoys it very much. Her appearance has improved greatly with the provision of some clothes that have been given to her. She is following her program willingly and is reported to be doing a very good job."

Margaret was clearly enjoying herself in these two programs. "It's so nice to have someone who cares about you," she told a nurse.

On May 15, another note cited how much "happier" Margaret had been since working in pottery: "hygiene had greatly improved and she seems to take pride in her personal appearance now. Very sociable."

On June 15, Margaret's behaviour started "fluctuating," although her attendance in the pottery program was still regular. Then on July 5, Margaret left the hospital without permission and went downtown with a former patient. Later she told her nurse she felt she wasn't being allowed enough independence. Her punishment was to stay on the ward the next day. After that, her attendance in the pottery program began to falter. "July 14 – This patient is once again becoming uncooperative with her programme and feels that she should leave hospital."

Staff decided, perhaps as punishment, to move her to an assembly-line program where her job was to fill bags with candy all day. When she told staff she was bored, they moved her into a job packing boxes with Christmas cards. Her work there was noted as being "sloppy and slow," and her hygiene was poor. Margaret responded by acting out.

> July 29 – Margaret left [Occupational Therapy] this morning and did not return to the ward until near supper time. She stated she could not take the job that she was doing, which was doing up small bags of candy. She talked this problem over with [a staffer] and about how bored she was becoming. She was advised that she must continue on a program regardless and because of this she will change her job to that of fixing and packing Xmas cards. Margaret stated that she would try her very best to be on time and be punctual.

The next month, on August 22, the director of the program suspended Margaret, citing her frequent absences and poor punctuality. He also made the sudden and extreme decision to discharge her from the hospital. In an unusual response that reflected the severity of the decision, staff objected and said that Margaret needed to stay in the program because each time she'd left she had experienced "extreme deterioration." The director fought to overrule them, writing on August 28: "Margaret was able to live in the community and certainly able and responsible enough to meet the workshop requirements. On the face of the above and Margaret's behaviour, Margaret should be discharged from the hospital and certainly discharged from the workshop. Margaret needs a reality approach and should be held increasingly responsible for her behaviour and meeting commitments. During the past several weeks there were periods when Margaret showed her best known grooming and clothing judgement."

It appears the doctor was overruled – Margaret was allowed to stay both in the hospital and in the program. It didn't last long, however, and on November 3, 1975, the decision was reversed and Margaret was moved into another boarding home, this one on Leeming Street. Her discharge summary reads:

> The patient is well known to the hospital, having had an enormous amount of admissions. She has shown a paranoid personality with considerable defiance and lack of motivation to change her style of life. For the most part, she has only made a marginal improvement and has really never worked or live self-independent for any substantial period of time.
>
> Her tendency, outside hospital, is to gradually lose control of her hygiene, her eating habits, to withdraw into a social withdrawal, together with mutism. At these stages, she is usually admitted to hospital and once again responds rather rapidly to Phenothiazines, however, in hospital she does not show much motivation to change her style of life.

The report ends with a comment that accurately foreshadowed what was to come: "Despite the fact she is now leaving the hospital, the outlook is rather poor."

IT'S NOT CLEAR what happened to Margaret over the next several months as the notes are incomplete. Three months later, on February 26, 1976, she was found living in a filthy home that neighbours described as an "extremely neglected environment with alcohol parties." She was sick and emaciated, and had a venereal disease. Her mental health had deteriorated to the point where she was slipping into a catatonic state.

According to one report, "the patient was very erratic in taking her medications, would often give them away, lose them. etc."

The doctor who treated her reiterated what many medical staff and social workers had stated before: "The wisdom of this patient living on her own in the community should be considered very carefully. Vigorous attempts have been made to remotivate her and achieve ordinary levels of grooming and social behaviour and these have met with entire failure. It is abundantly clear that without extensive supervision this patient is entirely unable to function in a self-sufficient fashion in the community."

On March 4, 1976, one week later, the same doctor wrote, "Bearing in mind her social deterioration, together with a catatonic-type of withdrawal and the positive finding [of venereal disease], and the recommendation from Public Health that they were concerned about her way of life, she was admitted to hospital."

Two weeks later, on March 18, another doctor, noting the "deplorable living conditions" she'd been found in, asked whether Margaret should "remain in some type of extended care setting in view of the repeated and many total abysmal failures of her to continue working in the community and surviving there, even with the maximum supports from all services."

As with all of Margaret's other readmissions, much attention was given to her when she was first brought in. One doctor weighed in on whether her earlier diagnosis of schizophrenia had been accurate and questioned whether she may have transient situational disturbance, which occurs when someone is unable to adjust to or cope with a particular stress or major life event. Another doctor still diagnosed her with a personality disorder. The different diagnoses may have been a reflection of high staff turnover.

In *Out of the Shadows*, Torrey wrote about the lack of continuity of care within psychiatric institutions: "Continuity is extremely important for the mentally ill both because of the complexity of their illnesses and because many such patients find it difficult to relate to an ever-changing panoply of case managers and other mental health professionals."

ONE MONTH AFTER being readmitted, the same doctor who had warned against Margaret ever being discharged signed the forms to discharge her into a boarding home. The rationale, according to her files, was that despite Margaret having a serious mental illness and proving incapable of living independently, he left the decision in her hands. On March 31, 1976, the doctor wrote: "The prognosis here appears poor in view of the multiple admissions and her poor social adjustment and her outpatient difficulty in being independent and self sufficient living in downtown Hamilton. Despite the fact that she deteriorates while living in the community, it appears that at present she feels she has the right to do so, and that she will from time to time continue to have admissions to hospital when she has deteriorated to the state of withdrawal and weight loss."

Given her repeated comments about wanting to stay, it's questionable whether Margaret knew that she was signing herself out of the hospital. Doctors had the legal means to keep her – through Involuntary Status – and ample evidence that she needed to stay, including cautionary notes from doctors, social workers and nurses. The doctor who signed the final order to discharge her had treated her for years and would have seen her dirt-encrusted fingernails and lice-filled hair whenever she'd returned from her boarding home stays. By allowing her to walk out of the hospital again, they were, in very real sense, sealing Margaret's fate.

On March 31, 1976, only one month after being found sick and emaciated, and with a venereal disease, Margaret was discharged from the hospital. What happened to her over the next several years is a complete mystery. While her previous records for just one year of hospitalization often included well over one hundred pages, the seven years between 1976 and 1983 were wrapped up in just three. It was as if when she walked out the hospital that day she disappeared into the mist.

The information on those three pages stated that when she left the HPH, she went to live at a boarding house on Leeming Street. The only other notes were prescriptions for various medications, including Ativan, which was used to treat anxiety disorders. There was also a scribbled note stating "Follow up H.P.H Special Clinic," but no further notes on whether Margaret actually came to the clinic. Although the hospital was supposed to provide follow-up care, the file simply reads that no records were available during this period.

WHAT WAS MARGARET's life like during those seven years? Where did she sleep at night and how had she survived? Since boarding homes were the only option for many former psychiatric patients, she likely stayed in a few of them but also relied on friends' couches and slept on the streets. Like most homeless people, during the day she likely sought refuge in coffee shops, malls and free meal programs, while at night she searched for a quiet alley-way. All the strings of her parachute had been cut and she was in full-out free fall.

THE NEXT NOTES in Margaret's file show the tragic turn her life had taken. On March 23, 1983, she was found in the basement of an apartment building lying in feces and covered in lice. She had been eating garbage out of a dumpster when the superintendent noticed her and called police, who took her to the HPH. Margaret was in a wretched state, filthy, malnourished and severely withdrawn. As the report states: "39 year old dishevelled lady brought in by police. Police had been called by the superintendent to have her removed from the locker rooms. From their understanding, she has been living off and on for three months in the locker room. The smell was quite intense as feces was everywhere. She was not talkative – has been feeding herself garbage. Not very verbal."

A further note, at the bottom under Special Precautions, read: "Possibly has lice."

Although the superintendent said she'd been living there off and on for three months, Margaret told doctors she'd been there for the past two years because she'd been unable to find a place to rent on the two hundred dollars she received from welfare. She'd been helped by friends, she said, and had used church meal programs to survive. In her usual upbeat tone, she told doctors she had been "getting along fine like this," and that she had only agreed to come to the hospital because of the cold weather.

Margaret was now thirty-nine. Doctors readmitted her, began a flurry of tests and started her back on her medications: chlorpromazine, and benztropine for her tremors. Despite her appalling state, she was listed as Informal status, which meant she had the right to leave the hospital at any time. Her health and behaviour indicated otherwise and suggested she needed a lengthy hospital stay to recover from her ordeal. Margaret had become extremely withdrawn and reclusive, would stay in her room for hours and refused to participate in any workshops or programs. She complained about having nightmares, which kept her awake at night.

When she wandered onto the ward, she would pull up her gown and expose herself or masturbate while staff and patients were in the room. Nurses caught her slapping herself in the face, and another time she was found soaking her head under a tap in the sink while letting water run all over the floor. She smoked excessively. Staff moved her to a single room that could be locked from the outside so they could control her movements. A note from March 27 showed how far her mental health had declined: "Loud banging noise heard coming from patient's room – door slammed. Patient apparently had thrown garbage against bedside table and had cleared out garbage. She said 'just straightening it out. Leave it alone!' Affect irritated, avoiding eye contact. walked out of room, pacing hallway and returning to room to check area."

THE HOSPITAL DIDN'T wait for her to recover. Two weeks after being found in the dumpster, Margaret was approved for another move to a boarding home. An April 8 report stated: "Margaret continues to be secluded on the ward and does not participate in ward programmes. She seems quite happy to have a roof over her head and three square meals. There has been really no change in her behaviour and mental status since being here. We have attempted to get her some second-hand clothes from the Pines. She is to be placed in a boarding home on Herkimer on Tuesday after a Welfare assessment."

That decision was abruptly changed when, three days later, Margaret tried to drown herself in the bathtub. A nurse caught her just in time. Maybe Margaret had been told that she had to leave and this was her desperate attempt to buy herself a bed. Maybe she was trying to end her life. It's confusing how staff could not have seen that Margaret needed to be hospitalized. She had told doctors she felt like she was "going off the deep end," and there were times when her behaviour was so out of control that she had to be put in restraints. She suffered from visual and auditory hallucinations, and doctors described her as going into a "catatonic stupor." After the drowning incident, her status was changed to Involuntary, which meant she was considered a danger to herself and couldn't leave the hospital.

The only thing Margaret wanted to do was smoke. She was up to more than two packs a day and when she ran out, she would wander around scavenging through ashtrays, looking for old cigarette butts. If there weren't any, she'd beg the other patients for one. Her behaviour had fallen to a new low. One night during dinner, she slapped herself in the face then took a mouthful of food before slapping herself again, repeating this until nurses physically restrained her. Another time they caught her hitting some plants, and during an interview with a doctor, she started laughing hysterically for no reason, like she was in on her own private joke.

Whatever had happened in those last seven years had ravaged her mind. Although she was on regular doses of medications and had begun to stabilize somewhat, she continued having wild outbursts. The tremors in her leg had also become severe. "She appears to have gross tremors on her lower extremities, swinging her leg back and forth quite vigorously."

Margaret again made it clear to staff that she wanted to stay in the hospital and told them that she found the responsibility of looking after herself too great. This time doctors agreed, and on April 25, they extended her Involuntary status with a certificate of renewal. Staff started her on a token program in which she could earn points for good behaviour. They hoped it would lead her to improving her hygiene and participating in activities. She could use the points she earned to "buy" cigarettes and meals. A note on May 4, however, stated that Margaret's "behaviour continues to be inappropriate." On May 6, her doctor wrote that he still had concerns about allowing her to leave the hospital: "Margaret continues to be dishevelled and behaves inappropriately on the ward. It continues to be felt that with her behaviour we will be unable to place her in a boarding home in the community."

Margaret had begun going to a workshop but stopped after a while, telling staff that "her nerves were bad." She also wasn't sleeping well. One doctor wrote, "Continues to have nightmares but refused to elaborate on what they were about."

MARGARET WAS IN a Catch-22. She wanted to be in the hospital where she could get better, but whenever she started to improve, the hospital would make plans to ship her out. Even the slightest improvements in her health put her on the short list to be discharged. Sure enough, the same doctor who, one month earlier, said that Margaret should not be moved out of the hospital, wrote that she was now ready to leave. As with her last discharge, he left the final decision in Margaret's hands: "We have left it open to her that if she did not wish to participate in this [token] programme which would enable her to be placed in a boarding home, that she could leave at any time."

On May 13, another doctor wrote, "No significant change in behaviour or mood." That same day, the doctor who wanted to release her wrote that "her appearance and behaviour have markedly improved. We plan to continue her on this program and if she maintains this level of improvement we will arrange for placement in a boarding home."

ON MAY 19, 1983, Margaret's status was changed to Informal, allowing her to leave at any time. On the form, in the space for her home address it read: No Fixed Address. The next day, Margaret repeated her concerns to staff about not wanting to leave: "She feels she would like to have someone look after her as the responsibility of this is too great for her."

ON MAY 20, a social worker was instructed to find Margaret a boarding home placement, and over the next eleven days, despite showing little improvement, discharge plans continued.

A medical report dated June 1, 1983, written as she was leaving the hospital stated: "thin, anxious-looking 39 year old lady with extreme scarring on her face from a cystic type of acne. There was evidence of a rash on her arms which was raised and indurated. The patient was dirty and dishevelled looking."

Margaret was moved into a boarding house on Main Street East and was to be monitored by a hospital social worker for one month on a "leave of absence" status with a referral to be made to an outpatient team. "The hope was that Margaret would be picked up by them," said a note in her file.

The boarding home operator was put in charge of managing her money and was told only to give it to Margaret if she kept up her hygiene and behaved properly. A few days later, the operator called the hospital to say that Margaret wasn't eating, that she was overly anxious and that she complained that the food smelled like dead bodies. Staff advised the operator to give Margaret some tasks to do around the house. There were no notes on how well this worked out.

ON JULY 14, 1983, Margaret was officially registered by the hospital as an outpatient. The leave of absence period, which was supposed to be a trial period to see how Margaret fared in the community, was littered with signs that things weren't going well. She missed appointments over the next few weeks, and when she did come to the hospital, she complained about feeling agitated and restless. A few times she failed to come home at night. During one of her appointments, a nurse noticed that she looked sick. Doctors altered her medication. Staff praised the boarding home operator for her "tolerant" attitude toward Margaret.

Four days later, Margaret showed up at the hospital asking to be readmitted. She was told she either had to go to St. Joseph's Hospital or return to the boarding home. She went back to the boarding home. Margaret's records over the next several months consisted of mostly handwritten notes by staff that revealed a long trail of missed appointments for injections and dental appointments, some of which had been set up to repair her broken teeth.

On one occasion, she went to the St. Joseph's Hospital emergency ward complaining of leg pains and was diagnosed with deep-vein thrombosis, a condition in which a blood clot forms in one or more of the deep veins in the body. There were no notes as to what care she received. On August 3, 1984, she was sent for emergency dental work after complaining to a nurse at the hospital about having a swollen cheek.

Margaret was thirty-nine. It had been almost twenty-three years since she was first admitted to the hospital. She'd been on a steady diet of drugs: antipsychotics chlorpromazine, clozapine and risperidone; benztropine and diazepam; tetracycline for infections; Gaviscon for her stomach problems and various treatments for her severe acne, plus drugs to counter the side effects. She would consistently take her medications in the hospital, but once she was moved into boarding homes, that would end in short time.

During the periods that she had lived outside of the hospital, she had been assaulted, lived in a garbage-filled dumpster, become pregnant, been found covered in feces and been picked up on the streets of Winnipeg where she was found penniless and destitute. Under the care of the system that was supposed to have made her better, she had instead become much worse.

Many times, she had been blamed for being sick and for not acting appropriately – first by her father, then by her social worker Scott and finally by doctors who'd chastised her like she was a misbehaving child. Although she had been diagnosed with schizophrenia, there appeared to be no recognition that her mental illness might be the cause of her behaviour.

For more than two decades Margaret had kept going, but at this point she was just barely hanging on.

Soon the pattern of missed appointments and declining hygiene began to repeat itself. While there was the occasional comment about Margaret "making a good recovery" or being "cooperative," for the most part, she had begun her downward slide. A doctor added Artane to her list of medications to control the tremors in her legs and Ativan for her anxiety. One day, a social worker came to her boarding home and found her asleep in her bed at noon. She wrote in her notes that Margaret "continues to refuse any structured activity."

On December 19, 1984, a doctor wrote that Margaret had "remained quite stable over the last nine months," and that she was considered well enough to be discharged from the hospital's follow-up care. That meant Margaret would, from here on, be managed by the boarding home operator and a family doctor. There is mention of a family doctor, but no notes on any appointments being set up. Despite the problems Margaret had experienced since being released, the hospital doctor wrote that, "in my opinion, Margaret is functioning at her optimal level and present living and medication arrangements should continue indefinitely."

JANUARY 8, 1985. That's the date on the last page of Margaret's four-inch-thick medical file contained in two binders. The notes on the page offered a brief outline of her life over the previous two years, painting a picture of a non-compliant patient who refused to participate in any workshops or programs and was habitually sloppy. She was described as problematic, as someone who had gotten sicker because she refused to abide by hospital rules. The words failed, abysmally, to show the real picture of who Margaret was and all that had happened to her within the hospital's walls.

After twenty-four years of being moved in and out of the hospital and into boarding homes, of being caught in a revolving door that always landed her back on the streets, Margaret was being released for the last time. Her 869-page medical file ended with two words: "Discharged today."

Part Three

ON THE STREETS

1985–1995

Margaret outside the Wesley Centre, wearing the coat given to her by Lynn Ferris.
Courtesy of Bill MacKinnon.

CHAPTER THIRTEEN
Princess of the Streets

1985–1989
Hamilton

Dark and lonely streets that reeked of exhaust fumes and dog pee and tasted like hard gravel are where Margaret laid her head most nights. Since being discharged, she had become a nameless bag lady occupying the alleyways and alcoves of the city. And while she occasionally stayed in boarding homes or with friends, the streets were more and more her full-time home. Margaret had dropped to the bottom of the barrel; she had no home, no family, not even a hospital number. She belonged to no one and no one was looking out for her. She had joined the ranks of the nameless homeless.

But she was also a survivor, and had become masterful at finding places to eat and sleep. She would curl up in the lobby of a bank kiosk, or on a bench at an all-night laundromat or in an open store doorway. For a while, she stayed in a spot beside the former Hamilton Board of Education building downtown. It was dark there so no one could see her.

One night she discovered that the entranceway to an art gallery was left open at night and was fully heated. She slept there for several weeks before word got out and other homeless people began to join her. At one point, there were as many as four or five people crowding into the small space.

That ended when Margaret urinated into the heating duct. The rancid smell coming up through the ducts greeted staff in the morning. After that, the entranceway was locked at night. She proudly related this story to several friends and shelter staff.

Life was like that for Margaret. She'd catch a break then it would all come crashing down. One step forward, two steps back. And still she kept going. She had become the princess of the streets.

When the warmer weather came, Margaret took up residency on park benches, like the one she found at a small park on King Street East, on the outskirts of downtown. She liked that it was out of the way and not crowded, so she had her own little space. During the day she would sit on the bench and smoke, often engaging in full conversations with herself. At night, the same bench became her bed. Although she rarely stayed in one spot long, that park was her home for several weeks. After that, she moved to the lawn by the downtown courthouse, sometimes alternating with the doorway of the nearby post office. After a few nights, the smell of urine would draw complaints and Margaret would be told to move.

One winter night she slept in the lobby of a new four-storey condo on Main Street East, near Tisdale. As it happened, it was the same condo where Pat Saunders's sister lived. Saunders had told her sister all about Margaret, and when she turned her TV to the channel hooked to the condo's security camera and saw a raggedy woman curled up on the lobby floor, she immediately recognized her. She grabbed a few sweaters and a blanket, and took them down to her, along with some food.

Margaret thanked her and went on her way.

"[My sister] told me Margaret looked terrible," said Saunders. "She couldn't wait to see her again so she could help her some more."

But Margaret never came back. Maybe the condo manager kicked her out after a resident complained. Those were the kinds of things that kept Margaret on the run. The world had rejected her for years, but now Margaret was rejecting the world. She turned her back on any services that could have helped her and never went back to the hospital unless she was taken to the emergency department by ambulance. The visits would be short, likely one or two days maximum, and usually came about because she'd been assaulted, like the time she got beat up at Gore Park.

It was a warm, sunny day and crowds had gathered in the small downtown park to enjoy the weather. Margaret was hanging out with her friend Bob Dixon when a guy strutted past wearing a new T-shirt, his head held high as if to show off his new shirt.

"He was a cocky guy," said Bob, who remembered how the guy was "always boasting about one thing or another."

People kept their distance from him as he had a reputation for being violent, but, to everyone's surprise, Margaret suddenly ran up behind him, grabbed his T-shirt and ripped it right off his back. No one knows why she did it, but she paid a price.

"He knocked her to the ground and kicked her hard right in the head," said Bob, grimacing. "Blood was coming out all over the place. It was awful."

Someone called an ambulance and Margaret was rushed to St. Joseph's Hospital. When Bob went to see her, all she talked about was how exciting it was to ride in a "brand-new ambulance." Bob shook his head as he recounted the visit. "She was always like that. She never complained. I couldn't believe how excited she was over this ambulance."

KATHERINE KALINOWSKI, CHIEF operating officer of the Good Shepherd Centre in Hamilton, the city's largest social services provider, knows how serious the homelessness crisis is. As she stepped to the front of the First Unitarian Church of Hamilton on a chilly Sunday morning in November 2018, she didn't have to look far to see the problem she was there to talk about. Behind her were two large windows that looked onto a grassy area leading to the back of the church, where some homeless people had pitched tents.

Church members were so concerned about the welfare of the homeless people that they started a committee to try and help them. The stretch of land was part of an area where an estimated thirty to one hundred homeless people were living near the escarpment, and by the rail tracks and bayfront.

They were aware that gentrification had contributed to the rise in homelessness as those more upwardly mobile were moving into lower income areas, which led to rent hikes. After several meetings, the committee concluded that while they couldn't solve the problem of homelessness, they could treat those living in the valley with dignity and humanity. This committee continues to meet to develop strategies on ways to accomplish this, including allowing them to stay there safely and providing them with food and blankets.

As Kalinowski stepped up to the microphone that day, she joked that she'd talked about homelessness so much she was sick of hearing her own voice. She was a tall, dark-haired woman with a deep voice that resonated with compassion. Launching into her talk, she emphasized the importance of applying a gendered lens to homelessness as homeless women weren't getting the services they needed. The bed shortage problem was but one example of that, she said, stating the 2017 turnaway rate at their homeless women's shelter, Mary's Place, was 2,630. That's the number of times shelter staff had to turn away a woman for lack of space. Staff always tried to put women up on a temporary basis, on a couch or even a chair, but it was not always possible.

"We turn away women at shelters hundreds of times every month," Kalinowski told the crowd.

While they tried to ensure women had somewhere else to go, she said it was always a worry because the shelter situation for women in Hamilton was so bad. It had improved slightly over the past few years, when Mary's Place was given funding for more beds and the YWCA program received funding for the second year in a row, but the increase hadn't kept up with the need.

In Hamilton, like many other cities, there exist far more beds for homeless men than for homeless women, which is why shelters for homeless women are consistently over capacity, especially during the winter, despite more beds being opened during those months. There are currently 194 beds in the men's emergency shelter system, including Mission Services, Salvation Army and Good Shepherd, compared to forty beds for women at Good Shepherd's Mary's Place, the Native Women's Centre Mountain View and St. Joe's Womankind program.

On any given night in the winter of 2018–19, the twenty-two beds at Mary's Place were full while another eight women were crowded onto couches and chairs. In December 2017, to provide more beds, the downtown YWCA, Mission Services and St. Joe's Womankind partnered over the winter to open Carole Anne's Place, which was supposed to be a ten to twelve bed shelter; however, they quickly realized they were going well over those numbers. Indeed, in the first two months after opening, they saw more than one hundred women access the program, and most nights they accommodated as many as seventeen women.

THERE ARE MANY things that push a woman into homelessness: mental illness and addiction, loss of job and/or their home, and domestic violence. On the streets, life can be even more difficult for women than it is for men. The average age of death for homeless women in Canada is thirty-nine, compared to women in the general population who die, on average, at age eighty-one. A study of almost two thousand homeless women conducted in Toronto in 2004 showed that young homeless women had ten times the mortality rate of other young women, and that most died from AIDS, drugs, alcohol abuse or suicide.

Still another Toronto study, this one from 2008, showed that depression and anxiety were extremely common among homeless women and that women were twice as likely to receive a mental health diagnosis as homeless men.

Why haven't these issues been addressed? Kalinowski believes that a huge part of the problem is that the public still perceives a homeless person as a "down on his luck" alcoholic male. During the Great Depression of the

1930s, a typical homeless person was a transient male who hopped freight trains and travelled from town to town. Some were drifters while others tried to find jobs. They were often referred to as hobos. But over the next several decades, the face of homelessness changed dramatically. Today it includes youth, women, veterans, Indigenous people, seniors and even families. Some groups are overly represented, specifically queer youth and Indigenous people.

For women, often the root cause of becoming homeless is poverty, said Kalinowski, who told the story of a woman who was married with two kids. She'd had a good job then got divorced and found her finances stretched. Although working full time, she was still having difficulty paying rent. Then her child got sick with a simple ear infection and, with no drug plan, she had to make the choice between paying rent and buying antibiotics. And so she borrowed from the rent money. Then another child got sick and she lost so much time off work that she wound up being laid off.

No longer able to pay her rent, she was evicted. If a woman lacks family support, she's often one step away from having to move into a shelter, and when that happens, it can also mean having to give up her children. The Good Shepherd's Women's Services operates a Housing First program that assists women who have experienced long periods of homelessness and who struggle with complex barriers to maintaining stable housing. There's also the SOS Program, which provides intensive support to women for up to two years and has been shown to be successful in helping women who have experienced chronic homelessness. But as Medora Uppal, director of operations at YWCA Hamilton, said, too many women are being left out. Although shelters like Mary's Place try and ensure that women who are turned away have a safe place to go, some are still being left out in the cold and too many are finding themselves in unsafe situations.

Violence is a common threat among homeless women and, according to the 2007 *Street Health Report*, one in five homeless women has been sexually assaulted or raped in the past year. The report, which included research by

Dr. Stephen Hwang, research scientist at the Centre for Research on Inner City Health in Toronto, also revealed that 37 percent of homeless women reported being physically assaulted in the past year, 21 percent reported being sexually assaulted and 43 percent had been sexually harassed while using a shelter, soup kitchen or some other form of housing.

Those numbers are even more disturbing when taking into account that sexual assaults are consistently under-reported, likely more so within the homeless community.

Homeless women like Margaret, who have a mental illness, are even more vulnerable to violence, according to a study by United College London and King's College London (England) that showed women with severe mental illnesses are up to five times more likely than the general population to become victims of sexual assault and two to three times more likely to suffer domestic violence. The findings were based on a survey of 303 randomly recruited psychiatric outpatients who had been in contact with community services for a year or more. Sixty percent had a diagnosis of schizophrenia.

As for incidences of violence inside psychiatric hospitals, a Canadian study included a random sampling of eighty-five women in five Toronto hospitals interviewed over a period of one year, including fifty women in provincial psychiatric wards and thirty-five in general hospital wards.

The study showed that one-third of the women reported incidents of either minor or severe physical or sexual assault during their hospital stay. All severe incidents took place in the provincial hospital setting, suggesting that one in every four female provincial patients may be at risk. "The severity could not be ascertained for the majority of sexual assault incidents since they involved male co-patients making sexual contact when the women were either asleep or in some way not fully conscious. Even on the wards, therefore, women were found to be at risk."

IN THE FALL of 1985, Margaret had a long-awaited visit from her mother and her brother Jim. Margaret may have been staying in a boarding home or with friends at the time, and she hadn't seen Jim since 1978, just before he and his family moved to the Ivory Coast in Africa to do missionary work. Jim and his wife, Barbara, were working as missionaries through the Baptist General Conference. They had three children – Ben, who was eight, and twin boys Brian and David, who were two. Five years later, they moved to Minnesota for a year then relocated to Paris where Jim studied at the Sorbonne. It was during their year in Paris that cracks began to appear in their marriage, and they divorced in 1986, shortly after moving back to the States.

Margaret would have known little, if anything, about her family's lives, and because of that, the visit may have been a bittersweet reminder of how disconnected from them she'd become.

MARGARET OCCASIONALLY STAYED in a boarding home, but the stays were short and sometimes ended because she'd had a fight with a landlord or she couldn't afford the rent. She might've tried finding a bed at a domestic violence shelter or the Wesley drop-in. Other nights, a friend's couch might've sufficed, if available; couch surfing is common among homeless people. The only institution she would venture into was the Barton Street jail, where she became so well known to police they nicknamed her Maggie J. When I first met Margaret at the Wesley, she had just come out of a two-week stint in jail, likely for mischief or public drunkenness.

"I had a really good time," she told me. "I ate so much food. I love to hang around in there."

IN THE 1970s, boarding homes in Hamilton, where Margaret and hundreds of other former psychiatric patients lived, were renamed second-level lodging homes. Hamilton was the first municipality in the province to open these lodging homes, in response to years of complaints around the poor quality of food, lack of supports and unsafe conditions. The homes were typically located in older two-storey homes in the inner city, and, under new regulations, operators were supposed to follow a set of health and safety rules that required them to provide meals, laundry service, assistance with medication, twenty-four-hour supervision and support to residents in the form of activities.

Residents were to have their own rooms and share the bathroom, kitchen and rest of the house with other tenants, and social workers and outreach workers were to schedule times to check in on them. Although licensing was a means to regulate the quality of accommodations and types of care provided, inspections were complaint-driven and happened infrequently. As a result, many former psychiatric patients who were moved into the homes continued having problems. The homes were later renamed residential care facilities and are still today plagued with problems. In September 2019, two facilities in Hamilton were shut down due to ongoing complaints.

Staff like Helen Kell and Pat Saunders, who worked in the mental health field, say it was normal for psychiatric patients who had been discharged from the hospital to stay briefly in a second-level lodging home then leave of their own accord and never return to the hospital.

Within the homeless population, the group known as the "chronically homeless" are those who have lived on the streets the longest and are more likely to suffer from disabilities, addictions and mental and physical health problems. According to the Homeless Hub, the chronically homeless use a high level of emergency services and institutional supports, and their episodes of homelessness "become more entrenched and ingrained in people's daily lives due to their long duration, which may be continuous or episodic."

Margaret would soon become a member of that group.

DURING THE RECESSION of the 1980s, Hamilton's welfare rolls swelled to record highs and agencies in Hamilton, including the Good Shepherd Centre, Mission Services and the Salvation Army, began to add more beds to their shelters to meet the growing need. Wesley Urban Ministries started a mobile van service that drove around the downtown at night and handed out soup, hot coffee and blankets. The agency soon realized that what people needed even more was a place to get out of the cold, and in 1984 they opened the overnight drop-in shelter on Rebecca Street.

While the building was old and the basement musty, the location was ideal as it was close to the downtown, near the bus station and right behind the police station, so help was close by if a fight broke out. It was also within walking distance to most of the other shelters, which made it easy for people to "do the rounds." Many preferred the Wesley because they were allowed to come and go as they pleased, and it was coed; other shelters were only for men, so couples were split up.

In the late 1980s, homelessness in Canada was declared a crisis. Most blamed the lack of affordable housing. A 2016 report by the Canadian Alliance to End Homelessness called *The State of Homelessness in Canada* stated, "Homelessness emerged as a problem as a result of a large disinvestment in affordable housing, structural shifts in the economy (resulting in, for example, a rapid decline in full-time, permanent, well-paying jobs) and reduced spending on a range of social and health supports in communities all across the country."

The government's withdrawal of investment in affordable housing was a major tipping point, but the push to empty psychiatric hospitals is why so many homeless people have a mental illness.

JOHN'S HOME WAS a blue plastic tarp near a garbage-filled ravine on the outskirts of downtown Hamilton. Outside his flimsy plastic tent were small beat-up chairs, an old mattress from a fold-out couch, blankets and a radio. John told the *Hamilton Spectator* in a December 2017 article that he had spent time in jail and had also lived in a crack house where his belongings had been stolen. But why would anyone prefer a freezing patch of land near a rail line to a warm bed at a shelter? For many people reading John's story, they would conclude that it was just another example of how many people were homeless by choice.

Media stories on homeless people who refuse to use shelters have reinforced the myth that no amount of coaxing could convince some to come inside. But a closer look into their stories reveals the multitude of reasons why many have turned their backs on shelters. Some have severe mental illnesses and can't manage confined, loud spaces while others find it impossible to abide by their strict rules. Others have been the victim of theft and/or violence at shelters one too many times, or they got fed up with the bedbugs. Still others were turned away so many times due to all of the beds being full that they stopped trying.

Some have a beloved dog, which may be the only thing that helps them get through their days, and most shelters don't take animals. A 2019 University of Windsor study showed that one in four homeless people have a pet and rather than give them up, they rough it out on the streets.

Then there are the Margarets, those who are so mentally and physically incapacitated that they've lost the ability to make rational decisions. They may have had negative experiences inside a psychiatric ward that convinced them not to go anywhere near a building that resembled institutional care. Through their portal to reality, they believe it's better to be on their own, even if that means sleeping outside in the winter.

When it comes to homelessness, the use of the word *choice* is inappropriate. Homelessness is never a choice. It's the desperate act of a person who has run out of all other options. As stated in the 2009 report *Homeless in Canada* by Charity Intelligence Canada: "No one in their right mind would choose to be homeless with its violence, stress and degradation. Sometimes sleeping on the streets is safer than being in a crowded emergency shelter. Homelessness reflects a failure in us and organizations to provide appropriate and responsive care."

Many homeless people with a mental illness would welcome the opportunity to stay in supportive housing that provided addiction and mental health services; however, it needs to be tailored to their needs. It also needs to be provided before their health deteriorates to the point where they're teetering on the edge of death, like Margaret was, and before they become impossible to reach.

Trying to help a chronically homeless person once they've hit rock bottom is a huge challenge, as Steve Lopez discovered. Lopez is a columnist for the *Los Angeles Times* and in 2005 wrote a series of columns on a homeless fellow named Nathaniel Ayers, who had schizophrenia and lived on LA's skid row. Lopez formed a friendship with Ayers then discovered that he was a Juilliard-trained classical bass student who could play several instruments beautifully. In Lopez's book *The Soloist: A Lost Dream, an Unlikely Friendship, and the Redemptive Power of Music* (which inspired the 2009 movie of the same name, starring Robert Downey Jr.), he documented his months of trying to help Ayers as well as the many setbacks. There were many times that he questioned his naïveté in thinking he could help Ayers, who eventually agreed to connect with a non-profit organization in Los Angeles called the LAMP Community, which helped people living with severe mental illness. Still, it was often one step forward and two steps back.

There are similarities between Nathaniel Ayers's and Margaret's stories, specifically that Ayers had also been diagnosed with schizophrenia and ended up homeless. What both stories reinforce is the importance of reaching homeless people before they've progressed past the point of no return.

"ARE YOU BEING a good girl?"

That's how Constable Michael Joy greeted Margaret when he saw her, and he saw her often in his job with the Hamilton-Wentworth Regional Police department. Joy was on the force for more than forty years, from 1970 to 2014, and would see her when he walked through the downtown or when he was driving his cruiser. Joy came to know Margaret well as she would frequently wander the streets or set herself up in a park on his route. He knew about the lack of supports for homeless people and he kept an eye on her to make sure she was all right.

"I would pull over and ask her if she was being a good girl, and she'd always say, 'Ya,' and I'd say, 'Okay, have a good day.'"

Joy was more than familiar with the kind of challenges police faced when it came to dealing with homeless people. Police are often the first line of contact for a homeless person and, during a cold alert, officers try and make sure there's no one left on the streets. If they see someone in distress, they sometimes put them in their cars; however, there are few places to take them. One police officer from Hamilton reportedly drove around for four hours one night with a homeless mentally ill man in the back of his cruiser who refused to go to a shelter. When the sun came up, the officer bought the man a cup of coffee then let him back out onto the streets.

When the shelters are full and there's nowhere else to take them, police have been known to charge homeless people with minor offences, like disorderly conduct or trespassing, to get them off the streets. Torrey wrote in *Out of the Shadows* that the practice in the US of charging homeless people with misdemeanours is so common that it's referred to as "mercy booking": "It appears . . . that jails and prisons have increasingly become surrogate mental hospitals for many people with severe mental illnesses."

On the other side, there have also been reports of harsh treatment by police against homeless people. Although people who are homeless are more likely to be the victims of crime than the perpetrators, they frequently complain of harassment by police. In a 2009 University of Toronto study, homeless people said they have been picked up for sleeping on a bench or shoplifting food, which are related to survival.

The closures of psychiatric beds combined with a lack of housing and community supports have also led to huge increases in the number of people with mental illness in our prisons. Ivan Zinger, correctional investigator of Canada, wrote in his 2017 annual report that Canada's prisons are so overburdened with prisoners suffering from severe mental health issues that he questioned whether mental illness had become criminalized. Offenders with mental health issues are also grossly overrepresented in solitary confinement because of the lack of specialized units available.

Zinger said that the situation is especially bad for women because there are no stand-alone treatment facilities for federal female inmates. The only emergency measure available to female inmates is an all-male treatment centre where they would be kept separate from male inmates. It is partly for that reason that female inmates are more likely to be placed in maximum-security units.

As Andrew Solomon wrote in *The Noonday Demon: An Atlas of Depression*: ". . . the result of deinstitutionalization has in many instances been to shift people from hospitals to prisons. And in the prison, where they received inadequate and inappropriate treatment, they cause a terrific amount of trouble."

In Michael J. Dear and Jennifer R. Wolch's book *Landscapes of Despair: From Deinstitutionalization to Homelessness*, the authors wrote: "It is hardly surprising that many individuals are quickly reinstitutionalized – back to jail, asylum or hospital. The others who manage to remain on the outside often survive on the margin – poor, lonely and isolated."

Former psychiatric patients became such a familiar part of the criminal justice system that cities like Hamilton set up special units where inmates with mental health problems can access a psychiatrist.

The chaotic and unpredictable environment inside most prisons is hardly an appropriate place for people suffering from mild anxiety let alone auditory hallucinations. Despite the high number of inmates with mental health problems, mental health screening remains almost non-existent in prisons and guards receive little to no training on how to work with someone who has a mental illness. With no treatment programs and few medications available, it's little wonder so many end up in segregation cells.

In 2013, Christina Jahn alleged that she was placed in segregation for 210 days at the Ottawa-Carleton Detention Centre, despite having a mental illness as well as addictions and cancer. She filed an application with the Human Rights Tribunal of Ontario and the Ontario Human Rights Commission (OHRC) intervened. As part of the settlement, the ministry agreed to review how to best serve women inmates who had a mental illness and put in place mental health screening for all inmates.

While the review looked promising, three years later nothing had been done. That prompted the OHRC to launch legal action against the province for breaching the agreement. Since then, reports have shown that conditions for prisoners with mental health issues have actually gotten worse, and a 2017 report by Ontario's official adviser on corrections, Howard Sapers, showed that the use of segregation among inmates with mental health issues had actually increased over the previous eighteen months. There was a breakthrough, however, in January 2018, when Ontario Corrections announced that inmates with mental health disabilities would no longer be placed in solitary confinement, barring exceptional circumstances.

CONSTABLE JOY STILL remembers being called to the east end park where Margaret lived for several months. People in the area had come to know and worry about her, so when they noticed her acting bizarrely one day, they called the police. The message that was passed along to Joy was that Margaret was "out of control." When Joy and another officer arrived, Margaret was running around the park bench, wildly flailing her arms about and yelling as if she were being chased. When they were unable to calm her down, they grabbed her by her arms and, with Margaret flailing about, dragged her across the lawn and wrestled her into the van. It was then that Joy realized the reason for her erratic behaviour. Hundreds of fleas were jumping from her hair and clothing. Many of them were landing on him.

The officers managed to get her into the van and took her to the hospital where she was put in a separate room and cleaned up before being released. Joy and the other officer returned to the station to have the van deloused, then showered and picked up new uniforms.

"You would see the homeless out there all the time and there was always a concern for their welfare but really there was nothing we could do," said Joy.

As for Margaret, he said, "She put up a good fight with her illness but it was sad."

CHAPTER FOURTEEN
Kindness of Strangers

1989–1990
Hamilton

The streets run all night. There are no walls to shut out the cacophony of sounds or the glare of lights, and for women, no doors to keep out the rage of drunken men. For Margaret to have lived on the streets as long as she did, she must have honed her survival skills to that of a soldier on high alert. Every day was a constant search for food and shelter, and if she didn't find herself a bed, she would push through the darkness until the light returned. Then she would repeat it all again, night after night. An unrelenting fight to stay alive, all through the fractured mind of schizophrenia.

The longer the streets were her home, the sicker she became. The sicker she became, the more disconnected she grew from any supports that could have pulled her back and the easier it became for society to turn its back on her. Margaret developed her famous strut. People started referring to her as "feisty" – "Margaret won't take any crap," they'd say. But others saw her cockiness as a front to make her look tough. At the Wesley, she became known for smashing people in the face with the melamine coffee cups, likely a defensive reaction.

Occasionally, Margaret might collect a disability pension of a couple of hundred dollars a month; however, as she had no permanent address or ID and could not open a bank account, a chunk of that would have been eaten up by cheque-cashing services. Some took as much as 25 percent.

Because of her illness and because she was a woman, Margaret would have been easy prey for thieves at the end of the month when her cheque came in. Maybe she learned to go into hiding during those days. She told friends she'd had her money stolen numerous times and that she'd been sexually assaulted more than once. Money was still a chronic problem for her. A 2008 study by Toronto's Street Health showed that 42 percent of homeless women had an average income of less than $2,500 per year. They cited such barriers as not having proper identification, negative experiences with previous caseworkers and lack of knowledge on how to navigate the system.

Margaret outside of a convenience store. She was rarely seen without her cigarettes. Courtesy of Bill MacKinnon.

THE CRUEL AND unrelenting hardships faced by homeless women can be deadly. In January 2019, a fifty-eight-year-old homeless woman in Toronto was killed when she was run over by a garbage truck in a downtown alley. Hang Vo was known to frequent various shelters in Toronto and had been sleeping on a grate for warmth. One week later, also in Toronto, a thirty-five-year-old homeless woman died after becoming lodged in the opening of a donation bin located near Bloor Street and Dovercourt Road. Witnesses told police they heard Crystal Papineau screaming for help at around two in the morning.

When officers arrived, her body was half out of the bin. She was pronounced dead at the scene. The night she died, temperatures had dipped below zero, and all of the city's women shelters were full. Advocates said her death was another reminder of the need for more supports and housing for homeless women. The same month that these two women died, it was announced that a four-storey, fifty-seven-bed YWCA-run shelter for home-less women would open in Toronto. The Davenport Road shelter was part of the City of Toronto's commitment to open one thousand new shelter beds by the end of 2020.

But the beds filled up quickly, reinforcing the high demand. Street nurse and homeless advocate Cathy Crowe, co-author of *Dying for a Home: Homeless Activists Speak Out* and author of *A Knapsack Full of Dreams*, told the CBC during a January 2019 vigil for Crystal Papineau that there was a much bigger issue that contributed to her death.

Crowe said there were more than one hundred women sleeping on floors and in chairs at overnight drop-ins in Toronto every night, and that another one thousand people were being squeezed into respite and out-of-the-cold centres. Advocates, including Crowe, called on Toronto mayor John Tory to declare a state of emergency when it came to homelessness. The mayor declined.

"The situation here just begs for national outrage," Crowe told CBC.

MARGARET'S MOTHER, VERNA, was still living in an Assemblies of God re-tirement village in Springfield, Missouri, and would periodically send her a few dollars. It's not known what address she used but it may have been one of the shelters that Margaret frequented. Margaret would use the money to buy coffee, cigarettes and lottery tickets. Whether she ever won anything or if she even checked her tickets isn't known. It's also not known whether her mother knew the full extent of her daughter's desperate living situation.

Even though Margaret would have had enough money at the beginning of the month to rent a room, she was so mentally incapacitated that she was beyond the point of being able to find one. She would think nothing of urinating on the sidewalk or throwing her shoes into the garbage if she decided she didn't like them. Her years of hospitalization; of being shunted from boarding homes to shelters, to emergency departments and in and out of jail, had worn her down. She was now completely reliant on crisis services, like emergency shelters and hospital emergency wards.

MARGARET'S PATH TO homelessness had been circuitous – from her family's home to the hospital, to boarding homes, back and forth to the hospital and finally to the streets. The pattern had repeated itself many times over until the streets became her permanent home. The longer she lived there, the more she relied on the kindness of strangers. Fortunately, there were many people who cared about her. People like Carol Green, whose small acts of kindness reflected the larger public concern about homelessness. Green met Margaret in 1984 in the coffee shop where she worked. She would see Margaret come in to warm herself and it always upset her because she would be wearing thin, tattered clothes. Green would buy her a cup of coffee and let her warm up, but she always worried when Margaret left.

One night after Green's shift ended, she walked over to Margaret and asked if she could sit down. Margaret said yes, and it marked the beginning of a friendship that carried on over the next two years. Whenever Margaret wandered in, Green would take a break and share a coffee with her. She would try and find out where Margaret was sleeping and whether she had enough to eat.

"She always said she had somewhere to go, but I knew she didn't. I really worried about her," said Green.

One day Green popped the question to her husband about taking Margaret in. They had a big house and their four children were gone, so why not? He agreed without hesitation. When Green made her offer to Margaret, she immediately turned it down.

"She didn't like to rely on anyone. I remember that about her," said Green.

LYNN FERRIS KNEW Margaret was a fighter. She had to be to have survived as long as she had as a woman alone on the streets. She also knew that

Margaret was fiercely independent and that she didn't like asking for help. Ferris had worked as a supervisor at the Wesley from 1991 to 2001, and from the moment she met Margaret, she felt a special affection for her. She loved Margaret's feistiness and her sense of humour, and admired her survival smarts.

"She always referred to me as the nice girl with the black hair even though I told her my name many times," said Ferris, laughing.

Ferris remembered the way Margaret would come in from the cold and cradle her coffee cup in her hands to get warm. She would always sit with her back to the wall so no one could walk up behind her. Then there was her famous strut.

"There was something regal about it," said Ferris.

It saddened her to see how street life was wearing Margaret down. She would cringe when she saw Margaret coming in wearing thin clothes and looking more sickly as time passed. "She was always filthy and hungry when I saw her. She had to be strong as a woman to deal with all of that but we could see how sick she was."

Whenever Margaret came by, Ferris would make sure she got a hot bowl of soup and warm clothing. But often Margaret's fashion sense overrode practicality, and in the winter she would come in wearing high heels, short jackets and skirts with bare legs. Ferris would pick out some warm clothes from the Wesley's donation box and give them to Margaret, but she'd only take them if they were her style.

When Ferris's mother died, she gave Margaret her mom's rust-coloured suede coat with a fur collar as she knew Margaret would love it and it would keep her warm. She was right. Margaret wore it constantly and had an extra bounce in her step when she had it on.

"It was funny seeing her in it because my mother was around the same height, so sometimes from behind I would think it was her," said Ferris.

Because Margaret was such a regular at the centre, the one summer they had a shortfall in funds and had to close for two months, Ferris made sure to tell Margaret personally, knowing she would be upset. "She started laughing maniacally and began pulling her hair out. It was so disturbing to see how distressed she was and there was nothing I could do. It was really, really sad."

FRANCINE SMALL MET Margaret in 1993. She had just started working at the Wesley and was twenty-three years old and fresh out of college with a diploma in social work. Her job as the Wesley's emergency services worker was to get to know people at the drop-in and find services to help them. But it was her first time in a homeless shelter, and she felt so intimidated that most nights she would hide in a corner and try to disappear behind the fog of cigarette smoke.

"It was a real eye-opener," said Small. "Nothing I had learned in college could have prepared me for what I saw there."

No one scared her more than Margaret, who she described as being larger than life. By now, Margaret was so well known around the shelter circuit, she'd earned the nickname Princess Margaret. "She would walk in with this swagger about her and heads would turn. Everyone knew when Margaret was there. She was like a woman from another era. She was so self-assured and never appeared to be scared."

Small also knew about Margaret's reputation for whipping the hard cups at people and she didn't want to be next. One night, while Small was standing in a corner, she looked across at the crowd and quietly confided to another staffer about her fear of the clientele and how overwhelmed she felt. She didn't realize Margaret was standing beside her.

"She said to me out of the blue, 'Why are you so sensitive? It's not going to work for you here.' I was shocked and it made me realize she was watching me. She was watching everything and she was absolutely right. I thought, 'Oh my god, she's right.'"

After that, everything changed.

"I became more sensitive to the clients, in the sense that I realized they were just people," said Small. "Margaret taught me that, that they were still just people. That's not something that you can learn in school but Margaret taught me that."

Small slowly began approaching people and talking to them, and found out about their lives before they became homeless. She was surprised to find that some had been married and had good jobs while others, like Margaret, could play musical instruments. The biggest lesson she learned was that all they really wanted was to be treated with respect. Two years later, Small was moved to a new position in the Wesley's housing department. Her new office was in a building far away from the drop-in shelter so she didn't see much of Margaret, although there were still regular reminders of the desperate lives homeless people lived. Often when she came to work, people were camped out in a field across the street – some in tents while others slept on the ground. The Wesley served a hot breakfast in the building where she worked and they wanted to be first in line.

One Christmas, Small and a few of her musician friends volunteered to perform at the Wesley Centre's holiday party. A large crowd of mostly home-less and transient folks were waiting in the room and when they arrived Small and her friends jumped onto the stage, eager to cheer everyone up. They broke out in song and played joyful Christmas tunes, prancing around the stage as they sang, confident they were treating the audience to a great time.

"We were feeling all proud of ourselves that we were doing this and we were up there singing 'Jingle Bells' and the crowd was just sitting there doing nothing. There was no reaction at all. We didn't know what was going on. Then a guy yelled from the back, 'You're depressing me.'"

They were so shocked that they stopped singing and walked off the stage. Huddling together backstage, they tried to understand what had just hap-pened. "That's when we realized, Christmas is not a happy time for a lot of people and they didn't want to be reminded of what they were missing. One of the musicians walked back out with his guitar and started playing the blues and the crowd loved it. It made me realize you need to ask people what they want and they will tell you. I don't think we do enough of that and it's not something we learned in school."

Small is now fifty and living in Montreal where she is a part-time profes-sor in sociology at Dawson College. She sees homeless people regularly in her neighbourhood, and her interaction all those years ago with Margaret still forms the foundation for how she treats them. One night a homeless woman came up to her and asked for spare change. The woman's teeth were rotten and she looked sick. As Small was reaching into her purse, a fellow walked by and stopped to chastise the woman for eating too much candy.

"So many people see people on the streets and put the blame on them for being homeless," said Small. "When I see people on the streets, I can feel it in my heart how much they are struggling. My empathy for women like this comes directly from working with Margaret. She taught me not to assume things about people."

Across Canada, the kindness of strangers plays out night after night and helps to keep thousands of homeless people alive. Strangers volunteer with hundreds of agencies and organizations, each one part of a huge nationwide network that feeds, clothes and shelters this most vulnerable group. These armies of volunteers help out at shelters, make hot meals, provide support at day drop-ins and help run soup vans. They cook and serve meals in church basements; collect donations of food, clothing; and raise money for agencies and churches. Agencies who run programs on shoestring budgets say they couldn't operate without volunteers. It's especially difficult when they see people, like Margaret, getting worn down year after year because there are no services to help them. They know that the bowls of soup they serve are a small thing compared to what they need.

If you counted up the number of staff and volunteers across Canada working at charities and agencies that help the homeless community, the number would be in the hundreds of thousands. Each and every one of them is doing what they can to keep homeless people alive for one more day.

The volunteers are people like Jeff Ng who, for sixteen years, has helped distribute food and clothing to homeless and low-income people in

Hamilton. Every Wednesday night, rain or snow, he and a group of about twenty-five volunteers from Parkview Church in east Hamilton set up tables in various parking spots or open areas, and redistribute donated food and clothing. They would see more than one hundred homeless people, low-income families and working poor every night. Their first stop is from 8:00 p.m. to 9:30 p.m., then they head over to another parking lot in the east end and help another one hundred people from ten till eleven thirty.

They also have a furniture warehouse and a small food bank at the church for people who need free items. The meals they provide are often the only healthy food that some people eat all week. By the end of the month, Ng estimates they've reached eight hundred to one thousand people.

"We are a small group and we rely completely on donations," Jeff told me.

Many of their clients are new immigrants, while others are people coming out of shelters, low-income families and homeless people. Their group has struggled to keep up with the growing demand, especially over the past year, and even though theirs is a much-needed service that provides a critical lifeline to the most vulnerable people in the city, they receive zero funding from any government source. Sadly, the volunteers count their successes by the number of people who don't freeze to death overnight. However, as Cathy Crowe wrote in *Dying for a Home: Homeless Activists Speak Out*, there's a downside to all this kindness. "What we have witnessed in Canada is the government's prolonged reliance on volunteer groups to provide increasingly complicated types of aid, with no sign of proper funding for the social service sector, let alone housing relief."

IT'S A SUNNY but cold winter afternoon in downtown Hamilton and a man is slumped on the sidewalk like a rag doll. His legs are splayed and his hood is pulled over his head. There's a large dark spot on his jeans where it looks like he's wet himself. Beside him is a rickety grocery cart that's stuffed with garbage bags, likely filled with everything he owns. His "bed" is outside the Hamilton Urban Core Community Health Centre, which provides health services to low-income and homeless people. It's located on a busy street where there's a steady stream of cars and pedestrians.

No one stops to see if he's all right. It's as if he's invisible.

This scene can be found in almost every city in every province and territory across the country, many times over. Despite the serious threat that homelessness poses to a person's health and the high costs it exacts on municipal and provincial health and social services, homeless people have simply blended into our landscape.

When did this immunity to human suffering start? How did we become so complacent about people sleeping on our streets? Hamilton social worker Suzanne Foreman worked with homeless people in Hamilton for years, including at Wesley Urban Ministries from 1992 to 1997, first in the street youth program then as a housing counsellor.

Foreman has short, grey hair and an honest smile, and spoke with compassion about homeless people. She believes a lot of people have bought into the media spin that many homeless people actually live in three-bedroom bungalows in the suburbs and that panhandling is an easy way to make a few extra bucks.

"There is a real disconnect between how homelessness is defined statistically and how the average person with a residence sees the issue," said Foreman.

She believes the public's apathy toward the homeless population is also about a lack of trust in our leaders. "Everybody wants somebody to do something, but distrust of political and health care systems, not being willing to speak up or rock any boats for fear of jeopardizing one's own stability, and being overwhelmed by daily encounters [with homeless people] have caused people to simply look away."

Or perhaps the image of a homeless person hits too close to home.

"I suspect some people look away because they are frightened. Employment and health issues have become so precarious for many that I think the reality of homelessness has started to hit too close to home. 'There but for the grace of . . .' and so on." Foreman worries most about the invisible homeless, those living in their vehicles or on somebody's couch or in a cardboard nest in Hamilton Cemetery. They suffer the most, she said, because they are so hidden. "They are exhausted and disillusioned. It is a desperate situation that can bring out both the best and the worst in people. I have no ready answers."

CHAPTER FIFTEEN
Bob and Margaret

She was different from any girl I would have picked for my wife,
but she was my wife.
– Bob Dixon

1989
Hamilton

Bob Dixon is a short, stocky fellow with a perpetually worried look that says he doesn't want trouble. His round belly is packed tightly inside an old yellow T-shirt that has a small hole in it near his navel. His belly jiggles like Santa when he laughs, which he does frequently when he talks about Margaret.

Bob is seventy-nine and lives in a long-term care home around the corner from the old Wesley Centre where he met Margaret in the late 1980s. He shares his small room with another man, separated by a thin curtain. There's an old wooden dresser at the foot of his bed and a bedside table crowded with his medications. A medical mask hangs on the wall that he wears for his sleep

Bob Dixon talking about Margaret. Photo by Denise Davy.

apnea. His hands tremble slightly as his lifts a cup of water to his mouth, which is cotton-ball dry, likely a side effect of the medications he takes for schizophrenia and epilepsy.

Sometimes Bob uses a wheelchair to get around, which he sat in during many of our visits. I settled into an upholstered chair in the corner and listened to him recite his memories of Margaret.

IF LOVE EVER needed a purpose, it found it in Bob and Margaret. The two met at the Wesley one night and formed a friendship based on mutual need – Bob needed a companion and Margaret needed a home. Over the weeks, as Bob came to know Margaret, he grew to admire her. During that year, Bob showed Margaret a level of kindness that she'd never experienced. Their story started in the late 1980s. Bob had his own apartment and was living comfortably on a monthly disability allowance. He also had a little cash from his part-time cleaning job at the Wesley. Bob chuckled when he explained how he was hired because they liked the way he was able to talk to the clients.

"To tell the truth, I was scared of them. If they'd said 'jump,' I would have jumped."

Bob enjoyed his life but he was lonely. He was in his late forties and any women he'd dated "just didn't stick around."

"They went out with me once then they would always turn me down."

Bob was a top student and "smart as a whip" in school, said his brother, Ross Dixon. He also had a heart of gold, said Ross, remembering the time when he was a kid and Bob went in search of Ross's bike when it had been stolen. Shortly after Bob graduated from teacher's college, Ross said his brother had his first episode in which Bob saw serpents who would come to him with messages from God. Bob was diagnosed with schizophrenia. He spent some time in a psychiatric ward where he was put on antipsychotic medication, which he's been on ever since and are effective in controlling his illness. He lived with his parents well into his adult years, until they died and he got his own place. He's lived in this Hamilton long-term care centre for about six years.

There were many times that Bob's friends at the Wesley heard him complain about feeling lonely. One night a staffer suggested he approach Margaret. Bob balked at the idea. His first impression of Margaret, when she was standing in line at the Wesley waiting to get a sandwich, was not good. She was wearing a ragged red sweater and old blue shorts. Bob said her hair was filthy and her face looked like "a red mass of acne." Word among staff was that she'd just gotten out of jail.

"I thought to myself, 'What's that!' She looked like a real mess," said Bob, shaking his head.

But dates for Bob were few and far between. He approached Margaret while she was sitting on the bench and invited her home. She accepted. They slept in the same bed. The next morning, as they headed to the Wesley for a coffee, Margaret told him she'd been sleeping at an all-night laundromat on a wooden bench in the front window but that the owner had kicked her out because she'd "made a mess."

Bob knew that likely meant she'd urinated on the floor, as Margaret was prone to do. It was obvious that Margaret had mental health problems, but Bob never asked about it. He'd had his own experience with hallucinations. As it happened, the night before, Bob had been visited by a serpent who told him that his wife had slept in a laundromat. Listening to Margaret tell her story, Bob took it as a sign.

"When she told me about the laundromat, I thought right away, 'Well, Margaret is like my wife. She was different from any girl I would have picked for my wife, but she was my wife.'"

FOR THE NEXT year, Bob provided Margaret with a level of stability she'd never known. He fed her, let her listen to his music and bought her cartons of her favourite Du Maurier cigarettes so she wouldn't have to roll her own. Margaret had never met anyone like Bob, who showed her more kindness than she likely felt she deserved. When Bob finished a shift at the Wesley, he and Margaret would head downtown together to get a coffee. They were an odd couple: Bob with his short, stocky frame and worried face; Margaret, lanky and scrawny and wearing ragged clothes. Within their own limitations, they'd created their own version of an old married couple. It wasn't everyone's definitions of happiness but it worked for them, at least in the early months.

"She was quite happy so long as she had her cup of coffee," said Bob, smiling.

Bob learned that Margaret had worked at a company called Appleford Paper Products where she typed dockets. It was likely a part-time job set up through the hospital.

"I didn't know what dockets were but I was impressed," said Bob.

Then there were her musical skills. "Boy, she could play a mean piano," said Bob, smiling. "I was at a Christmas service at the Wesley with her when she got up from the table, walked to the front of the room, and sat down at the piano and started to play. I was never so surprised in my life. When I saw her go up there, I thought, 'Oh no, she's going to make a fool of herself again,' but instead she played all these Christmas tunes. And she told me she could play the accordion. I asked her if I bought her an accordion would she play it and she said, 'No.'"

Margaret loved listening to Bob's Bing Crosby *White Christmas* CD, which he had ordered after hearing it on the radio. It quickly became Margaret's favourite and she would ask him to play it again and again. Bob would oblige. "It was one of the few times she would sit quietly," said Bob. "She would put her head back and just listen."

Margaret opened up to Bob about how she'd been assaulted by male patients at the hospital. She told Bob she'd managed to fight them off, but that other times she hadn't been as lucky.

"She told me she was laying on the grass beside a house in broad daylight once when an Indian fellow jumped on top of her and raped her. Margaret didn't have a choice," said Bob. "She would have been beaten to a pulp if she hadn't given in to him and she knew that."

Old habits died hard, however, and even though she now had guaranteed shelter, she would sometimes take off for days. Bob would walk the streets looking for her and sometimes catch her eating food out of a dumpster. He would try and convince her to come home and, if she refused, he would give her money or bus tickets. One cold winter day Bob found her outside without boots on and went home and retrieved his new fur-lined boots with the zipper and took them to her. Unfortunately, Margaret wasn't always very appreciative.

"I asked her what had happened to the boots and she said she threw them away. I went and looked in all the garbage cans because they were really good boots and they were brand new. I never found them."

Another time, Bob found a long fake fur coat in a donation box and grabbed it then walked through downtown looking for her. She wore it for a few weeks, but when she saw a homeless woman at the Wesley wearing a short-waisted fake fur coat, she traded it for ten dollars. Bob shrugged in resignation. "It couldn't have been as warm as the other one but she liked the style."

Despite Margaret's scrawny size, she was "all muscle," said Bob. "She was throwing a fit at the Wesley Centre one time and I was trying to calm her down when she up and – wham-o – hit me right in the head here with a cup." He leaned forward and pointed to a long white scar on his forehead. "I was two hundred pounds or so but she could take me and push me right across the floor. One time she threw me across the room. Boy, was I surprised."

It was also surprising in light of how sick she was. A few years before she moved in with Bob, Margaret had been diagnosed with breast cancer. Although it was in the early stages and would have responded to treatment, Margaret refused because of her mistrust of doctors. The only time she went close to seeing a doctor was when she accompanied Bob to see his psychiatrist. "She wasn't very pleasant to him," said Bob, smiling.

While it frustrated him that Margaret wouldn't get medical help, he accepted it. "She wouldn't go back to the psychiatric hospital because she told me they'd given her shock treatments up there and she said she didn't want them anymore. She said they just seemed to grab her by the throat and they hurt. Whenever I asked her to go she said, 'You go.'"

Bob soon discovered that Margaret's domestic skills were sadly lacking. Whenever she cooked her favourite Kraft Dinner meal, she'd let the water spill over the pot and onto the stove then tell Bob to clean it up.

"I tried to tell her to clean it up but she refused."

She wouldn't bathe for days and her body odour was rancid, and even worse, when she had her period, she would let the blood run down her legs and trail behind her as she walked. Bob remembered one time they were riding the bus together when Margaret's period started, and she had no underwear or pants on under her coat. "I was praying to God to please keep your legs crossed." Margaret stood up when they reached their stop. "There was this red bloody mess on the seat. I thought, 'Oh my god,' I just wanted to get out of there."

For the first few months, Bob picked up her cigarette butts, swept food off the floor and wiped up her spilled beer. He had to constantly remind her to be careful with her lit cigarettes and feared she would set fire to the apartment as she regularly threw lit butts and matches on the couch and onto the floor.

"I didn't mind picking up her cigarettes for a couple of nights, but it kept going and going. I never knew if there was going to be a fire."

As time wore on, her behaviour became wilder. Once she was standing at the kitchen sink filling an electric kettle and not wearing any pants. Bob walked up behind her and playfully grabbed her behind. She sent the kettle flying across the room where it hit the wall and smashed into small pieces. Bob patiently picked it up and tried to fix it but to no avail. He threatened to kick her out and, on a few occasions, followed through. But he always took her back.

Another time, while they were watching TV, Margaret suddenly got up, bounced across the room and poured her beer into an ashtray, letting it overflow onto the floor as she laughed uproariously. Still another time she was in the living room drinking beer with another homeless woman when the woman yelled, "Let's throw a bottle through the window." Bob jumped up and grabbed them both and ordered them out. Cleaning up after Margaret was wearing thin, but what upset him most was when she accused Bob of stealing her disability money.

"It was Margaret who used to go in and take my money. I had a box of quarters and she always took them," said Bob.

As tensions grew between them, Margaret starting sleeping on the couch. One morning Bob woke up to find the bedsheets covered in brown stains. Margaret told him she'd gone to the bathroom in the middle of the night and hadn't wiped herself.

"I said to Margaret, 'That looks like shit,' and she said, 'It is shit.' She didn't wipe herself or anything. I had to show her how to use the toilet paper to wipe herself and then I had to show her how to put a new roll of toilet paper on."

He shook his head, frustrated. "One day she got the little roll and flushed it down the toilet and plugged up the toilet."

As much as Bob liked having a "wife," he was slowly realizing that Margaret's wild ways couldn't be tamed. "She wouldn't do anything you told her to do or asked her. I could understand it to a point, but I got to the point where I couldn't take it anymore."

Bob often wondered why Margaret's parents didn't visit and why they weren't more concerned about her. Margaret still called her mother collect at her nursing home in Springfield, Missouri, but Bob said, "The impression I got was that Margaret was an outcast to her family. She rarely talked about her dad and her talks with her mother were almost always combative. It would always end up in an argument every time."

Bob didn't know what they would argue about. He just knew they didn't get along. "I don't think her mom understood Margaret's life, that she was actually sleeping outside with a blanket in the snow. It's hard for anyone to understand how she lived. I had a hard time understanding it myself."

IT'S UNLIKELY VERNA had any idea just how horrific her daughter's life was. There was a secrecy around anything to do with Margaret, and relatives said Margaret's name was often spoken in whispers. Her nephew David, Jim's son, lives in Kunshan, China, outside of Shanghai, with his wife, Diana, and their ten-year-old son, Elliott. David, forty-four, said his aunt was a mystery to them.

"She was always a story I heard, either in hushed tones or as an after-thought in some reminiscence from my father or uncle," wrote David in an email. "I knew of her through stories of her illness and her homelessness. I think my father [Jim] went to Canada to visit her once, but I don't remember her well-being to have occupied a space in our family growing up. Maybe my father was trying to escape in his own way, too. I knew she wasn't being cared for in a nice hospital. I knew she had issues related to her health that were being ignored."

Because they knew so little about her, David said there was a tendency to make up stories, like Margaret had HIV or that she was a heroin user. There was never any way to find out the truth.

"My grandfather, her dad, died before I was born and my grandmother never spoke of her. She may have been the family pariah, a shame on the name of those that chose to 'tough it out,'" wrote David.

David's twin brother, Brian, lives in Oostburg, Wisconsin, with his wife, Courtney, and their ten-year-old son, Theo. Like his father and grandfa-ther, Brian became a man of the cloth and works as a pastor at the First Presbyterian Church. He said they knew so little about Margaret and were never even told where she lived. Brian offered to look through the family's photo collection for photos of Margaret because his parents kept extensive records of all family members. He was sure they'd have several. But after going through four large boxes of "meticulously curated material" that his father had put together, representing a thorough record of the family, he found only three small photos of Margaret.

"The genealogical records my dad compiled have files on virtually everyone, including some cousins and uncles and aunts, but not a single mention
of Margaret," Brian wrote in an email. "There are
actually letters from [Abe] to what seem to be
obscure parishes in the Swedish countryside asking for information about our lineage and yet not
a single manila folder with the name 'Margaret'
on it. She was, it seems, a mystery even to her
own family."

Jacobson Christmas card.
Clockwise from top left corner:
Abe, Verna, Margaret, David,
John and Jim (centre). Courtesy
of Jacobson family.

One of those photos was a Christmas card
with pictures of Abe and Verna and the four
children. It was taken during their missionary
years. Margaret looked to be around twelve. It
read: "Serving with Joy." Those words were ironic,
Brian wrote, because the photo showed Abe with
his lips firmly clenched into an expression of impatience while Verna looked
on with a mix of disappointment and fatigue.

"I found [the photo] to be humorous in a dark sort of way," wrote Brian.
"It declares that the family serves with joy while the father and mother look
anything but joyful. In fact, the truth is I don't ever remember seeing a picture of my grandfather smiling or laughing."

Although Margaret was never talked about, Brian never stopped wondering about her and thought many times about the possible reasons for her
mental illness. He believes it was a combination of nature and nurture, that
she may have been genetically predisposed but that her stressful upbringing
also contributed to her becoming so ill.

I've come to believe that because my grandparents were austere and
authoritarian, that the combination of a loveless upbringing within the
rigours of the mission field combined to exacerbate whatever social anx-
ieties and genetic predispositions toward mental illness existed in both
Margaret and John.

This is perhaps too simple an explanation, and is merely speculative, but based on the little information I have, it's the best I've been able to do.

Speculative yes, but there's likely some truth to it given how harsh Abe was on his children. Margaret likely felt the most pressure as the oldest. Brian remembered his grandfather as someone who withheld love from his children and David remembers as a child hearing stories about abuse in the Jacobson household. He said his grandfather was known to call Verna "Dumb Dutch."

> He [Jim] often said that no one in the household ever said "I love you." Indeed, growing up I never heard my grandmother utter those words. Not to us, her grandkids, and not to my father or mother. She was never unkind, just not particularly affectionate.
>
> My father [Jim] said that he felt love from his dad when he would rap his knuckles with a ruler to correct his piano playing. That was a way that he felt his father was wanting the best for him.

Indeed, Margaret had been a disappointment to Abe from the moment she was born, as he had let it be known he had wanted a boy. Throughout her childhood, Abe set such high expectations for his children that she never felt good enough. When she got sick in her teens, Abe blamed her for an illness she couldn't control. When he was forced to leave his missionary job, which he loved, he did the one thing that hurt her the most – he left her behind.

Even from her hospital bed, Abe's disapproval haunted Margaret like a ghost. He would fill his letters with Biblical passages designed to show how she'd failed him and the Lord. Her sickness was her punishment, he told her. Margaret had been taught all her life to believe in the word of the Lord above all else – who was she to question her missionary father.

ONE AFTERNOON AFTER Bob and Margaret had left the apartment, the landlord went up to check on things as he'd heard some noises and suspected there were problems. Seeing the mess of burn marks and food stains, he confronted Bob upon his return and said that either Margaret left or he would evict them both. Bob was worried about Margaret but he didn't want to become homeless himself. He had no other option but to tell her to go. Margaret took it in stride and left promptly. A few days later, she returned and asked for the cartons of Du Mauriers Bob had bought her. Bob hesitated as he knew she'd either lose them or they'd be stolen, but he relented and gave them to her, all eight cartons. A few days later, Bob ran into Margaret at the Wesley. She had lost all eight cartons.

Shortly after, Margaret moved in with a tall, heavy-set, dark-haired fellow named John, who was a regular at the Wesley. While Bob was relieved that Margaret had a place to stay, he was worried because John was known for his explosive temper. One day John came into the Wesley boasting about a big engagement ring he'd bought for Margaret and said they'd planned to be married. Only a few days later, John showed up raging about how Margaret had thrown his new television set across the room. There was no more talk about the engagement. The next day, Margaret came to the Wesley sporting a large black eye. The day after, she had two.

A few weeks later John went to jail, though not for hitting Margaret – she hadn't reported the assault. He had been charged with breaking into the Wesley. Margaret asked Bob if she could trade the ring with him for a couple of packs of cigarettes but Bob didn't have the money on him. With John gone, Margaret had the apartment to herself and would play the radio full blast day and night. When a tenant asked her to turn it down, she refused, so the tenant kicked in the door and turned it down for her. The landlord then told her to get out and Margaret returned to the streets.

Bob shook his head, thinking back to the year he lived with her. "I did it for a year and I thought I could help her, but then I couldn't stand it the way she was. I couldn't do it anymore."

AFTER MARGARET MOVED out, Bob continued looking after her. Whenever he went out, he would make sure he had a few dollars and some bus tickets in his pockets, and would seek her out and give them to her. One snowy day he found her walking barefoot and gave her twenty dollars to buy a pair of shoes. Later someone told him that Margaret had purchased a pair of high heels with the money, worn them for a day and thrown them out. During one particularly brutal winter, Bob found out through folks at the Wesley that Margaret was sleeping on the streets. He wandered around until he found her then took her to an army surplus store where he bought her a sleeping bag for seventy-two dollars. It was a thick fleece-lined bag designed for sub-zero temperatures. One week later, Bob saw Margaret at the Wesley without the bag. "I asked her about it and she told me she left it at the spot where she was sleeping," said Bob.

Bob (right) giving Margaret bus tickets. Courtesy of Barry Gray, *Hamilton Spectator*.

He headed over to the post office entranceway and retrieved it then carried it back to her, with a reprimand that she wasn't to leave it unattended. A few nights later, the scenario repeated itself. Bob again saw Margaret without the sleeping bag and again had to retrieve it. This time, there was a large wet mark inside that smelled like urine. He asked Margaret about it.

"She said, 'I did that.' She said she was too cold to get out and go to the bathroom so she just went in the sleeping bag." The next time Bob saw her, the zipper was broken.

"I said to her, 'To hell with it.' I can't keep doing this."

A few months later, Bob heard Margaret had rented a room in an old hotel downtown, so he went to visit. The room was small and gloomy, and the floor was cluttered with dirty clothes, rotten food and old cigarette butts. Margaret shared a bathroom down the hall with other tenants and had a sink in her room. On this day, she didn't feel like making the walk to the bathroom so she jumped up onto the sink, her scrawny legs splayed out like a bird on her perch, and urinated.

Bob's round stomach quivered as he laughed, remembering the sight of her.

"I've never seen anything like it," he said, shaking his head. "I was afraid that sink was going to come right off the wall."

ON THE WALL beside Bob's bed are four framed photos: one of Leonardo da Vinci's *The Last Supper*, another of his parents, a small one of Bob with his brother Ross and one of Margaret. It's the black-and-white photo that ran with the *Spectator* story and she is wearing the ten-dollar faux fur coat and holding a piece of white bread as she stared down at the table. She'd torn a hole out of the centre of the bread.

"She was good for me because she took away some of my loneliness," said Bob. "And I guess I was good for her and took away some of her loneliness, too. I loved her in my own special little way and I told her."

He smiled. "She was brilliant. I have to say, she really was brilliant."

CHAPTER SIXTEEN
The Black Hole

She cracked another client's face open with a coffee mug.
– Wesley staffer

1993–1994
Hamilton

When Margaret opened the door to her apartment, she looked haggard and several buttons on her shirt were undone. Through the opening Bob could see a dent in one of her breasts. He had heard that Margaret was

Margaret during a visit to the ladies' drop-in at the Wesley. Courtesy of Bill MacKinnon.

now living with other homeless people in a new apartment and wanted to check on her as she had been complaining about being tired and that her eyesight was getting worse. He noticed she was having difficulty breathing and seemed increasingly frail.

"Her clothes were so dirty and ripped all the time, I really worried about her," he said.

When Bob asked about the dent in her breast, Margaret told him her breast cancer had spread to her lymph nodes. After decades of neglect and rough living, Margaret's body was exhausted. She had been on the streets for close to ten years and had a hacking two-pack-a-day cough, advanced cancer and venereal disease. Physically, she was as ragged as her clothes and her mental health was also deteriorating – regular screaming fits had the misfortune of getting her kicked out of shelters. That meant more nights on the streets.

When Bob would ask Margaret why she was acting up, she would often blame the shock treatments, saying, "It's the ECT monkey that's with me."

Despite her staggeringly poor health, Margaret still refused to see a doctor and any suggestions to go to a clinic were shut down immediately. Perhaps even through the unfocused lens of her schizophrenic mind, Margaret knew she was dying and wanted to go out on her own terms.

Margaret had entered the "black hole," a term used in a 2003 report by the City of Hamilton called *The Homelessness Continuum: A Community Plan for Hamilton* to describe the stage when a homeless person's health is so compromised, they are close to death. The same phrase was used in a 1996 report completed after three homeless men froze to death in downtown Toronto. That tragedy prompted such outrage that it resulted in the opening of Seaton House, a four-storey shelter that grew into Toronto's largest shelter. It had a capacity for up to seven hundred men, although at times it housed as many as nine hundred. During discussions at Seaton about the health problems, staff used the phrase *black hole* to describe the final stage of a homeless person's life.

The City of Hamilton report stated that homeless people with a mental disorder or disability were the most vulnerable within the homeless population and prone to becoming chronically homeless and/or falling into poor health.

Although these reports date back several years, they're still relevant today for their insights into the health stages experienced by homeless people.

The first stage, according to the 2003 report, is when a person becomes homeless after experiencing a crisis, such as the loss of a job and/or money. A person will likely fall into the second stage if they are struggling with a severe mental illness or chronic alcohol or drug problems, which make it harder for them to get off the streets. The final stage – the black hole – occurs when a person has been on the streets for fourteen or more years and has experienced, according to the report, "such profound social decomposition that they are literally in the throes of death." This last group suffers from "acute deterioration of their health, require more frequent and/or intense services or interventions, and often use significantly more health services." They are the most likely to have chronic depression or schizophrenia, often complicated by alcoholism or such health problems as diabetes, cirrhosis of the liver and/or level four cancers.

A 2012 report by the Homeless Hub titled *The Real Cost of Homelessness* shows that homeless people are twenty-nine times more likely to have hepatitis C, twenty times more likely to have epilepsy, five times more likely to have heart disease and four times more likely to develop cancer. The rates of diabetes, hypertension and asthma are far greater among this group than among the general population and their health problems go undetected for longer periods. The chronically homeless are the most vulnerable among the homeless population to sliding into ill health and succumbing to chronic illnesses as well as addiction, incarceration, mistreatment and early death. Poor dental health and foot problems are extremely common, violence is a constant threat and a high number become injured as a result of falls or being struck by cars.

They also struggle with weather-related issues, like frostbite and heatstroke, from exposure to the elements, and a high number die from alcohol abuse and unintentional drug overdoses.

According to research by Dr. Stephen Hwang, who is also director of MAP Centre for Urban Health Solutions at St. Michael's Hospital in Toronto, a small group within the homeless population have multiple complex health care needs and visit the emergency department eight times more than people in the general population. The four-year study was conducted by St. Michael's Hospital and included almost nine hundred homeless adults who had more than 8,500 ED visits. The most interesting discovery was that 60 percent of those visits were made by only 10 percent of the participants, who averaged twelve trips to the ED a year. Compared to the low-income population of Toronto, homeless participants in this study visited an ED more than eight times as often.

Their health issues are so complex, according to Dr. Hwang, because their ability to function mentally is severely compromised. As shown in a 2007 report by the Canadian Institute for Health Information (CIHI) called *Mental Health and Homelessness*, mental diseases and disorders are the most common reasons for a homeless person to be admitted to the hospital, and mental health and behavioural disorders account for a larger share of emergency department visits and hospital stays among homeless people than among the population as a whole.

As Rael Jean Isaac wrote in her book *Madness in the Streets: How Psychiatry and the Law Abandoned the Mentally Ill*: "Above all, the mentally ill on our streets merit primary attention because, apart from children, they are the most vulnerable and helpless of the so-called homeless population, and thus can make the greatest moral claim upon community support."

Although many communities have specialized health services for homeless people, like the Hamilton Urban Core Community Health Centre, some stay away from them due to lack of trust or fear of authority figures. Some have had past negative experiences while others have more pressing needs than their health, like finding a bed for the night. As a result, many use emergency departments only when their problems have worsened.

Even if a homeless person is able to access medical care things can fall apart during the recovery period when they may need bedrest and regular medication. Instead, they get caught up in looking for food and a place to sleep.

DESPITE MARGARET'S COMBATIVE relationship with her mother, she continued calling her, although she still didn't confide about her problems.

Margaret had been hiding the sad details of her life from her parents since she was admitted to the hospital at seventeen, perhaps trying to be the perfect daughter. Verna was living in Maranatha Village, a retirement home run by the Assemblies of God in Springfield, Missouri, and her own health was failing. She liked to talk about her years of work as a missionary although she refused to accept credit for any of her accomplishments, giving it all to Abe. According to a church report: "She equated everything that was done in Antigua to the success of her husband's ministry. Any contradiction on my part was severely reprehended."

Sometime in 1993, a pastor from her church visited Verna and noticed that her health and memory were deteriorating. In the spring of 1994, Verna's diabetes flared up. Her son Jim, who lived nearby, began making daily visits to her apartment. In May, he arrived and found his mother lying unconscious on the floor. He called the ambulance and she was taken to the hospital. Tests showed she hadn't been taking her medication. During Jim's daily visits, he would sit beside her bed and read the scriptures and pray for her. Even with Jim's prayers, Verna's health continued to fail. On June 16, she suffered a series of strokes and died. She was seventy-eight.

Last respects were paid at her bedside followed by a prayer by the pastor. Like her husband, Verna had requested her body be donated to scientific research. In Jim's letter to the West Indies School of Theology, notifying them of his mother's death, he wrote, "All that knew her will rejoice with me in knowing that she now knows the ultimate joy of the presence of God in Heaven."

Margaret didn't find out about her mother's death until several weeks later. The news came in the form of a letter from Jim: "She may not have recognized me, I don't know. She was not able to eat, or speak intelligibly." Later, Jim would send Margaret a scrapbook filled with family photos and cards. He included a letter in which he shared the news that he had remarried and moved to Las Cruces, New Mexico. He was planning to get back into ministerial work: "We want to be part of the caring church for the downtrodden."

Verna's death represented the end of any long-held hope Margaret had for being reunited with her mother. They'd had a complicated relationship, and many times her mother had given her criticism when she needed compassion. But Verna was still her mother, and in some childhood photos they looked to have had a certain bond. Margaret even resembled her mother in some ways, with her pointy chin, round nose and high cheekbones.

Two months after her mother's death, Margaret received news that Jim had died. He had passed away on February 25, 1995, of an aortic dissection caused when the layers of tissue that make up the heart become thinned. He was forty-eight and left behind his wife, Susan, and their eighteen-year-old twin sons from his first marriage, David and Brian. Margaret had only seen her brother a few times over the past thirty years, but his death meant one more link to her family was gone.

MARGARET CONTINUED VISITING the Wesley drop-in for a hot lunch and to escape the cold. Suzanne Foreman would often see her while she was meeting with clients and remembered one of their last encounters.

"She was looking for cigarettes and I gave her one of mine and lit it for her," said Suzanne. "I stood for a minute as she inhaled and then she told me to piss off."

Before she left, Foreman gave Margaret her business card and told Margaret to call her if she ever needed help. She put it in her pocket and walked away. Despite how hostile Margaret was toward her, Foreman wanted to keep the lines of communication open in case Margaret needed help.

"Each time I saw her I would nod hello and keep walking. When she nodded back, I would say hello and offer her a smoke. She was indeed an angry woman."

One day Foreman was talking to another staffer in the Wesley cafeteria when Margaret pointed at her and said, "Yeah, that one."

"I went over to where she was sitting and she asked me about [Wesley United Ministries] housing. I started my spiel and she interrupted with 'Yeah, no, that's no good.' I asked her what she was looking for and she smirked and said 'Peace of mind.' She never volunteered much of her story and I didn't ask, but when I saw her we would have a companionable smoke together, with a bit of chatter about inane things if she was in a talking mood."

Once Foreman found Margaret lying beside a downtown building. She was disoriented and looked like she may have been assaulted. Foreman helped her up and escorted her to the Wesley's Rebecca Street building where she got her a cup of coffee.

"I tried a couple of times to talk with her about safe housing but she would have none of it," said Foreman.

Her lasting image of Margaret is of her wearing a "very ratty fur that was several sizes too big for her slender frame," and walking that famous walk, which gave her an "odd touch of affected elegance."

"When she walked away, she would toss her head and shift that fur as if she were royalty. She had such a carriage about her and I often wondered if there was some kind of alternate reality in her head that gave her the illusion of control instead of constant vulnerability."

While many noticed Margaret's royal strut and thought it part of her feistiness, Foreman saw it differently. She saw it as a front, to hide the vulnerable side of her that had been hurt and victimized so many times. It was a side she chose to keep well hidden.

"The affectation of dignity was heartbreaking to watch," said Foreman. "But I admired her for it."

One time Margaret was taken to the emergency department at St. Joseph's Hospital and staff called Foreman after finding her card in Margaret's pocket. She had needed stitches for a cut lip. Foreman didn't ask what had happened. "We had a coffee in the cafeteria there and then walked back downtown, but she didn't want to go to the WUM [Wesley United Ministries]. She just wanted to sit in the park for a while in the sun."

Foreman knew that Margaret had her pride and that she would push away people who tried to help her. They sat for a while then Margaret suddenly turned to Foreman and spit out, "Piss off you."

Foreman was surprised but not offended. She knew about Margaret's illness and her rough life. "I didn't see her for a long time after that," she said.

Like so many who'd known her, Foreman had a special place in her heart for Margaret:

> I had a million questions about her life that I knew she wouldn't answer if I were to ask directly. It was easier to let her take the reins of the conversation but it was the long moments between sentences when she actually made eye contact that spoke the most.
>
> They were full of pain and defiance. She could look right through a person as if someone invisible who was standing behind them was more interesting. There were some days of complete incoherence when she would babble and rage unintelligibly until whatever storm she was in had passed or blown itself out.

IT WAS DECEMBER 22, 1994, and the freezing temperatures and heavy snow had prompted the Wesley to open one hour earlier, at 8:00 a.m. Even at that hour, the basement had filled up quickly. The overcrowding had upped the tension level at the shelter and there'd been more fights lately. As a result, staff had clamped down on the barring policy that meant any signs of violence and a person would be shown the door.

"We had to let clients know they were responsible for their actions," said Bob Stevens, a long-time staffer at the Wesley.

Stevens had been working long hours at the drop-in centre and was looking forward to some time off over the holidays. He'd been a front-line worker there for years and knew Margaret well. He admired her determination and saw a kindness in her weathered face. Although Margaret kept to herself, she liked Stevens because he'd helped her out a few times. One night she'd asked him for boots, and when he couldn't find any in her size, he told her he'd keep an eye out for some. When a pair came in about a week later, he gave them to her. She seemed appreciative.

Another time, Margaret wandered in around two in the morning with

her coat covered in ice and snow. She was annoyed and kept ranting and raving about how cold it was. Staff backed off, knowing how volatile she could
be, but Stevens stepped forward to help her. "I knew to let her calm down
and I told the other staff I was going to get her a coat [from the emergency
supply]."

Stevens gently approached her and told her he didn't want her to catch a
cold then offered her the new coat. She took it and changed coats. Stevens
hung the other one up to dry. "The other staff, the newbies, couldn't believe
it, first, that I had approached her and, second, that she took the coat. They
asked what I said and I told them. I think Margaret knew I cared about her
and that I had her best interests at heart."

Stevens liked Margaret but also knew that when provoked, she could be
violent, which is what happened the night of December 22. Margaret was
sitting on one of the benches when, out of the blue, she picked up one of the
hard, plastic coffee cups and whacked the face of a homeless woman sitting
across from her.

"I don't remember why she did it but she cracked another client's face
open with a coffee mug," said Stevens.

The injury was so severe that staff had to call in someone with medical
experience. What could they do with Margaret? They knew she was ill and
that it was her mental illness that was causing her to act up. It's likely the
many times Margaret had been assaulted factored in as well – she was in
constant defence mode.

"We didn't want to throw her out in the cold but we couldn't let her stay,
as it would look like the policy didn't apply to her," said Stevens.

All of the supervisors were working at the Wesley's Christmas Store
handing out gifts to needy families, so staff had to make a decision on their
own. They agonized about what to do and knew that if they treated Margaret
differently from their other clients, it would undermine their authority. They
finally decided: she had to go. Stevens approached her and politely asked her
to leave. She refused. Stevens asked her again and she again refused. After

several unsuccessful attempts, he felt he had no choice but to call the police. No one could have guessed that things were about to get much worse.

Two police officers arrived and politely informed Margaret she had to leave. When she refused, they took her by her arms and tried to stand her up. She pulled back and began kicking them then screamed so fiercely she filled the whole room, said Stevens. The officers yanked her off the bench and began dragging her across the floor, her legs flailing in all directions, as she continued screaming at the top of her lungs.

"She was like a wild animal," said Stevens, who had a sickening feeling in his stomach as he watched the scene unfold.

Stevens knew it was freezing cold outside and that a deep layer of snow had blanketed the ground. Evicting her meant she likely had to spend the night outside. But he had no choice. For Margaret, the cold may not have been the reason she fought back so aggressively. As Suzanne Foreman said, she still had her pride, and at the Wesley, where she was well known as the princess of the streets, being dragged out came with a load of humiliation.

The memory of the incident still haunts Stevens. Many years later, he ran into one of the officers from that night and it was the first thing they talked about. They both felt bad about having to throw her out.

"It was so horrible, which is why I remember all of the details," said Stevens.

IN THE LATE 1700s, Victorian workhouses were set up in England under the premise that they would provide jobs and shelter for people who had nowhere to go. Instead, they became hellish places of despair where food was dished out at starvation levels, people worked brutally long hours at back-breaking jobs – like crushing stones – and infectious diseases spread like wildfire. Even children weren't spared the cruelty of workhouse life, many were taken from their mothers and made to work.

Jennifer Worth worked as a midwife at a convent in east London and recounted some of the stories she'd heard by inmates in her memoir *Call the*

Midwife: Shadows of the Workhouse. "Workhouse life bred and fostered its own insanity," wrote Worth, adding that some were so "stifling to the human soul" that they "destroyed the last shreds of human dignity."

"I once heard, in the 1950s, what used to be called 'the workhouse howl' emitted from the throat of a woman who had been a workhouse inmate for about twenty years in the early twentieth century. It was a noise to make your blood run cold."

Some of the conditions Margaret lived in while homeless weren't far off from the punishing despair and misery of workhouse life. Surviving on the filthy streets, sickly and without hope, she suffered indignities that no human should experience. What kept her going? How had her spirit not been broken by what she'd been through?

"I think her anger fuelled her survival in some ways," said Suzanne Foreman. "Whether she used it consciously as a survival tool is anybody's guess."

CHAPTER SEVENTEEN
The Snowy Walk

1995

Hamilton

The showers at the Wesley drop-in shelter provided Margaret with one of the few joys in her life. She would strip down naked, lay on the tiles and let the steaming water wash over her skinny, malnourished body. She would often lay there for more than an hour, and sometimes the only way staff could get her out was to turn off the water. Oftentimes the cook would yell, "There's no hot water. Somebody get Margaret out of the shower."

Margaret visits a Wesley drop-in. Courtesy of Bill MacKinnon.

After nearly a decade on the streets, Margaret knew the ropes. She knew which agencies offered hot meal programs at what time of the day, which shelters had drop-ins and which ones had beds. Despite being thrown out of the Wesley many times, it was still her favourite hangout, partly because of the showers. It's where she went on December 6, a cold, snowy day when the temperatures had dipped to minus six, with wind chill. She'd spent most of the day there, hanging out with Bob Dixon, and as the 4:00 p.m. closing time approached, she waited for Bob to finish cleaning so he could lock up.

Earlier, Bob had discovered Margaret smoking in a shower stall, which was against the rules.

"She told me to sweep up the ashes so they wouldn't know," said Bob.

Bob obliged then finished the rest of the cleaning while Margaret wandered outside. She walked over to a heating vent where hot steam blasted into the cold winter air then she opened her coat and stood in front of the vent, letting the warmth spread over her body like a welcoming hug. The Wesley overnight shelter wouldn't reopen until midnight so Margaret had eight hours to kill. Perhaps she knew, as she soaked up the warm steam, that it would be a while until she would be warm again.

The city's first homeless shelter for women, Mary's Place, had opened six months before on East Avenue North, but Margaret either didn't know about it or had given up on shelters as they were almost always full. At the domestic violence shelters, she'd been asked to leave so many times for unruly behaviour that she stayed away. Staff at the YWCA had tried to accommodate her more than once by setting up a cot by the elevator but it was an even farther walk. Her bed for the night, once again, would be a rickety bench at the Wesley.

Bob walked outside and saw Margaret standing by the vent. Looking at her in her thin brown coat and pants, he began to worry. He knew he couldn't take her home because he risked being evicted – the cigarette burns on his rug and couch were standing reminders of her behaviour. Just then, a Wesley staffer pulled up and offered him a ride to the bus stop. Bob climbed in. As they drove off, he looked back at Margaret, standing alone on the street, and thought, "Boy, women have really got it bad."

He had no idea how fitting his words would be that night.

As the car disappeared down the street, Margaret began her snowy walk. She'd survived hundreds of cold nights before, but that night's brutal weather added another level of urgency. She likely walked east along Rebecca Street then up Ferguson to King Street, the city's main artery, which is lined with stores and restaurants. There would have been a steady stream of traffic with people heading home from work.

A few blocks west, crowds of women would soon be gathering outside of city hall for the sixth annual memorial service to commemorate the anniversary of the Montreal massacre, one of the worst mass murders in Canadian history. In 1989, a gunman opened fire on female students at a university, killing fourteen women and injuring another fourteen women and men. In Hamilton, as in other cities across Canada, speeches would be read, then throngs of women would begin their solemn march through the streets, holding placards and carrying candles in remembrance of the women who had died and the hundreds of others who had lost their lives at the hands of a violent partner.

Even with all of the public awareness that had been prompted because of the massacre, violence was still an ongoing threat for women. Margaret knew that better than most. John had left her with two black eyes, she'd been raped at least once and was assaulted so horrifically in Gage Park that she had to be taken by ambulance to the emergency department. It's likely she didn't know about the march and, even if she had, wouldn't have joined. She had her own survival needs to deal with. If she didn't find a warm place to stay, she could freeze to death. She likely walked past the tattoo parlour, a few clothing boutiques and the Tally Ho restaurant, where she and Bob often went for coffee. She must have stopped at a few places, or maybe huddled in a doorway for a while, as she didn't arrive at the Mr. Sub shop until two hours later, even though it was a fifteen-minute walk from the Wesley. Along the way, someone must have placed a blanket on her shoulders.

It was shortly after 6:00 p.m. when she arrived at the Mr. Sub shop. A few hours later, after several 911 calls, Margaret would be rushed to the hospital and pronounced dead.

THAT MARGARET SURVIVED on the streets as long as she did was a testimony to her survival skills. Homeless people, especially the chronically homeless, die at a much younger age than the general population. According to a 2009 *Homeless in Canada* report by Charity Intelligence Canada, the average life expectancy of a homeless person in Canada was thirty-nine. That age varies depending on the source – for example, a 2014 BC study said that the average age of a homeless person's death was between forty and forty-nine years old, compared to the average British Columbian who died at around eighty-two. That number is consistent with international and national research, including a 2012 UK report called *Homelessness Kills*, which found that the average life expectancy for homeless individuals in the United Kingdom was forty-seven years.

Statistics on the numbers of deaths also varies. According to the 2009 *Homeless in Canada* report, some 1,390 homeless people die every year in Canada. The actual number is much higher since homeless deaths aren't counted in most cities. There are also other reasons to doubt the number – for example, hospitals in BC don't consider a person to be homeless once they've been admitted, so their deaths would not be reported. As the report states, "If someone contracts pneumonia while living on the streets and then dies after being admitted to a hospital, they are not counted by the coroners as homeless."

The BC study by *Megaphone Magazine* (quoted above) was part of a report called *Dying on the Streets: Homeless Deaths in British Columbia*, which looked at the homeless death rates in BC between 2006 and 2013. It included data from the coroner and showed that homeless people were twice as likely as the average British Columbian to die by accident, suicide or homicide and, as other studies showed, many deaths were connected to drugs and alcohol.

More than one third of homeless deaths were due to substance abuse, according to studies. Homeless people are also at a seven-to-nine-times-higher risk of dying from alcohol-related diseases and are twenty times more at risk of dying from drugs than the general population.

WHO ARE THE homeless people who have died? In Hamilton, they are Rick Vance, who was sick with a hacking cough when he walked into the James Street Baptist Church in Hamilton one winter night in 2004. The church was one of many locations for the Out of the Cold program, which provided hot meals and shelter for the homeless community. Rick was a regular there and was well liked. Volunteers were concerned about his cough when he first came in, and when they didn't hear him hacking, they thought he'd fallen asleep. Later, they checked on him and discovered he had died. It turned out Rick had pneumonia. He was forty-two.

Sometimes the street takes people much younger. Donald Dupuis was known by his nickname, Hightower, so called because of his six-foot-plus height. Donald mostly lived in abandoned buildings around the downtown with other homeless people. His last home was an abandoned hotel on King Street East that had become a hangout for street kids and transients. One night a fire broke out on the third floor when Dupuis was asleep. Donald didn't make it out alive. Firefighters said he was sitting on his bed putting on his shoe when he lost consciousness due to smoke inhalation. Donald died on July 3, 1996. He was twenty years old.

Some defy the odds, like Stan Kowalski, who had been without a permanent residence for years when he died at the age of eighty-two. Stanislaw was born in Poland during the war and it was rumoured he spent time in Nazi and Soviet concentration camps. He moved to Canada in 1950 and worked on sugar beet farms and tobacco farms but rarely stayed at one job long. The older he got, the more he moved around. He ended up in Hamilton, where he would occasionally move into a boarding house but never stayed long because he didn't like having his own place.

Stan eventually moved into a remote shack outside of town, which is where he was found one cold winter day, suffering from gangrene and frostbite so severe that both his legs had to be amputated. Stan's new life was lived in a wheelchair. Stan died on November 21, 1997. He was found face down in a parking lot, covered in newspapers.

THE LACK OF solid data on homeless deaths has been a major hindrance to agencies and charities, and prevents them from understanding the full scope of the problem and, in turn, providing the appropriate services to prevent further deaths. Without it, they don't have the big picture that shows what homelessness looks like. Even in Toronto, Canada's largest city, where an estimated nine thousand people are homeless, officials have been slow to make change.

That's despite advocates who have been fighting for change for decades. On December 12, 2018, a group of homeless advocates held a press conference to announce the formation of a new group called the Shelter and Housing Justice Network (SHJN). They asked the City of Toronto to declare a state of emergency around homelessness. Doing so would mean that the city could leverage help from other levels of government.

Street nurse Cathy Crowe, in an interview with Matt Galloway on CBC's *Metro Morning*, said that over the past twenty years, the homeless numbers in Toronto had grown from five thousand to almost double that. All of the shelters and respite centres were full, said Crowe, and the conditions inside most were appalling, including one shelter that was dealing with an outbreak of the strep A bacterial infection.

"When that happens it's hellish," said Crowe.

THE BATTLE TO secure death statistics on homeless people dates back to the mid-1980s, when the Toronto Disaster Relief Committee (TDRC), a research, advocacy and public education group involved in issues affecting homeless people in Toronto, began recording the deaths of homeless people for a memorial. The group named over six hundred homeless or formerly homeless people who had died since the mid-1980s, according to a 2010 Toronto Public Health report. The lowest number to die in one year was twenty-three (in 2008) while the highest was seventy-three (in 2005). Others ranged from thirty-three in 2009 to sixty in 2006.

In 2007, after years of lobbying, the City of Toronto finally agreed to start tracking homeless deaths. Before that, there was no mechanism to report deaths to the Shelter, Support & Housing Administration or to city council. While this was a huge step forward, it turned out they were only recording the deaths of people in city-run shelters and not those who had died on the streets or elsewhere, which is why the numbers were so low. Between 2007 and 2015, they recorded 217 shelter-related deaths.

In 2016, the city began including homeless people who had died outside of the shelter system and, after more pressure, public health officials agreed to launch a program that would track all homeless deaths throughout the entire city. From January 1, 2017, to June 30, 2018, they counted 145 homeless people who had died. Of those, 110 were male. It was a far cry from the twenty-three deaths recorded in 2008 and showed the importance of having a solid tracking method.

In Toronto in 2018, following the deaths of two homeless men, the province agreed to hold two inquests: one involved Grant "Gunner" Faulkner, a forty-nine-year-old father of three daughters who died January 13, 2015, when the hut he was living in near McCowan Road and Sheppard Avenue in Scarborough caught fire; and the other involved Brad Chapman, forty-three, who died on August 26, 2015, of an opiate overdose. Brad's family hoped the inquest would examine how homeless people who struggle with addictions are underserved by city and provincial social service nets.

The jurors put forward a combined total of ninety recommendations, which included transferring responsibility for health in correctional facilities to the Ministry of Health, developing a province-wide electronic health record for all individuals in custody, improving delivery of health care for people who are incarcerated and ensuring better planning for those discharged from corrections. There was no legal requirement for them to be implemented.

The fact that homeless people die at much younger ages and at much higher rates than non-homeless people suggests there's an urgency to pinning down the death numbers. With no central registry and no tracking of homeless deaths, people's names and histories have been lost. In many cities, the only recording of homeless deaths has been on makeshift memorial walls created by agencies and churches. Outside the Church of the Holy Trinity in downtown Toronto, a Homeless Memorial has been set up and is maintained by the church and concerned citizens. A service is held beside the memorial on the second Tuesday of every month, and an online memorial shows the sad list of names of people who have died over several years. In December 2019, following the death of yet another homeless person, Toronto councillor Kristyn Wong-Tam told the *Star* that the problem had gone beyond being a crisis and that thirteen more homeless people had died in Toronto over the last thirty days.

"That's almost 1,000 since they started to name homeless deaths," Wong-Tam told the *Star*. "These are the ones that we know. If that doesn't indicate that we are in an emergency then I really don't know what words to use at council."

In 2011, a memorial wall was erected at the Wesley Centre in a quiet corner on the second floor. It's where Rev. Thomas Davies worked and where he often met with his homeless clients. Davies, who was the chaplain for Wesley Urban Ministries, said money was so tight that he was only able to have the wall constructed because a woman who attended one of his services donated one thousand dollars. A fund was later set up so people could donate one hundred dollars to pay for a memorial service led by the Wesley Urban Ministries chaplain when someone dies.

The wall was designed very simply, with a black background and gold-coloured brick-sized plaques. Most of the names were provided to him by his clients. The wall quickly filled up, and for many it's become an important way for people to remember a lost friend. Similar memorial walls have been erected in cities like London, Halifax, Victoria and Edmonton. It's a sad statement, said Davies, that almost everyone he's talked to has known someone who died. Also sad were the ages of the people. "I've yet to bury anyone over the age of fifty-five," said Davies.

The Wesley Centre memorial wall includes the name of Ronnie Geng, who died in 2010 and was better known by his nickname Listerine Man because of his addiction to mouthwash. By the end of 2011, there were 143 names on the wall, and by 2016 that number had grown to 214. Their names were added as people remembered them. Some had died many years earlier. Nicknames are common among homeless people and are also included, as with Edward "Moses" Ashbee, Len "Newf" Squires and Tony "Me Old Trout" Evoy.

Behind every name, there are stories about people like Jonathan Field, who was known for his love of playing bass guitar. Signs of a mental illness first surfaced when he was in his teens, when Jonathan told his mother he thought people were out to get him. He was never diagnosed, and like many people with mental illness, Jonathan self-medicated with drugs and alcohol. It was the only way he knew how to drown out the voices in his head.

For a while, things went well. He ran a flyer distribution business and even played in the occasional band. He had a girlfriend and they had a daughter together. His parents always worried that he couldn't stay at anything long, and soon enough, his business ended, as did his relationship. Not long after, he took to the streets where he pawned his guitar to buy alcohol. His parents would drive to Hamilton from their home in Whitby whenever he called and would find him a room. Things would work out for a while, then he would end up back on the streets.

Jonathan was in his thirties when he booked himself into a detox program. It was there that he was diagnosed with schizophrenia – finally, a label for the noises inside his head. He was admitted to a psychiatric hospital and put on medications, which helped him stabilize. Without proper follow-up, however, he ended up back on the streets and slowly went off his medications. In his last few years, Jonathan often stayed at the men's hostel at Mission Services where they eventually put him up in an apartment across the street.

On November 17, 1992, his body was found there. He was thirty-eight and had been dead for more than a day.

The memorial services have allowed people to share their stories about individuals who have died. That's important, said Davies, because so many homeless people die alone in unmarked graves, their stories left untold. Some people who visit the wall will sit on the floor and touch the plaque. For them, it's a healing place. But for others, it's a place of dread. "They wonder if they're next," said Davies.

In Toronto, the homeless problem has spilled into the ravines, parks and highway underpasses, which now double as tent cities. Hamilton had several tent encampments after COVID-19 hit, though nothing on the scale of Toronto. City workers regularly clear out the couches, chairs and tents from underneath the Gardiner Expressway. A few months later, however, more couches and chairs will appear and workers will return to clear them away. Like many cities, Toronto's homelessness crisis has been magnified by gentrification, the urban renewal of lower-class neighbourhoods, which has driven up rental costs and pushed out tenants. Toronto's skyrocketing rental and housing costs have even impacted people who have healthy incomes, and bidding wars, which are the norm, have pushed costs up even higher.

It's a war that few people are winning – least of all, those who have been pushed out of their homes and are now counted among homeless people.

CHAPTER EIGHTEEN
A Lonely Burial

1995
Hamilton

On December 13, under a cloudy colourless sky, Margaret's body was driven across town by funeral coach to Woodland Cemetery, a one-hundred-acre tree-filled cemetery that overlooks the bay. The Truscott, Brown and Dwyer Funeral Chapel on King Street East, which has been in the same location since 1950, handled the city-funded burial. Because it was paid for by the city, there would be no mahogany casket, no visitation services where people could share their memories of Margaret and no funeral service. Instead, her body was placed in a simple, unfinished wood casket and quietly driven to the cemetery where no one was waiting.

On the way to the cemetery, the funeral coach likely passed by some of the coffee shops where Margaret had hung out and the alleyways where she'd slept. At Woodland, the coach wound its way along the narrow asphalt lanes, past the trees and tidy rows of grey and black granite stones. Margaret's final home was section ten, row thirty-nine, grave eight. Cemetery staff dressed in blue coveralls had used special equipment to break through the frost and dig the hole. They unceremoniously lowered the box into the ground and tossed dirt on top.

The year Margaret died, 3,872 people died in the City of Hamilton, most leaving this world to a ritual of grieving and tender words. Crowds would have gathered beside loved ones' gravesites and tears would have been shed in their memory. At Margaret's burial, no one was there to say goodbye. Police had failed to notify anyone of her death so no one even knew that Hamilton's princess of the streets was gone. With no belongings to her name and no will to go over, it was as if she had never been born.

On December 15, Bob Dixon wandered into the welfare office to pick up his disability pension and innocently asked if Margaret had been by. Good friend that he was, he thought he'd do her a favour and pick up her cheque for her. Staff knew Bob and were aware of his long-time friendship with Margaret. They also knew Margaret had died because her file had already been closed.

"I hate to tell you this but Margaret passed away," Bob recalls being told.

Bob's face turned red with shock and he stood frozen to the spot. As he tried to digest the words he'd just heard, his memory reached back to the last time he'd seen Margaret, his only "wife." He had watched her walk down the snow-filled street outside of the Wesley Centre as he drove off.

"You could have knocked me over with a feather," said Bob, who asked the staffer what had happened.

She didn't know. All she could tell Bob was that Margaret had already been buried because they'd closed her file. Bob immediately left the office and walked to the Wesley Centre where he shared the news with staff and clients. Margaret was beloved by many at the Wesley who had known her for more than ten years, and the news spread quickly. Lynn Ferris, who Margaret always referred to as the "nice lady with the dark hair," shut the door to her office and broke down and cried.

"She was such a big part of that place and embodied why we were there," said Ferris. "She was more than just a client. She was a person I got to know and she was why I wanted to work there. Whenever I did something for Margaret, when I made sure she had a safe place to go, and I saw how appreciative she was, it was the reason I went to work every day."

Ferris made some calls to find out more details on how Margaret had died. What upset her more than anything was hearing that Margaret had cried out for help as she struggled to pull herself up from the floor.

"She never, ever asked for help so she must have been in real need," said Ferris. "I remember one night she came in and she had a wound on her foot and she let me care for her. That was huge that she let me help her. It meant a lot to me."

Ferris sent out the following memo to staff: "Night staff received a message from Bob Dixon (friend of Margaret's) that she died Dec. 6/95. She collapsed in a restaurant and was taken to a hospital where she died. She was buried Dec. 14/95." (Woodland states the burial was on the thirteenth.)

THINKING BACK TO that moment when she learned of Margaret's death, Ferris encapsulated what so many thought of Margaret: "Margaret had done the best she could with what she had. She suffered and she never asked for pity. If she got angry it was because she was frustrated or it was the voices in her head."

Years of working with homeless people and seeing too many die had worn Ferris down. She had stopped going to their funerals years earlier. "I told my coworkers I couldn't take it anymore."

She would make an exception for Margaret.

NEWS OF MARGARET'S death rippled through the homeless pipeline like a tsunami. After more than a decade on the streets, Margaret was well known and well loved by staff and clients at shelters and among people in the community, including store owners and those who saw her in coffee shops. With her raggedy clothes, she was hard to miss. Many had come to know Margaret personally while others knew of her through word of mouth, or they had read about her in the *Spectator* articles. Staff said that after the feature article on Margaret ran, she took on a bit of celebrity status and seemed to have an extra bounce in her step when people told her they'd seen her in the paper.

Rev. Bill MacKinnon called to tell me the news. He had worked with homeless people for years, including as director of services at Wesley Urban Ministries, which is where he met Margaret. "I know you cared about her and would want to know," he told me.

I wrote a story on Margaret's death and the response from readers was immediate. My phone rang off the hook from people who had known Margaret and were distressed to hear that she had died. It turned out there was a small army of people out there who cared about her and had tried to help her in their own small way. Some were strangers who had gotten to know her from seeing her on the streets and in coffee shops. They shared their heartbreaking stories about how they'd tried to help her by giving her spare change or buying her a cup of coffee. They were heartbroken to read what had happened. They saw the injustice in what had happened to her and were saddened and angry at how she'd been treated.

One woman cried into the phone as she talked about her frequent meetings with Margaret in the downtown area. Like Carol Green, this woman had convinced Margaret on several occasions to let her buy her a coffee and had offered her a place to say. Like Carol, Margaret had turned her down.

Brother Richard MacPhee had met many homeless people in his thirty years as executive director of Good Shepherd Centre, but Margaret had been special. "You could see the tragedy of life in her face, but you recognized the gentleness of life in her smile. That smile gave you a glimmer of the real person inside her," he said.

While fond memories and affection were shared, there was also a growing anger around how Margaret had died, and that police had taken so long to get there then failed to notify anyone. Hamilton Police Service responded by saying they had followed protocol around conducting a sudden death investigation, which stated there was no specific time period in which they must wait before a person is buried. The policy also stated that when they had "exhausted" their efforts to locate next of kin, a report must be forwarded to the regional supervising coroner who then issued a writ of burial. It did not appear that any efforts – let alone "exhaustive" ones – had been conducted.

Margaret had also been well known by staff inside Hamilton's jail and by police officers, and Lynn Ferris said any number of people at the Wesley Centre could have identified her, including Bob Dixon, who had contact information for her brother David. As it was, David didn't find out about his sister's death for several days.

"I remember thinking that it was good that my mother was no longer alive to hear that news," David wrote in an email.

IN THE MONTHS following Margaret's death, the anger many felt grew beyond the loss of a friend and toward the larger issue of homelessness. Vigils were held around the city, both at the gravesite and at spots she had visited. Some organized fundraising events to pay for programs to help other homeless people while others started petitions demanding more services to prevent further homeless deaths. Another petition was set up to demand an inquest into the circumstances around her death and to shed light on the wider problems faced by homeless people, especially those with mental illness.

One letter submitted to then coroner Dr. Bonnie Porter was from members of a church and outreach group, and was signed by Dr. Guy Mersereau, a psychiatrist who had worked with homeless people and who'd cited concerns around Margaret's life and death, from the poor ambulance response time to lack of shelter beds and help for her mental illness. "Who will speak for her now? And who will speak for the others like her? For many of her problems were hardly unique to her, and the winter has only begun."

The letter ended with a plea: "Her life and death deserve more, much more. She deserves at least some of the attention to these problems which was denied her in life."

Despite the massive outcry, nothing happened. The coroner's office said that what had happened to Margaret was an isolated incident and that a recent inquest into the deaths of three homeless people in Toronto had already looked at problems around homelessness. Staff who worked at the shelters, including Lynn Ferris, were frustrated. They stared into the tired, weathered faces of people like Margaret every day and knew that it was only a matter of time before another person died.

They knew homeless people were largely ignored because they weren't able to fight for their rights. They'd felt the frustration of knowing that people and politicians just didn't care. I caught a glimpse of that attitude in my own newsroom. After I wrote my first feature on Margaret, the editor who oversaw the Saturday page, where my story was to run, refused to publish it saying readers would be offended by the sickly homeless woman staring out at them. Looking me straight in the eyes, he said, "Why would I want to run that photo [of Margaret] in the paper? When I see people like that, I cross to the other side of the street."

I was shocked at his narrow-mindedness and tried to argue that homelessness was a massive problem in cities across Canada, and that shining a light on one homeless person's life could educate readers on how people ended up living on the streets and what their lives were like. His reply was that my story would only make people feel guilty and he refused to "subject our readers to that." Because his section was the only one with ample space for a lengthy feature, my story sat in limbo for four months. I joked to colleagues that my feature on the homeless community had become the story with no home, but inside I was fuming that one person's judgmental opinion was blocking a story on such an important issue.

When I mentioned my predicament to another editor, he saw the value in my story and made space for it, making it the lead story on the front page as well as giving it a full page inside. Reader reaction was swift and proved the Saturday editor wrong. Many called the newsroom in tears saying they knew Margaret from seeing her on the streets and were angry that there were no services to help her. Many asked the same question I had when I met her: How could this have happened to anyone in a country like Canada? Those who had come to know her by seeing her in coffee shops and panhandling had developed an affection for Margaret and saw her as a person they would cross the street to help, not avoid.

But my editor wasn't alone in his judgmental attitude. Many negative stereotypes exist about homeless people, from the belief that they're just lazy to the myth that they've chosen that lifestyle. In 2015, a national homelessness charity called Raising the Roof launched a public awareness campaign called Change the Conversation to dispel the myths and stereotypes of the homeless community. It involved homeless people reading mean tweets about themselves, some of which were so callous that the readers broke down in tears. A few samples:

> I was enjoying a latte when I saw a hobo girl across the street. I almost vomited. Get back on your side of the bridge. No one likes you.

> If home is where the heart is, are homeless people heartless?

> I hate it when it gets cold out because all the homeless people get on the bus.

Former NDP leader and homeless advocate Jack Layton also addressed this attitudinal problem in his book *Homelessness: How to End the National Crisis*, writing that blaming homeless people is a diversionary tactic and noting how it's easier to criticize them than it is to fix the problem. As Layton wrote: "As mass homelessness has become the new reality in Canada, starting in the 1990s, some tried to pin the blame on the homeless themselves. You've heard the line: the homeless are 'lazy, crazy or stupid' or to be more polite, it's all a matter of individual pathology."

AT THE WESLEY Centre's drop-in the day after Margaret died and before anyone had been told, an odd thing happened. Whenever Margaret came to the Wesley, staff always knew it was her as she would lean on the buzzer so that it let out a long, continual buzz.

"We'd all smile when we heard it [the buzzer] and say 'Margaret's here.' It was like Norm from *Cheers*," said Lynn Ferris.

The day after Margaret died, the buzzer went off four times, every few hours, and each time in the same long buzz as if the person was leaning on it. Staff automatically thought it was Margaret and they'd bounce up the stairs. But when they opened the door, no one was there.

"It was bizarre," said Ferris. "It was like her spirit was telling us to look for her."

THE DAY AFTER Bob Dixon found out Margaret had died, he asked a friend to drive him to the cemetery. He was still numb from the news and didn't know where she was buried so he walked over to the only fresh grave that didn't have flowers on it and stood there quietly looking down at the lonely mound. "I didn't know what to say. The only prayer I could think of was the Lord's Prayer."

He respectfully pulled off his wool toque, held it to his chest and recited the prayer. Bob had always been a man of few words and knew when it was time to go.

"Then I heard a little voice say, 'I think that's it.'"

ICY GUSTS OF wind swept across the field as a group of us gathered around Margaret's unmarked grave. It was January 8, a few weeks after she had died, and about twenty of us had come to say our goodbyes. We were there to give Margaret the loving send-off she deserved and was denied. Her death weighed heavily on Rev. Bill MacKinnon, who had worked closely with homeless people in Hamilton for years. He was a grey-haired, serious-looking fellow and a smile didn't come easily to his face. Someone passed around copies of the lyrics to "Away in a Manger," a song Margaret played at a Wesley Christmas concert, and we all sang together.

> Away in a manger, no crib for a bed
> The little Lord Jesus laid down his sweet head
> The stars in the bright sky looked down where he lay.
> The little Lord Jesus asleep on the hay.

THE FRIGID WIND made it even more difficult to stand in one spot. But for everyone there, the cold was a brutal reminder of what Margaret coped with every winter. It was also a reminder of the inadequacies that riddled the system.

"It's cold and uncomfortable, but the reality is that's what Margaret's life was like before she died," MacKinnon told the group.

Standing beside Bill was Oman Huhad, a social worker with Hamilton Public Health Services who worked with the chronically homeless. His office was often the back alleys and doorways where homeless people slept. Then there was Steve Buckle, who knew Margaret from his work with the region's needle exchange program. Margaret never did drugs but Steve would see her on the streets during his regular walkabouts. Violet Wakeman met Margaret sixteen years earlier while helping out at the Good Shepherd Centre. She told the group that she had convinced Margaret to go to an Alcoholics Anonymous meeting, but not because Margaret was drinking.

"I thought that, if nothing else, it would be a place where she could have some free food and a warm place," said Wakeman.

Standing quietly beside Wakeman was Bob Dixon. No one knew Margaret better than Bob, and no one had helped her more. He was also the last person there who'd seen her alive.

"Margaret hated the cold with a passion," said Dixon, shivering. "And she loved to be warm and drink coffee, and I hope that's what we're going to do after we leave here."

Cold was a central theme in the comments, and it was how MacKinnon closed the ceremony. Looking around at the group, he said solemnly, "At last she's finally out of the cold."

THE DAY MY story on Margaret's memorial service was published in the *Spec*, I received a call from someone who was upset that Margaret didn't have a gravestone. Fabian Bortolotto had never met Margaret, but when he read that the city didn't cover the cost of a gravestone, he stepped forward to help.

He thought it wrong that Margaret had been treated so unfairly all her life and wanted to make sure she wasn't forgotten after her death. Bortolotto was co-owner of European Monuments in Oakville and wanted to donate a marker for Margaret's grave. I thanked him and put him in touch with Lynn Ferris, who told him about Margaret's love of roses. Bortolotto had a flower engraved on the marker with the words:

Affectionately known as "Princess Margaret"
A big sister to the Hamilton poor and street persons

A short walk across the field from where Margaret is buried sits the gravesite of Mary Popovich, another homeless woman who lived a sad life and died tragically. The two likely would have known each other as they frequented the same haunts. Like Margaret, Mary was a well-known street person who had been diagnosed with schizophrenia and had been in and out of psychiatric institutions most of her life. Her last known discharge had been from the Queen Street Mental Health Centre in Toronto several years earlier. During the day, Mary would often sit on the front steps of the Wesley Centre with her overstuffed grocery cart. Staff would take her tangerines to help with her dry mouth, which was a side effect of her epilepsy.

In her last days, Mary had open sores on her legs and a hacking cough, but, like Margaret, she refused medical care. She didn't like the shelters and often stayed with friends, which is where she went the night of October 23, 1992. The friend in question had a small second-floor apartment in a rundown home on Barton Street East. Sometime in the night, Mary went outside for a smoke on the balcony and fell asleep. The next day, her frozen body was found hunched over on a black vinyl office chair on the balcony. No one had noticed when she didn't come back inside. She was sixty-five.

The coroner cited respiratory failure as the probable cause of Mary's death, which surprised no one since Mary was a heavy smoker and had been diagnosed with bouts of pneumonia, emphysema and bronchitis. But those who knew Mary blamed the system for providing too few supports. After she died, people promised more would be done to prevent other deaths. They put out donation cans at shelters to raise money for a gravestone, but because people who visited shelters had so little money, it took several months to raise the money. Those who had attended the graveside service held for Mary in October of 1993 vowed that another homeless person would never die on the streets of Hamilton again.

Margaret died two years later.

INSIDE THE MISSION Services building in east Hamilton, laughter spills out from a group of women gathered around a table. At another table, a lone woman lies sprawled across its surface with her hood pulled over her head. She looks to be sleeping. This is Willow's Place, a drop-in program for homeless women where they can come and have a meal, use laundry facilities and take a shower. To the women who come here regularly, it's a second home where they can access services and meet other women. Being homeless can be lonely, and here they can connect with others.

Mission Services was formed more than sixty years ago and started with a small shelter for men on James Street North. Over the years, they added more services for women, who make up a growing number of the homeless population. It was also in recognition that homeless women face different problems than men, said Mission Services' executive director Carol Cowan-Morneau. According to a 2011 report by Hamilton's Social Planning and Research Council called *Not to be Forgotten: Homeless Women in Hamilton*, on any given day in the city, more than seven thousand women are at risk of becoming homeless. There are also more precariously housed women than men.

Despite the fact that women make up 27.3 percent of the homeless population in the city, there are fewer shelter beds for women and services for homeless women are greatly lacking.

Many programs for homeless people are coed, like Out of the Cold, which started in Toronto in January 1987 in a small storefront on St. Clair Avenue. In Hamilton, the first Out of the Cold site opened at James Street Baptist Church, shortly after the Toronto one. Many more churches have followed and now provide breakfasts and dinners six days a week from ten locations from November to the end of March. Although the program is coed, few women come out. Like many programs, they fear the violence and harassment.

While men's shelters are adequate to fill the need, women's shelters are constantly operating at or over capacity. Some of the women at Willow's Place today have come directly from Carole Anne's Place at the downtown YWCA, a program that provides overnight shelter to homeless women in the winter. Money is always tight for these programs.

In November 2019, the program received a last-minute funding reprieve from the city after staff pleaded to councillors for $228,000 in emergency funding to keep their doors open. The funding was for Carol Anne's Place and Willow's Place. Councillors were told that when the shelters are full, women end up sleeping in shipping containers, stairwells, alleys and sheds, while some resort to sex work to stay out of the cold. City councillors agreed to provide the emergency funding to keep the two programs running over the winter.

"We have women who have disclosed horror stories of how they're being physically and sexually assaulted at night on our streets," Sheryl Bolton, director of community service for Mission Services, told the *Spectator* on November 8, 2019.

Despite the need for services, women's shelters across Canada continue to experience alarming occupancy pressures. While the first men's shelter in Hamilton opened in the 1950s, the first shelter for homeless women (Good Shepherd's Mary's Place) didn't open until forty-five years later, in 1995.

Experts say it's important to have separate shelters, like Mary's Place, which opened with ten beds. It was filled to capacity almost immediately. Twenty years later, a new twenty-bed Mary's Place opened on Pearl Street;

this one included medical care and counselling services, and the beds filled up again. A funding increase in 2017 allowed them to add another five beds; however, it's still not enough to meet the need and during the pandemic they were forced to reduce their occupancy to follow social distancing rules.

On a typical day at Mary's Place, within an hour of a woman leaving, a new woman comes in to take her place. The night that Margaret died, even if she had known about Mary's Place, it likely would have been full. Staff at women's shelters know that the services they provide are only dealing with the symptoms of a problem and not the causes. They know that many women who experience homelessness are dealing with mental health and/ or addiction issues or trauma related to gender-based violence. Katherine Kalinowski, who is also chair of the Women's Housing Planning Collaborative (WHPC) in Hamilton, said many women come to shelters due to lack of family supports and even when housing is provided for them, there is still a need for supports that go beyond the provisions of bricks and mortar.

"Having a place to live is only the beginning for many people," said Kalinowski. "Having a community where you are treated with dignity, respect and you have a sense of belonging is essential."

CHAPTER NINETEEN
"If Margaret Had Kept Me"

1998

Hamilton

The woman at the end of the phone sounded articulate, but what she was telling me didn't make sense. As a newspaper reporter, it was common to receive odd phone calls from the public. So when the caller told me she was engaged to Margaret's son, I suspected it wasn't true.

It had been three years since Margaret had died. There had been little information in my article that identified her son, whom she had named

Jeremy visits his mother's grave.
Photo by Denise Davy.

Jeffrey. He would be twenty-six now and his adoptive parents could be living anywhere, not just in Hamilton. I had considered trying to find him, but with no paper trail, it would have been impossible. His adoptive parents would have been given a report on his background but it was unlikely it would have included any details on his birth mother, even her name.

The caller explained that she was engaged to a fellow who had been adopted through the Children's Aid Society (CAS) of Hamilton, and that he'd recently been given a copy of the CAS

240

adoption report. She'd read my story and had connected the dots to her fiancé, largely based on the birthdate and that Margaret had named her son Jeffrey. The adoptive parents already had a son named Jeffrey so they had renamed him Jeremy.

When she asked to meet, I was reluctant because of how far-fetched this seemed; however, when she told me I was their only link to her fiancé's birth mother, I agreed. I couldn't stand in the way of someone getting to know their birth parent. We arranged a time for them to come to my house, but as soon as I got off the phone, I questioned whether I'd done the right thing. The chance of this person being Margaret's son was slim. Even worse, what if it was him? What could I tell him? That his mother had lived on the streets, that she was neglected and abused all her life? There was another reason for my hesitation. The sadness that Margaret had felt all those years ago when she talked about losing her son was something I was now experiencing. A few months earlier, my teenage son, Ryan, had been killed. He was my only child. My whole world had been turned upside down. An iceberg of shock had encased me in the first weeks and helped me through those early days, but it had begun to melt and most days I felt like I was drowning in grief. In short, this was not a good time for this to be happening.

But I kept going back to that point – if he was indeed Margaret's son, I was their only link to her. I couldn't deny them this meeting. When I opened the door, any question was answered immediately. There was Margaret's face staring back at me, albeit a younger, male version of her. The same rounded tip of the nose, the same oval face, the slightly pointed chin and high forehead. They were all Margaret's. This was most definitely the boy she had given up for adoption twenty-six years ago. I felt an immediate connection with him, and we reached forward and hugged.

"I see the resemblance," I told him, smiling.

He and his fiancée settled into my navy blue loveseat and I sat across from them. Looking at Jeremy, I thought about how happy Margaret would have been to see her son all grown up and looking so healthy. Jeremy was pleasant

and soft-spoken, and had a friendly smile. Perhaps this is what Margaret
would have been like if her mental illness hadn't taken her down.

Jeremy told me he was adopted by a Hamilton couple who told him when
he was four or five that he was adopted. "I always remember being adopted. I
don't recall a 'sit down' moment." He also had a strange inkling that his birth
mom might be a street person.

Looking at me intently, Jeremy asked the question that had no doubt been
pressing on him for many years. "What was she like?"

I took a deep breath and told him how Margaret had opened up to me at
the Wesley and shared the difficult but fascinating details of her life, details
she had never shared with any of the staff there. I stood up and waved my
hands over my head to show them how she had bounced out of her chair and
waved at me when I left. They both laughed.

Then I told Jeremy that, although his mother had lived a difficult life, she
was still a strong, spirited woman and that there was something innately
sweet and kind about her. I wanted him to know that, despite everything
Margaret had been through, there was a remarkable humanity about her. She
had survived for years against unbelievable odds and, despite what had been
thrown at her, she was still a force to be reckoned with right up to her death.
That was her legacy.

Jeremy smiled faintly. I wished I had more to offer him. Then I remembered
the photos I had of Margaret, taken at the shelter by the *Spec* photographer.
On impulse, I asked if he wanted to see them.

"Of course," he said eagerly.

Upon seeing the look on his face, however, I immediately regretted showing them to him. His jaw dropped and he turned ashen as he stared down
at the photos of his mother with her leathery, pockmarked skin and matted
hair. One photo showed a close-up of her nicotine-stained fingers, a cigarette
dangling between them. I apologized and said maybe I shouldn't have shown
him, but he insisted it was fine. He wanted to know everything about her, he
said. When they left, I suggested some names of people they could talk to at

the Wesley who knew Margaret. We agreed to keep in touch.

Over the next several years, I heard through the grapevine that Jeremy and his fiancée had married and that they'd had a son. Life got busy for me, too. I adopted a beautiful baby girl from China, and a few years later, I returned there and adopted my second daughter. Time passed. Then an email arrived from Rev. Bill MacKinnon.

"The 20th anniversary of Margaret's death is coming up," he wrote. "Do you want to get together and have a memorial service at Margaret's grave?"

Absolutely, I told him. I would invite Jeremy, although it had now been seventeen years since our meeting. First, I had to find him.

JEREMY IS NOW forty-three and still looks healthy and fit. He seems happy and is living with his new family in a town outside of Niagara Falls. He and his wife separated several years ago but are still in touch, and I was able to locate him through her. Jeremy still sees his son, who lives with his ex-wife. He invited me inside his cozy bungalow, comfortably decorated in earth tones. His black lab jumped up on me so excitedly that Jeremy had to move him into another room. As we talked, the TV was tuned to a channel playing spiritual music. Jeremy's new girlfriend is someone he knew from high school. They'd had a daughter together, who was now four. Jeremy is working at a hardware store.

I asked him what happened after we met and he told me that he had launched himself into a frantic search to find out more about his mother. He visited shelters and talked to people who knew Margaret, including Bob Dixon and Bill MacKinnon. The more he learned about her tragic life and mental illness, the more he worried that he may have inherited her genes, especially since his father may have also had a mental illness. Those concerns proved to be well founded.

About a year into his marriage, he started experiencing what appeared to be the early symptoms of schizophrenia: he heard voices and talked about aliens landing. One night, driven by something inside of him that he couldn't understand, he drove to Hamilton, parked his car down a side street and pulled a green garbage bag overtop his clothes. Then he started to walk. He had no idea where he was going and ended up wandering the streets for hours. The more he walked, the more disoriented he felt. He ended up out front of the Salvation Army hostel on York Boulevard.

"Do you think you were trying to experience the way your mother lived?" I asked him.

He shook his head and said he didn't know. "I felt very lost, not comfortable. A lot of people thought I was ill. I don't know if I was. I did get to see that there was freedom in that life. I had nothing but I didn't care about anything."

He said he must have been acting strangely because the police picked him up and took him to the Hamilton General Hospital emergency ward where things got worse.

"They suddenly started bombarding me with questions," said Jeremy. "They said I was uncooperative. I'm not sure what they thought, that I was manic."

Jeremy remembered feeling like his mind was floating. A lot of what happened to him next was fuzzy. He remembered a lot of pushing and shoving, and the next thing he knew, hospital staff were putting him in restraints. He was taken by ambulance to the Hamilton Psychiatric Hospital and kept there for a few weeks. He thinks he was placed on the same ward as his mother.

Doctors started him on lithium and told him he needed to stay in the hospital until he was stable. It was there that he met a patient named Joshua who showed him "the way of the Lord." They had long talks in the hallways and the TV room, and, over the next two weeks, he said Joshua taught him about the spiritual war that was going on in the world and told him he didn't have to be part of it. It was like an epiphany, said Jeremy, who started reading the Bible and understanding the connections between his life and the stories therein.

"Moses had to be given up for adoption or he would have died," he told me. "If Margaret had kept me, she wouldn't have been able to care for me."

When Jeremy talked about the Bible, which he did a lot, he did so with the passion of a preacher at the altar. He became animated, his hands moving through the air and his eyes widening. He talked with persuasion, and regardless of what topic was being discussed he would bring it back to the Bible, often quoting from the scriptures. His email tagline is "Peace be unto you in the Name Yeshua the Messiah."

I asked him if he had considered the similarities between his religious passion and his grandfather's. He smiled proudly. Yes, it hasn't been lost on him, he said. "That whole family was about sowing the seed of light in foreign countries and here I am talking about the spirituality of people. Let's wake up and love each other, the greatness of life is right here in our hometown."

Jeremy has something else in common with his grandfather. He has thought many times about what happened to Margaret and believes that it wasn't only the stress of living in the British West Indies and having strict missionary parents that caused her breakdown. He believes, as Abe did, that Margaret's illness was connected to her inability to fully accept the Lord into her life, that what manifested itself as mental illness in Margaret was actually her wrestling with her belief in God.

While he was in the hospital, he thought about what it must have been like for his mother when she was there. He described the environment as oppressive and believes it likely added to her problems. Staff wouldn't have understood that the root of Margaret's problem came from her struggles with her religious beliefs. "The world, and even family, oftentimes do not 'get' the effects of someone wrestling with God," Jeremy wrote in an email. "The world would rather call them crazy and institutionalize them."

CHAPTER TWENTY

"It Was Tragic What Happened to Her"

December 6, 2015
Hamilton

On the twentieth anniversary of Margaret's death, a small group of people gathered around her grave at Woodland Cemetery to pay respects to a woman who deserved a life so much better than the one she lived. In contrast to twenty years ago, when the ground was a frozen blanket of snow, the grass was green and the temperature downright balmy. The landscape may have changed, but homelessness was still a crisis across the country. Community programs and supportive housing were still missing and their absence meant people were suffering.

Most of the people at Margaret's gravesite have worked in some capacity with the homeless community. They knew that every person living on the streets is a reflection of our collective failure to care enough to protect our most vulnerable citizens. Their sadness at not being able to do more was etched across their faces. Some brought red roses and one person was holding an elegant white lily. One by one, they walked up to Margaret's small stone and gently placed their floral offerings on the grass.

Rev. Bill MacKinnon stood before us. A few more grey hairs were sprinkled through his hair and beard now. He told us he kept his notes from twenty years prior and would read from them today. As he read, it was clear that the passage of time has changed very little. The homeless crisis was as bad today as when Margaret died, said MacKinnon. As he talked, wax from the white candle he was holding dripped down and coated his fingers. Margaret's dignity was stolen from her in the cruel ways that she was treated, he said. Several people nodded as he spoke. They knew the lack of services for homeless people meant many were being left out in the cold. Then, just as he did twenty years ago, MacKinnon invited anyone who wished to say a few words to step forward.

I took the candle and talked about my first meeting with Margaret and my plans to write more about her and homelessness. "I hope that I can show that Margaret's life mattered," I said.

I passed the candle to Jeremy. He smiled shyly, unsure of what to say, then glanced nervously at the group. When he introduced himself as Margaret's son, there was a gasp. No one here knew Margaret had a son.

"I know a lot of you knew Margaret and I want to thank everyone for the part they played in helping her," he said. He told the crowd that he hoped his being here would show that something good came of Margaret's life. He smiled and passed the candle to Suzanne Foreman, who smiled back. "I recognize the smile," she told Jeremy as she shook his hand.

One by one, the candle was passed around as people shared what they remembered about Margaret.

Helen Kell took the candle and smiled gently. "She was a real character. You couldn't help but like her," she told the crowd.

One person talked about the anger she felt when the petition for an inquest into Margaret's death was rejected. Bob Dixon's brother, Ross, told the crowd he had come in Bob's place because Bob wasn't up to it. An older fellow took the candle and said he never knew Margaret but felt compelled to come because his mother died the same way. He later handed out a card that read: "I am a person – not an illness."

Medora Uppal, who was director of women's services at the Good Shepherd Centre, took the candle and looked out solemnly at the crowd.

She's a petite, dark-haired woman with soft, pretty features, and she's worked in women's services for years. She reminded everyone that a few kilometres away, at city hall that night, a crowd of women would gather to mark the anniversary of the Montreal massacre, just as they had twenty years ago, on the night Margaret died.

"This memorial for Margaret and the gathering downtown for the murdered women in Montreal are reminders of the precarious lives women lead and how much more needs to be done to protect women," said Uppal.

As more people shared their stories of Margaret, a profound sadness filled the air. Then MacKinnon told the story about Margaret at a Christmas gathering when the crowd was about to sing "Away in a Manger."

"Margaret threw her head back and yelled, 'No crib for a bed,'" said MacKinnon.

We all laughed, grateful for the break from sadness. Then MacKinnon talked about how fitting Margaret's words were, given her daily battle to find a bed.

"It was tragic what happened to her," Foreman told me afterward. "There has been so much anger and outrage in the twenty years since she died but there hasn't been any change."

TODAY, I WIND my way along the path at Woodland Cemetery until I reach Margaret's grave. Section ten, row thirty-nine, grave eight. I try and visit when I can. The stone is almost completely buried under a tangle of grass and weeds but I remember its location by its close proximity to a maple tree. I kneel down and yank out the weeds as dirt burrows under my fingernails and muddies my palm. I wipe my hands on the grass then say a few words to Margaret and head over to another area in the cemetery, one that overlooks the bay where mallards bob in the water. It's close to a large oak tree that shelters the graves. Margaret and I share another connection – my son's grave is a short walk from hers.

On December 6, 2018, I retraced Margaret's last steps from the Wesley shelter to the sub shop where she spent her last night. It was the same time of day, around 4:00 p.m., when she made the walk twenty-three years earlier. By the time Margaret took her last walk on that cold winter night, the chronic twitching in her legs had become so severe her whole body shook and her mental illness was so full-blown she would erupt into screaming fits. The streets were filled with cars, just as they would have been years earlier, and many of the same shops were still there: a coffee shop, Chinese restaurant, barbershop and tattoo parlour.

She would have passed the stately St. Patrick's Parish where a life-sized bronze statue called *Homeless Jesus* was erected on a bench out front a few years after Margaret died. Jesus is lying down and wrapped in a blanket, the statue so lifelike that it has prompted calls to the Hamilton Paramedic Service from people concerned about the homeless person sleeping in the cold. But it's what has happened inside the church in the years since Margaret's death that's the bigger story.

Five years ago, church members started serving coffee and sandwiches to people who wandered into the church homeless and hungry. As the number of people grew, the church stepped up to meet the demand and slowly added more meals and more volunteers. They now serve more than three hundred meals a day, every day. Often, the lineups are so long they circle around the church. Those lineups provide a picture of how many people are still suffering and show how the numbers of people experiencing homelessness, poverty and housing precarity have grown. This program, like many others, responds to those who are homeless as well as those living on the brink of homelessness. A free meal every day is essential if you have no home and it can resolve the painful question of whether to pay the rent or feed yourself and your family.

Margaret's story prompts many questions about our attitude toward homeless people, especially those with mental illness. Why have our laws still not changed to protect homeless people with mental illness? A person can only be hospitalized against their will if they are deemed a threat to themselves or others. But the doctors who allowed Margaret to make the final decision to leave the hospital turned her right to self-determination against her. By allowing her to walk out when she was still so sick, they sealed her fate.

As Steve Lurie, executive director of Canadian Mental Health Association, Toronto, said, things would fall apart after Margaret left the hospital because she stopped taking her medications and had no support.

"Margaret is a classic example of where housing with supports would have worked," said Lurie. "The issue was medication noncompliance and there could have been a team that visited her, and if there was a barrier for her to get to the hospital for her shot then she could have had access to a team, which could have administered medication in her boarding home. She would have done fine. The question is, how do we create better bureaucratic and political will to make this happen?"

In the end, said Lurie, the lack of housing is very much a human rights issue. "People have a right to a decent place to live and the kind of services they need to realize their hopes and dreams. This is articulated in the UN Convention on the Rights of the Disabled and Canada is a signatory."

THE MARGARETS OF the homeless world are victims of a plan gone wrong. Rather than improving people's lives, deinstitutionalization shortened them by pushing them into situations where they were forced to fend for themselves, like being walked off a gangplank. Over the past three decades, mental health policies have moved away from institutional care and toward a system that relies more on community services. And yet we have not been able to patch up the damage from deinstitutionalization that moved psychiatric patients into communities lacking in supports and affordable housing.

The closure of all of those psychiatric hospital beds is still impacting people today. In 1965, there were 15,257 psychiatric beds in the province of

Ontario. By 2016–17, although the population had doubled, the total number of mental health beds in Ontario was 4,479. Unfortunately, the money saved from those bed closures is still not being funnelled into community supports, as shown in a BC study. Between 1994 and 1995, the operating costs of BC psychiatric hospitals and psychiatric units in hospitals totalled $424 million. By 1998–99, this had dropped to $234 million. A comparison of expenditures for community psychiatric services for the same period showed a decrease from $208 million to $200 million – the funding for community care actually decreased.

Transitional housing programs are one community support that's been found to be very effective. They offer an alternate level of support to people with severe and persistent mental illness or illnesses. The individuals have typically experienced several unsuccessful attempts at living on their own and are often at risk for repeated and prolonged hospitalization, according to the 2016 report *Turning the Key*, which included a sub-report by the Mental Health Commission that funded the report.

They are programs like Hamilton House, in Calgary, Alberta – an eight-bed transitional housing program, and a partnership between the Calgary Region of the Canadian Mental Health Association (CMHA) and Alberta Health Services. Staff include a program manager and supportive living coordinators, a full-time nurse who works in the home and monitors symptoms and medications, plus a dedicated psychiatrist who follows up with clients who don't have a community psychiatrist. The team works together to connect clients with community services to help them manage their mental health symptoms and, ultimately, reduce the need for hospitalization.

According to the *Turning the Key* report, there are 520,700 people living with mental illness who are inadequately housed. Among them, as many as 119,800 are homeless. And yet, according to the 2016 report, only 25,367 housing units in Canada were dedicated to people living with mental illness.

That's unacceptable, said Steve Lurie. "The problem is the government's failure to invest in housing and in services in the community. That's what contributes to homelessness," said Lurie.

Lurie said homeless people who have a mental illness need more than just bricks and mortar. They need supports, specifically recovery-oriented supports, because so many people living with mental illness also struggle with addictions. With the proper supports, he said Margaret likely could have coped in the community. "I think what Margaret needed when she was discharged is to have been part of an Assertive Community Treatment Team, which would have had daily meetings about how she was doing. If she wasn't taking her meds, they might intervene earlier or they might have to have a hospital admission."

Assertive Community Treatment (ACT) teams is a multidisciplinary treatment program made up of a social worker, a nurse, a vocational specialist, an occupational therapist, a psychiatrist, a peer support worker and an addictions specialist. They provide a wide range of services from psychiatric treatment to help with administering medications, as well as helping people access community services. The support provided is tailored to each individual's needs to ensure people get the help they require to live as independently as possible.

ACT has been highly successful and has even become a model for other community service work; however, like with many programs, the wait-lists are long.

"In Toronto, you can wait a year to get access to an Assertive Community Treatment Team and the wait times are going up," said Lurie, adding that it raises the question of whether hospitals should be discharging people if there isn't sufficient supply of housing or supports. "We're stabilizing people then we're discharging them into homelessness."

THE PRINCIPLE OF moving mental health and addictions care from psychiatric hospitals into the community only works if the right services exist, including supportive housing. But the throngs of homeless mentally ill people are proof that those services are woefully inadequate. Countless reports and studies have shown that we need to shift away from crisis management services, such as emergency shelters, soup kitchens and food banks, and move toward permanent solutions that prevent homelessness. Experts have been recommending this since the early 1990s, as shown in a report by the now defunct Hamilton District Health Council, which outlined housing and support requirements as a key recommendation for homeless people with serious mental illnesses. It stated that the supportive housing model could reduce hospitalization rates and improve mental health stability, and, in the long term, lead to a reduction in the need for crisis intervention.

Other reports, like the 2012 study *The Real Cost of Homelessness* by the Homeless Hub, a web-based research library and information centre, stated that if agencies shifted their "focus to prevention and housing (with supports, if necessary), we would not only be responding appropriately and compassionately to a problem that harms individuals, families and communities, but we would also be saving money."

The problem is that agencies are stuck in the loop of providing emergency survival services in order to keep people alive. With hundreds of homeless people coming to their doors daily, they fear that ending those services could be deadly. Meanwhile, the wait-lists for supportive housing continue to grow. In a ten-year period, the wait-list in Toronto grew from seven hundred people in 2009 to over seventeen thousand in 2019. The previous Liberal government was given a plan that would have developed thirty thousand supportive housing units in Ontario over a ten-year period; however, even though it was fully costed and represented only a small fraction of total health spending, the plan was never implemented. While the current Ontario government has pledged to match the increased federal funding for community mental health and addictions services, the only province in Canada to do so, the match funding has not begun to flow and there is no action plan for the development of supportive housing.

WHEN I BEGAN my investigation into Margaret's life, my goal was to find out how she had ended up on the streets. Something had gone terribly wrong for her to be sleeping outside and trying to survive in minus thirty degree temperatures. Then I widened my lens to the thousands of others who were homeless for the same reasons. Like Margaret, they were leading desperate lives because of bed closures, cuts in services, lack of community supports and massive shortfalls in affordable housing.

What many people, including politicians, still fail to recognize is that homeless people are living on our streets at a much greater economic cost than it would be to house them. It may appear that homelessness costs little to nothing but, according to the Canadian Observatory on Homelessness, the annual cost comes in at a whopping $7 billion.

Those costs include interactions with police, the criminal justice system, shelter costs and social supports like disability payments. They take into account that homeless people can end up in jail for nuisance charges, like trespassing, public urination and shoplifting. Social housing, in comparison, averages around $1,545 a month.

MALCOLM GLADWELL EXPOSED the cost of homelessness in his 2006 article in the *New Yorker* magazine called "Million-Dollar Murray," which told the story of a homeless man who lived in Reno, Nevada. Gladwell added up the cost of his visits to homeless shelters, hospitals, prisons and emergency rooms over ten years and it came to more than $100,000 a year.

What Gladwell discovered was that the highest costs were going to the chronically homeless. He cited data collected by a Boston graduate student named Dennis Culhane, who, during a research stint in shelters, found that 80 percent of shelter users were in and out fairly quickly, another 10 percent were episodic users who would come for around three weeks at a time and the last ten percent, the chronically homeless, were those who lived in shelters for years.

As Gladwell wrote, "They were older. Many were mentally ill or physically disabled, and when we think about homelessness as a social problem – the people sleeping on the sidewalk, aggressively panhandling, lying drunk in doorways, huddled on subway grates and under bridges – it's this group that we have in mind."

It is this group of chronically homeless, wrote Gladwell, who are consuming far more health and social services than anyone had anticipated, mostly because of their complex needs and reliance on high-cost emergency services.

Gladwell's article was cited in *The Real Cost of Homelessness* report, followed by the comment, "Lest we smugly believe this is an American story only, that with their high cost of health care and propensity to imprison people the costs quickly become inflated, it is worth pointing out that many of the same arguments have been made effectively in Canada."

The financial studies on homelessness vary depending on the city and province but all point to the same conclusion: there is a critical need to invest in homelessness prevention, mainly by providing supportive housing.

MANY PROVINCES HAVE done their own cost analysis of homelessness. In Calgary, the city calculated in 2008 that the annual cost of supports for the transiently homeless was $72,444 per person, while the cost of supports for those who are chronically homelessness was $134,642 per person. That included health care, housing and emergency services. In 2016 dollars, those numbers grew to $87,000 and $161,000, respectively. The report noted that by the time a person sought help, their health had seriously deteriorated and they needed extensive ongoing care. Despite their heavy reliance on services, many kept getting sicker.

One of the most extensive studies done on the cost of homelessness was in 2017 by McGill University health economist Eric Latimer and included 990 people who had one or more of six mental disorders: major depression, manic or hypomanic episode, post-traumatic stress disorder, mood disorder with psychotic features or current psychotic disorder, with or without concurrent substance use disorder. The participants lived in Vancouver, Winnipeg, Toronto, Montreal and Moncton, and were followed on a daily basis for nine months, between October 2009 and June 2011. The results showed that, on average, the annual costs for a person struggling with homelessness and mental illness was $53,144 per person.

In the three largest cities – Toronto, Vancouver and Montreal – the costs (excluding the cost for medications) ranged from about $56,000 per year, while in smaller cities like Moncton the cost was only $30,000 per year. That range was mostly due to spending differences on psychiatric hospital stays, which was much greater in Vancouver and Montreal than in the three other cities. Costs of justice-related services (not including incarcerations) were much higher in Toronto than in the other cities.

THERE ARE OTHER hidden costs of homelessness that aren't included in these figures, including panhandling, which increases in direct proportion to the number of people living on the street. In 1999, it became such a huge problem in Ontario that the province introduced the Safe Streets Act to try and stop panhandling, squeegeeing and other forms of solicitation. The act stated that any form of panhandling that was done in an "aggressive manner that is likely to cause a reasonable person to fear for their safety and security" was prohibited.

The wording of the act was vague enough that it allowed police broad discretion in its application, and in some cities, including Hamilton and Toronto, the issuing of tickets got out of control. In Toronto, the number of tickets issued to homeless people rose from 710 in 2000, to more than 15,324 in 2010. Over those years, according to a report in the *Toronto Star*, the total value of the 67,388 tickets issued during that time was estimated at more than $4 million. The cost to the Toronto Police Service of issuing the tickets was $936,019.

In Hamilton, one homeless person named Dwight Perry became a target for panhandling. According to a report in August 2017 by CBC Hamilton, the sixty-year-old homeless man had been given so many panhandling tickets that he owed more than twenty thousand dollars in fines. In March 2018, the court dismissed the charges and Perry's lawyer told the court, "After the dismissal of the charge today, one would hope that the province would exercise its discretion and no longer prosecute Dwight and others . . . to do so would, arguably, be an abuse of process."

While all of these numbers have focused on the economic costs of homelessness, the human lives that have been lost are priceless.

Advocates like Cathy Crowe, who has fought tirelessly to help homeless people, wonder how many more have to die before something is done. In her book *Dying for a Home*, she wrote about the three homeless men – Eugene Upper, Irwin Anderson and Mirsalah-Aldin Kompani – who froze to death within three months of each other in Toronto in 1996. In the same year, a few months before, another homeless man named Brent Simms had been killed when he was run over by a car while sleeping on the sidewalk. The deaths prompted the formation of the Toronto Coalition against Homelessness (TCAH), which successfully pushed for an inquest. At its conclusion, when the coroner's jury was asked, "By what means did the men die?," the answer was summed up in one word: "Homelessness."

THE BASEMENT DROP-IN shelter on Rebecca Street where I first met Margaret closed in April 1996, and a new centre opened at 195 Ferguson Avenue North. It was about seven hundred metres north and still within walking distance to downtown. Staff at the Wesley were glad to move, not only because they needed more space to help manage their growing number of clientele but because the cockroach problem at the Wesley had become unbearable. The new space filled up quickly, including the housing project for people who are hard to house.

Four years after the move, the Wesley opened the city's first twenty-four-hour emergency services drop-in shelter in order to meet the growing need. By 2005, the Wesley was running more than twelve programs from six locations. Meanwhile, the brick building that staff left behind on Rebecca Street was redeveloped into trendy condos called the Stone Lofts that come with twelve-foot ceilings and funky brick interior walls.

HELEN KELL LONG ago retired from the HPH and now works as a hairstylist in seniors' homes, but she is still helping people with mental illness. The difference is that before she helped patients inside the walls of a hospital; today she is helping those who live on our streets. It's symbolic of how the problem has been shifted from hospitals to the sidewalks.

Helen's "boys," as she calls them, are Bruce and Greg. They don't know each other and she found them in separate areas of the city but she supports them in the same way – by giving them food, clothing and money whenever she sees them. She knows the spots where they hang out so she knows where to find them to give them their goodies, and if they're not there, she'll drive around looking for them, even if it takes hours. She met Greg a few years ago while driving down a street close to her home on the Hamilton Mountain. He was sitting on the curb and she immediately pulled over as it was unusual to see homeless people in the suburbs. She sat down next to him and struck up a conversation to find out who he was.

"He told me he didn't like going downtown. He didn't feel safe," said Kell.

She gave him five dollars and told him she'd see him again, and she's been true to her word. Since then, she sees him at least once a week and gives him money and clothing, some of which she collects from friends. She also hits up her friends for their "free coffee" wins from Tim Hortons' Roll Up the Rim contest and throws in a few dollars from her own pocket.

Greg isn't much of a talker so it's hard to find out what he needs. Kell has tried to talk him into going to a shelter but he doesn't want to leave his grocery cart. "His whole life is in that buggy," said Kell.

One cold winter day she found Greg wandering the streets wearing only thin shoes and a light coat, so she went home and put together a large bag filled with boots, a poncho and gloves then added some chocolate bars and a ten-dollar bill. When she handed it to him, he slowly looked through the bag, took out what he needed – the boots and poncho – and gave the rest back. It's been more than four years since she started helping Greg and she's yet to miss a week. On those days when he's not at his usual spot, giving up on finding him isn't an option.

One winter she lost track of him for two weeks and was despondent. When she finally spotted him in a different neighbourhood, she stopped the car and ran over to him.

"It was like I'd seen my kid," she said, with a wide smile. "I said, 'Greg, there you are,' and he looked at me like he didn't know me. I told him, 'I'm the one who got the bag of clothes for you,' and he said, 'Thank you.'"

Then there's Bruce. Kell met him during one of her drives around the city and gave him ten dollars. He gets the same amount whenever she sees him. She jokes about the things she does for her "boys." "I always tell them, 'You know I could have retired years ago if I didn't support all you guys.'"

The stories of Greg and Bruce are similar to Margaret and Mary's stories and the stories of thousands of other homeless people. While they differ in the details, the common thread is that they're all homeless and have some type of mental health problem. All victims of the same half-finished plan.

ON FEBRUARY 20, 2008, Margaret's brother John died, two weeks shy of his sixty-third birthday. He left behind a substantial amount of money, which was distributed to close family members. They guessed that it came from his social assistance cheques and that he must have saved them up to give to them. John's nephew Brian, who is a pastor in Wisconsin, knew little about his uncle's life.

"All I have to go on is what's in the photo," said Brian. "Much like Margaret, John is mostly a mystery to me."

CHAPTER TWENTY-ONE
In From the Cold

Margaret taught me much about homelessness. She taught me that every homeless person has a name, that they are somebody's son or daughter and that they had a life before they became homeless. Most of all, she taught me that they are not there by choice but because of a complicated series of events that can be traced to a broken system and, too often, to a broken mind.

By understanding what happened to Margaret, we can understand what happened to thousands of others who are homeless because of the failure to replace hospital beds with community services and the failure to provide affordable and supportive housing. In short, the mess that exists today was entirely man-made and preventable.

Margaret's tragic life and early death also raise serious questions about our attitude toward the homeless community. The fact that the problem is still so prevalent speaks to our willingness to turn away from the people who need our help the most and to blame them for their problems. There is hope for a kinder future and it is found in the real-life examples of cities and countries that have taken on the task of ending homelessness and won.

The most successful are based on the Housing First model, which works to remove barriers preventing people from accessing supportive services and addresses the often overwhelming issues of addiction and mental health, as well as unemployment and physical health problems.

The Housing First program was introduced in 1990 by Sam Tsemberis – a Canadian psychology practitioner, and founder and executive director of Pathways to Housing – for people with serious mental illnesses, long histories of homelessness and often co-occurring substance abuse issues. The approach has been adopted by organizations across North America, all of which follow the same principle – people can only move forward in their lives if they have safe and supportive housing. Once they're housed, supports are set up that are tailored to their physical and mental health needs. Research shows that most chronically homeless people who are provided with housing will stay there, and that over time their mental and physical health will improve. Had the Housing First model been in place before deinstitutionalization began to unfold, we very likely wouldn't be facing the crisis in homelessness that exists today.

Funding shortfalls for mental health supports, not just those needed for homeless people, have been a reality for decades. In Ontario, approximately 1.5 million people have some type of mental health problem and, of those, one in five, or approximately seventy-five thousand people, are dealing with a severe mental illness. According to the Mental Health Commission of Canada, only one-third are receiving the services they need while the majority are relying on their families and are stuck on long wait-lists.

WHAT DOES ENDING homelessness look like? It looks like Finland where, in 2008, the country became the first and only EU country to adopt the Housing First model. The results have been astonishing. Between 2009 and 2016, Finland saw its homeless population drop by 18 percent, and they did it by increasing access to housing and providing people with individually tailored support services. The government used existing social housing, purchased apartments for use as rental apartments and built new housing.

Some shelters and dormitory-type hostels were converted into supported housing, including a large hostel for homeless people in Helsinki that had been run by the Salvation Army. The 250-bed hostel was renovated and turned into eighty independent apartments with on-site staff. Supports are there if people need them – for example, if a tenant has problems paying their rent or needs to apply for government benefits, a housing advisor is available to assist them. There are also financial and debt counselling services available. As reported in the *Guardian* in March 2017, "Finland has all but eradicated rough sleeping and sustainably housed a significant number of long-term homeless people."

Closer to home, Medicine Hat, a town of around sixty-four thousand in southern Alberta, has become a national role model for its work in ending homelessness. It started in 2008 when a study showed they were spending close to one hundred thousand dollars to keep one person on the street annually, largely because people were using high-cost emergency services, such as fire, police and EMS. That included health, social services, justice, hospital visits and jail time, as well as the police costs to manage the homeless community.

They realized they were just managing the homelessness crisis by feeding, clothing and sheltering people day after day instead of eliminating it. The town compared the one-hundred-thousand-dollar figure to the twenty thousand dollars it was estimated to cost to house one person for one year and decided to make some changes. In 2009, the town signed a pledge that no one would spend more than ten days in an emergency shelter or on the streets before they were put in touch with support agencies or placed into supportive housing. Within three days of someone turning up on the housing society's radar, the person would be seen by a support worker, and within ten days they would have permanent housing.

The plan called Starting At Home was based on the Housing First model, and was consistent with the principles that had been outlined in a provincial report called *A Plan for Alberta: Ending Homelessness in 10 years* by the Alberta Secretariat for Action on Homelessness. The goal was to focus on quickly moving people experiencing homelessness into independent and permanent homes. Once people were in a place of their own, the underlying factors that led to them becoming homeless would be addressed.

Mayor Ted Clugston was skeptical at first and described the plan as being too ambitious. In one media interview, he commented that trying to end homelessness was like trying to bring about world peace. "It was these elusive goals that everybody wants to do, but can never do," Clugston told a reporter during a CBC radio interview.

When Clugston heard about the dollar savings, however, it convinced him they needed to give it a try. All evidence showed that the old-school approach of telling a homeless person to "get clean" before they could apply for housing wasn't working and, without supports, it was inevitable a person would fall back into a cycle of drug use and poverty.

That cycle was keeping them dependent on hospital emergency rooms, shelters and jails, and driving up costs. As Clugston told the CBC, "This is the cheapest and the most humane way to treat people."

The town adopted a five-year plan with a goal to house 290 homeless people, eliminate half of all emergency shelter beds, reduce the average length of stay in shelters to ten days and decrease the flow of homeless people into jails and hospitals. They knew it wouldn't work unless they addressed one of the root causes of homelessness and, to that end, they set up evidence-based mental health programs. The estimated implementation costs included a one-time capital investment of $7.5 million, which went on to create fifty units of permanent supportive housing with costs shared between the government and community at a seventy–thirty split.

The estimate to operate the units was approximately $1.7 million with an additional investment of $1.3 million annually until the end of the 2016 fiscal year. That would allow them to double their intensive case management and increase the rapid rehousing capacity by 50 percent. The total amount from 2014 to 2016 was $3.4 million.

The results surprised everyone, including the mayor. From when they started in April 2009 until December 31, 2016, they housed 1,072 people. That included 312 children. They also saw major decreases in other areas:

- a 73 percent drop in the number of days spent in jail by homeless people, from 11,294 to 3,050;
- a 33 percent drop in the number of days homeless people spent in the hospital;
- a 15 percent drop in ER use by homeless people; and
- a 10 percent increase in court appearances. The increase, they discovered, was because homeless people were now stable enough to go to court and pay their tickets.

By 2017, YEAR seven of the plan, they had housed 1,094 homeless people, including 777 adults and 317 children. In some cases, they had even managed to house people before the ten-day pledge. The programs also connected people with supports and provided housing grants. Those who were part of the program saw improvements in people's mental and physical health, and cost reductions in crisis health services. Some people found jobs, 5 percent went on disability support and 121 people took part in budgeting workshops. After six years of watching the program in action, Mayor Clugston had become a believer in the Housing First model.

"If you're addicted to drugs, it's going to be pretty hard to get off them if you're sleeping under a park bench," he told the CBC. "Years ago, we'd have people living in the shelter for years, now it's measured in days and weeks."

In 2015, Hamilton was selected to be one of the sites for a pilot community for the 20,000 Homes Campaign, a national initiative that pledged to find twenty thousand homes for vulnerable people by July 1, 2018.

It was likely chosen because the city had already seen some success in reducing homelessness. In May 2016, the city's Housing First update showed there had been a 35 percent reduction in the number of chronically homeless between 2014 and 2015, and in one year, they had surpassed their target and provided housing to 184 individuals. It's worth noting that this drop occurred in the same period that the housing and rental market was turned upside down with higher prices. They also saw a drop in the number of individuals and families accessing emergency shelters.

Of the thirty-three communities across Canada that were enrolled in the campaign, Hamilton reported the most dramatic drop. "What Hamilton's doing is showing what works to reduce homelessness," Tim Richter, president and CEO of the Canadian Alliance to End Homelessness told CBC.

The problem is still far from resolved. An estimated 15,400 people are on wait-lists for subsidized housing units in Hamilton. About one thousand of them are currently experiencing some form of homelessness.

Is it possible Margaret would have responded to the housing program at Medicine Hat? She would have been placed in supportive housing and provided with services tailored to her needs, specifically for her mental illness, within ten days of becoming homeless.

At William Tuke's York Retreat, she would have received compassionate care in a smaller family-like atmosphere. In Trieste, she would have lived in a community where a strong network of supports were available to her 24-7, allowing her to live independently. Within any of these models, Margaret may well have lived out her years happy and healthy. Even in her most worn-down state, she wasn't beyond reach. She had shown that when she was in a program she enjoyed, like pottery, and when she was treated with respect, she behaved well and was co-operative. With the right programs in place within a supportive environment, she likely could have thrived.

At Home/Chez Soi was the mother of all homeless housing projects. Described as one of the most ambitious in the world, the five-year research project was launched in Canada in 2008 with a price tag of $110 million. It was designed to provide housing to people who were experiencing both serious mental illness and homelessness. The Mental Health Commission of Canada was behind the federally funded program.

At Home/Chez Soi used the Housing First approach to establish five demonstration sites in Vancouver, Winnipeg, Toronto, Montreal and Moncton. They then followed more than two thousand participants for two years. Each site was focused on a specific subpopulation: Vancouver included people with problematic substance use; Winnipeg included urban Indigenous homeless people; Toronto and Montreal included ethno-racialized populations, including new immigrants, and Montreal added a component on vocational training; and Moncton looked at the challenges of providing services in smaller communities.

The Toronto site included 580 participants of which 41 percent had been homeless for more than five years. More than half likely had a psychotic disorder while the others had depression or some form of post-traumatic stress disorder, and many had drug and/or alcohol problems.

On average, the Housing First model was estimated to cost between $14,177 and $22,257 per person per year, depending on the person's needs. The study's conclusions, which were released in October 2019, found that, over the previous six months, 62 percent of the participants had been housed all of the time, which was twice as high as the 31 percent rate for other programs.

The result confirmed that while people with severe mental health issues, substance-use disorders and other illnesses needed a lot of support, which could be costly, providing housing with supports worked. The cost savings were lower than expected, however – for every ten dollars that was invested in housing first, $9.60 was saved in other government services.

THERE ARE MANY examples of programs that have proven the effectiveness of providing housing first. In southeast Calgary in October 2019, fifteen tiny homes were built to house homeless veterans as part of a project led by the Homes for Heroes Foundation. The veterans who were moved into these homes had served as far back as the Korean War and as recently as Afghanistan. Each home was 275 square feet and built within an area that included a resource centre, community gardens, memorials and on-site counselling, which was provided in recognition of the struggles experienced by many vets.

In Toronto, the House of Compassion provides supportive housing for twenty-one residents who have a severe mental illness. Run by a non-profit charitable organization founded in 1988, residents are provided with permanent housing and twenty-four-hour support staff to help with their daily living needs, including meal preparation and taking their medications.

For some homeless people, like Kasper Dewyk, boarding homes work well. I met Kasper in the winter of 1997 for a story I wrote for the *Hamilton Spectator*. He was thirty-seven years old and his shoulder-length brown hair was coated with grime from the parking garage floor where he slept. His hair stuck out at the sides like a mad scientist and his face and clothes were coated in a thin layer of grease. The skin on his wrists was raw where he had chewed it, a habit he'd developed to numb the voices in his head.

But his most distinctive feature was his large brown doe-like eyes that stared straight ahead, never blinking, like he was in a constant state of shock. Kasper had been diagnosed with schizophrenia in his early twenties, and after being in and out of the HPH for years, he was sent to live in a boarding home. Kasper was twenty-nine at the time and spent a total of five hours in the home before he walked out, telling staff he "couldn't handle the company of people." He made his new home in the second-floor stairwell of a downtown parking garage and slept there for almost eight years. The concrete was cold and littered with discarded cigarettes, but it gave Kasper the privacy he so desperately craved.

His only friend was Oman Huhad, an outreach worker with the public health department who had visited Kasper regularly for a year before Kasper would talk to him. Fortunately, Kasper was a man who liked routine, which made it easy for Oman to find him. Every morning, he would peel himself off his cement bed, have a cigarette then walk across the street to a coffee shop for his morning coffee. His next stop was at the MacNab Street YMCA for a breakfast of eggs and toast. During the warmer months, he spent his days parked on a bench outside a nearby church, and in the winter, he would often spend all day wandering through malls and coffee shops.

His family would see him sitting on the sidewalk and try to help, but he always refused. His sister, Yolanda, who lived in Dundas, only a fifteen-minute drive from Kasper's bed in the parking garage, said it was heartbreaking for their family to see him there.

"You can't imagine what it's like to drive by your brother sleeping on a bench," said Yolanda. "Even when a family cares very much about someone who has a mental illness, it's impossible to help them if they won't accept it. We talked to so many psychiatrists and social workers and they said he has to be either suicidal or homicidal. We were always waiting for that phone call that said he'd frozen to death on the streets."

Sometimes Yolanda and her family would drive around the city looking for him, and when they caught sight of him, they would quickly pull over. It was terrible seeing him looking so ragged and sick, she said.

"I would say to him, 'I can help you. You really need help. Do you want us to take you to the hospital?' But Kasper would shut down. I've had a thousand conversations like this with him and there's either no response or he'll pick up on some odd thing I mentioned."

Even when he did accept help, like the time they bought him an expensive winter coat, things didn't always work out. Soon after they gave him the coat, it was stolen from him at a shelter. Yolanda not only felt the frustration of not being able to help her brother but also the sting of judgment from people who told her they couldn't understand why she didn't take him in. They failed to understand what people like Kasper go through and how difficult it is to get them to accept help, said Yolanda.

"It is easy to turn our backs on people who are mentally ill because even though they're victims, we want to blame them. People look at them and see they're dirty and they think, why don't they just take a shower. But for people like Kasper to take a shower he would have to figure out where to go, how to fill out the forms, where he would get the money. He couldn't do it."

She understood why her brother turned his back on shelters and on some agencies. "Homeless people have been bossed around and bullied in shelters. They don't want them anywhere because they say they smell bad. So where was he welcome? The people at the Y who pay three hundred dollars a year don't want someone in there like him. So where was he supposed to go?"

That feeling of powerlessness is familiar to many family members who have a relative with a mental illness, many of who blame the Mental Health Act for preventing them from getting a loved one into care. They believe the act gives the person who has a mental illness too much power at a time when they don't know what's best for themselves. Meanwhile, patient rights advocates say the act is too subjective because it allows a doctor to involuntarily admit a patient based on their "belief" that they are a danger to themselves or others.

Then there are the doctors who say it places too many restrictions on them and prevents them from admitting someone. Some sign the form with much reluctance, fearing legal retribution, while others complain the forms are too time-consuming and complex. Dr. David Dawson, chief psychiatrist at the HPH from 1985 to 1995, said the act often made it challenging for him to admit patients who had mental health problems and to keep them there for any length of time. For example, if a patient requested a review board meeting in order to have the certificate removed, it could take an entire afternoon out of his busy schedule when he had several other patients to see. He then had to prove that the person needed to be admitted, which wasn't always easy and could require written statements and copious research.

OMAN HUHAD'S JOB was to help homeless people like Kasper who wouldn't use shelters, and provide them with the supports they needed, even if it was just a pair of shoes or a blanket. He would check on Kasper a few times a week and if he didn't see him at the coffee shop or the Y, he knew to look in the garage. On the day I visited, we met Kasper while he was eating his breakfast at the Y. Oman sat patiently beside him while he ate and gently asked him what he needed, suggesting blankets, clothes, shoes. It was a one-way conversation, but if Kasper needed something, he would let Oman know with a nod.

One winter, Oman had to go away. His family lived in Ethiopia and needed his help. Just getting to their remote village in east Africa would take more than a week, first by plane, then bus and finally by foot. Even if there had been a worker who could've filled in for Oman, Kasper wouldn't have trusted them. That meant Kasper would be on his own. Oman was worried because there'd been a heavy snowfall that winter. As it turned out, he had good reason to worry. The morning Oman returned, he found Kasper lying on the snowy sidewalk outside of the parking garage. He was barefoot, emaciated and his feet were raw and swollen. Kasper looked up at Oman like a lost child and muttered, "Kasper sick."

Oman was shocked.

"He looked so sick, he looked like someone from a Third World country," said Oman, who immediately called a taxi and took Kasper to the emergency department at St. Joseph's Hospital.

As they waited for the cab, Oman tried to squeeze Kasper's feet into his shoes but they were too swollen. At the hospital, doctors said the frostbite was so severe that gangrene had set in and they would need to amputate to prevent the infection from spreading. They also knew that a homeless man without feet would die a sad death. Kasper didn't want to lose his feet and told the hospital to call his sister to intervene. Yolanda had seen my earlier story on her brother in the *Spectator* and had tried to connect with him but he had pushed her away.

When doctors called her, she rushed to her brother's side. Her main concern was to keep her brother alive so she agreed to sign the consent form for the amputation. Kasper refused, however, and under the Mental Health Act, doctors had to oblige. They instead put him on a strong dose of antibiotics and hoped for the best. Once Kasper was hooked up to an IV, doctors added an antipsychotic medication to control his schizophrenic symptoms. He had stopped taking any medication years earlier due to the side effects.

Within days, Kasper's world began to look different. The voices in his head were quieted and, for the first time in years, he was able to read. He let nurses cut his grime-coated hair and trim his unruly beard, and a new Kasper emerged. Miraculously, the infection healed and doctors only needed to remove a small part of his right foot. But Yolanda said the real miracle was in what happened next.

"The day we went to the hospital to talk about Kasper's future was the day of the newspaper article on Ms. [Margaret] Jacobson's death," said Yolanda.

During the meeting to decide Kasper's fate, doctors mentioned the article as a cautionary tale.

"I think it was one of the things that helped keep him in there. They didn't want that to happen to him," said Yolanda.

Doctors allowed Kasper to stay in the hospital while he healed and extended his admission while he underwent weekly physiotherapy sessions for his foot. They slipped a prosthesis into his shoe and taught him how to walk so he had only a slight limp. Over the next several months, a team of doctors, nurses and social workers met regularly with Yolanda to discuss his progress. After he had stabilized, doctors kept him in the hospital until they found proper housing. As the hospital social worker said at the time, "He's slid through the cracks for so many years. We looked at his case and said, 'How can we make sure it doesn't happen again?'"

At one point, doctors asked Yolanda if she could take him. She had to say no.

"I'm not a terrible human being. I just know it wouldn't have worked. My children ended up cowering behind the sofa when he came to visit. They were terrified of him. One time he lit a fire on the driveway because we weren't home and he wanted to be warm. It wouldn't have worked," said Yolanda.

After a full year in the hospital, Kasper was moved into Brock Lodge, a subsidized residential care home on King Street East. The owners treated him with respect, he had the supports he needed and the other residents became like family and came to admire his savvy *Jeopardy* skills. Kasper loved it and lived there for twenty-two years.

Yolanda visited him every week. Each visit reminded her of how grateful she was that her brother was finally safe. In the end, Kasper's two-pack-a-day cigarette habit caught up with him and in February 2018 he was diagnosed with lung cancer. Kasper was a man with simple needs and when he was told he only had a few weeks to live, all he asked for was a Coke and a cigarette. One month later, on March 15, he died.

"He was never a whiner," said Yolanda. "He never complained about anything."

At a service to celebrate his life, family and friends had a chance to say goodbye to Kasper and to celebrate what they loved about him. A family friend named Vicky described him as a "gentle soul" who controlled his own choices.

"His death was peaceful and his life was not without purpose. He asked for nothing. Ever. Most of us can't imagine what courage and ingenuity it must have taken to survive," said Vicky. "Kasper lived life on his own terms and even when it was uncomfortable for people around him, he made his own choices. Courage has many faces and Kasper was, in fact, courageous."

Kasper was cremated and his ashes were buried beside his parents at a small cemetery in Cayuga by the Grand River. His service concluded with comforting words from a poem by John Clare called "I Am!"

> And sleep as I in childhood sweetly slept:
> Untroubling and untroubled where I lie;
> The grass below – above the vaulted sky.

CHAPTER TWENTY-TWO
"We Know How to Solve the Problem"

When the pandemic hit Canada in early spring 2020, it drew attention to the country's homelessness problem like never before. Funding was provided to help curb the spread of infection by opening new beds, making motel and hotel rooms available and converting arenas into shelters.

For those who staffed shelters and agencies, the pandemic created monumental challenges around how to continue helping the city's most vulnerable. Agencies recognized that homeless people are at far greater risk of succumbing to illnesses because so many have weakened immune systems due to their complex health problems. A study published in the *Canadian Medical Association Journal* in January 2021 showed that homeless people are over twenty times more likely to be hospitalized for COVID-19, over ten times more likely to require intensive care and over five times as likely to die within twenty-one days of testing positive.

Staff were suddenly thrust into new territory, trying to adjust to rules around social distancing, wearing masks and using hand sanitizer. They were difficult enough rules for businesses to follow but far more challenging when your clients live on the street and have a mental illness. And what about homeless people themselves? How were they supposed to stay home when they didn't have one? How could they buy hand sanitizer and masks when they barely had enough money for a meal? And how could they follow social distancing rules when shelter beds were mere inches apart? Overcrowded shelters were like a petri dish for the deadly virus to spread and breed, and in Toronto, more than three dozen outbreaks occurred in shelter sites from when the pandemic was declared in mid-March to the end of July.

Overnight, homeless people had lost their safe spaces where they could escape from the heat and cold: shopping malls, libraries and coffee shops. People stopped volunteering due to the fear of being infected. Then there were the extra costs to agencies to purchase masks and sanitizer.

"It put unprecedented pressures on our communities, on our social support systems and on the health care system," Katherine Kalinowski, chief operating officer for Good Shepherd Centre in Hamilton, wrote in an email.

It also put pressure on small-volunteer led groups. Jeff Ng, who had been part of the volunteer crew at Parkview Church in east Hamilton for sixteen years, said the new rules meant adjusting their safety protocol so they could serve meals from a distance while wearing masks and gloves. Unfortunately, it also resulted in fewer volunteers. While the church typically relied on a loyal crew of more than twenty-five volunteers every Wednesday night at their two locations, after COVID-19 hit that number dropped to six.

"There is very high anxiety level among the volunteers who fear getting infected," Ng wrote in an email.

Ng said the virus made it more difficult for volunteers to have a "friendly chat with our guests," which meant they lost a connection to some but they kept their perspective and remembered that while the pandemic was scary, so was starvation.

"The people who are marginalized in our community have more than just the virus on their minds. They are thinking about the food, about the cold and about trying to survive," wrote Ng. "We continue to serve with love, patience and humility knowing that it is for a greater good."

Despite these pressures, Kalinowski said that in Hamilton, people came together for the greater good. That included the city, community agencies and grassroots organizations, including the Shelter Health Network, doctors and nurses who worked with homeless people.

"I was in awe at the level of collaboration, innovation and responsiveness that was shown by organizations, institutions and government in Hamilton as they worked together to reduce the chances of infection," Kalinowski wrote.

HELPING HOMELESS PEOPLE as a volunteer can take many forms, from holding bake sales to raise money for programs to serving meals in churches. For me, it started in 2016 when I came across an article on a program in the UK called Helping Handbags Worldwide, which encourages women to fill their unwanted purses with sanitary products and toiletries, and pass them out to homeless women. A similar program exists in Scotland, in which donations for vulnerable women are given to organizations to hand out. Closer to home, there's the Purse Project in Ottawa, which collects gently used purses filled with toiletries and gives them to homeless women.

I contacted Kalinowski and asked about a purse donation project that encouraged women in the community to donate their gently used purses that they had filled with toiletries. The purses could be delivered to Mary's Place where staff would hand them out. Kalinowski liked the idea and the Purses for Margaret project was born. What began in my basement with purses collected from friends and family soon took off. Donations of purses and hygiene items, including pads and tampons, small shampoo, conditioner, lotion and soaps, arrived by the tubful, then my daughters and I would fill the purses and deliver them to the shelter.

I set up a Facebook page to reach a wider audience and was fortunate that the First Unitarian Church of Hamilton, of which I am a member, agreed to allow me use of their donation box for purse drop-offs. The project clearly touched a nerve as the response was overwhelming. In the first few weeks, purses poured in from individuals, groups and business owners who sent me samples as well as cash donations, which I used to buy items from dollar stores. Two drugstores donated several boxes of tampons and pads, and a dental clinic gave me a huge box filled with toothbrushes, toothpaste and dental floss, along with a cheque for $250 to purchase more items.

Rummage sales and thrift stores became great sources for used purses, especially on half-price days. On my birthday, I asked friends to donate purses and hygiene items instead of gifts. My first delivery to Mary's Place was made only a few weeks after I announced the project. My trunk was filled with sixty-four purses, all overflowing with toiletries.

It quickly became a "women helping women" project as women belonging to book clubs, church groups, roller derby teams, teachers' federations, softball leagues and soccer teams made donations. A major breakthrough came when a woman, who preferred to remain anonymous, generously offered to donate several hundred pads and tampons directly to Mary's Place every month on an ongoing basis.

Six months after Purses for Margaret was launched, the shelter had received well over two thousand purses. The community has continued to respond in other ways. In November 2019, I put the word out that Mary's Place was short on winter coats. Within two weeks, the shelter had received over two hundred coats, hats, mitts and scarves. Rabbi Hillel Lavery-Yisraeli from the Beth Jacob Synagogue in west Hamilton generously purchased several new parkas and donated them to the shelter. He repeated those donations in 2020. Other members of the synagogue stepped forward with handmade hats, mitts and scarves.

When I give talks on the purse project, there's always a mountain of purses and hygiene items tucked into a corner, ready for me to take to the shelter. More than three years after starting it, I am still being contacted by people wanting to know how they can help.

When I asked shelter staff how the women were responding to the purses, I was told that they are just as grateful for the items inside the purses as they are for the message they send.

"The purses show them there's someone out there who cares about them," said the staffer. For a group who is too often made to feel invisible, that's a priceless gift.

Anyone interested in starting their own purse project can check out the Purses for Margaret Facebook page at https://www.facebook.com/PursesforMargaret/.

ALTHOUGH THE VOLUNTEER landscape has changed during COVID-19 due to physical distancing restrictions, there are still many ways in which people can help. For those who are not in the vulnerable age categories or don't have underlying health conditions, many organizations still need help with food preparation, resource distribution and telephone support. Whether it's a large well-established agency or a small grassroots group, they are all in need of volunteers and many couldn't operate without them. When looking for an agency to volunteer with, Kalinowski encourages people to choose one that has a mission statement that resonates with them.

If you're unable to volunteer and still want to help, donations of food or money are always needed. Cash donations have become increasingly essential since the pandemic, as many have experienced a significant decline in donations. Many groups rely heavily on these donations to cover unexpected costs, like personal protective equipment and additional staffing.

"It is vital that we help keep the doors open at organizations who are working on the frontline," wrote Kalinowski.

Agencies, charities and grassroots groups almost always need clothing, especially in the winter when they need warm coats, boots, socks, hats and gloves, plus new underwear, especially thermals. They also need household items, like dishes and bedding, for people who are moving into housing. Kalinowski said that while donating cell phones, tablets and phone cards may seem exorbitant, they are an important lifeline for homeless people because they allow them to stay in touch with family or friends, and to seek essential services like income support and telehealth.

WHAT ABOUT GIVING spare change to a homeless person on the street? It's a personal choice, says MacKinnon, who has worked with the homeless community for close to thirty years. He knows many people feel conflicted about this, but for him it's an easy decision. He gives. He does it because it allows a person to buy themselves lunch or a cup of coffee, and also lets them know that people care.

He's heard the arguments against this – that homeless people use the money to buy alcohol or drugs – and he doesn't listen. "Maybe they will buy beer with the money, but if that's what they need, don't judge. It's a gift, and if there's something they need in the moment, who am I to say that's wrong," said MacKinnon, who is a chaplain at Alexander Place retirement home in Waterdown.

As for the belief that panhandlers don't actually need the money, MacKinnon says he's never met anyone who is doing it for fun. "It is a hard way to make a living. The person who has the nice house is one in a million and even if they're in housing, it's likely assisted housing and they won't have much left over."

When MacKinnon worked with homeless people at Wesley Urban Ministries, his predecessor, Rev. Art Verrall, told him people often asked him how he was able to distinguish between the panhandlers who genuinely needed to use the food bank and imposters. "He said that in his years of experience, ninety-eight percent of users have genuine needs and that he didn't have the time or interest to chase down the few who didn't. I have always followed his example on this topic," said MacKinnon.

Those words have stayed with him for years and are the reason why he says the worst thing you can do is to pretend you don't see them or tell them you don't have any money.

"The person knows that you probably do," said MacKinnon. And even if you don't have any money and can't give them change, make sure you make eye contact with them – the interaction is important. You will generally get "Have a nice day" or "God Bless" in response.

There's also the option of giving a gift card for a coffee shop or fast-food restaurant, like Tim Hortons. The cards allow a person to get a hot drink and food on their own terms. At the same time, it gives them access to a warm space.

MacKinnon doesn't agree with people asking a homeless person to dine with them. "So often I hear people say, 'I feel sorry for those people but I will NOT give them money but I will gladly take them to McDonald's and buy them a hamburger.' This is so patronizing. Maybe they don't want a hamburger. Nobody tells me how to spend my money so why should I assume I have the right to do the same to the panhandler? A true gift has no strings attached."

You can also offer them a blanket or warm clothes. Doing some research into local services before you talk to a homeless person means being able to provide them with information on where to go for help. While some people are leery about getting too close to a homeless person, the reality is that it's much more likely for them to be the victim of a violent crime rather than the perpetrator.

Sometimes, said MacKinnon, the best thing you can do is to simply look them in the eye and ask them their name. It's a sign that you recognize them as an individual, and that small act of kindness may even give them a sense of dignity – something rarely offered to a homeless person.

Steve Lurie has found his own way of helping – he gives to one or two specific individuals he's gotten to know over the years. One is a homeless fellow who lives in his area. Lurie gives him money whenever he sees him. When they first met, Lurie tried to encourage him to go into a shelter, but he always declined.

"It's sad but I respect his right to choose his life," said Lurie, who also volunteers his musical talents at a Toronto Out of the Cold program. Lurie, who plays drums, and his bandmates go into various churches and entertain the homeless community with an evening of music. He knows the gift of music can help lift people's spirits.

While donating and volunteering are important, experts agree the most effective way to help is to speak out. As Kalinowski said, giving a homeless person spare change will help them get through another day, but contacting your elected representatives can help put them into a permanent bed.

"It is so important that people use their energy and voices to draw attention to the crisis of homelessness," wrote Kalinowski in an email. She encourages people to write letters to the editor, call their elected representatives and engage civic and faith groups in calls to action. "Ending homelessness is a moral imperative. It is also just common sense."

People in leadership roles – including MPPs, city or town councillors and federal MPs – are in positions to make decisions and they need to be reminded of how critical the situation is. Communities like Medicine Hat, Alberta, have shown that change can happen when the right people are in those positions.

"Tell them homelessness is a national crisis and that funding is needed, not just for shelter beds, which offer only a temporary reprieve, but for supportive housing programs and community supports, which will get people off the streets for good," wrote Kalinowski.

She suggests making your letter or email personal by describing how homelessness has affected your community, or telling them about a chance encounter you've had with a homeless person.

"Politicians need to know that people care about homelessness, and they need to know there are viable ways to end homelessness rather than simply trying to manage it," wrote Kalinowski.

Starting a grassroots group that advocates for services for homeless people can be even more effective than advocating on one's own and can start with a get-together with friends and family where you spend a night writing letters to your elected officials. (You don't need postage if you send a letter to your MP on Parliament Hill.)

It's important to be educated on the larger issues around homelessness by contacting groups like the Canadian Alliance to End Homelessness (CAEH), which is an excellent source for statistics, studies and policies. Find out which political party has a plan in place to support homeless people and campaign for them or organize protests to make a public appeal for change.

Lurie agrees it is important to take steps toward making change. Every night in every city in this country, homeless people flock to shelters for help and while it's still important to support shelters and agencies, the reality is that more needs to be done to end homelessness.

"My advice is that we should stop putting band-aids on things," said Lurie. "Maybe giving money to the homeless makes you feel good but it's a band-aid. We know how to solve the problem. We're just not doing it. The reality is, if there were more affordable housing options and programs like Housing First, there'd be less homelessness."

When the pandemic first hit, many hoped the government would provide funds to create permanent solutions. That hasn't happened.

As Lurie said, Toronto set a target years ago to provide at least eighteen thousand units of supportive housing. His hope was that it would be acted on. "We know that the homeless and people living in congregate settings are at high risk, due to the inability to social distance. This is why this was also the time to commit to getting shovels in the ground," wrote Lurie.

Instead, the wait-list for supportive housing in Toronto continues to grow by another four hundred names every three months. "There has been very limited progress. It will take vision and commitment of all three levels of government, the private sector and the community sector working together."

Kalinowski said the speed and efficiency at which things were achieved during the pandemic proved the government can act quickly when it needs to, even with highly complex long-standing problems.

"COVID is a crisis but so is homelessness. They say necessity is the mother of invention. I can only hope that we can leverage the COVID crisis to take radical action on the homelessness crisis in Canada," wrote Kalinowski.

Change came too late for Margaret. In the end, it wasn't the fall in the sub shop or the cancer that killed her. It was the system of neglect that continues to mean a slow death for thousands of other homeless people. What happened to Margaret should be a catalyst for change. Knowing how much she suffered, we should vow that no other person in this country will have to endure the same pain and indignities.

MANY PEOPLE HAVE asked me why Margaret opened up to me on that cold winter night at the Wesley back in 1993. It was out of character for her to talk to anyone let alone share intimate details of her life. She was more likely to bash them over the head with a hard coffee cup. Some people have thought it was because she didn't want the tragedies that had befallen her to happen to anyone else. But Margaret couldn't have known that what was happening to her had impacted thousands of others, just as she couldn't have known that she was part of a global plan that went awry. Her schizophrenia distorted reality and, without any medication, her mental capacity was greatly compromised.

I think she talked to me because all I asked her was to tell me her story. It was a simple question that focused on her, not the fact that she was homeless. On most days, the majority of people asked if she was hungry or if she had a place to sleep – survival questions that reminded her of life as a homeless person. During the forty-five minutes we talked, when she told me about her childhood and the son she'd given birth to and how she could play the piano and had worked as a typist, she wasn't a homeless woman who lived in a constant state of crisis. She was Margaret Louise Jacobson. Her story was one that she rarely got the chance to tell.

In the end, all Margaret wanted was what everyone wants – to be treated with respect. My hope is that she felt a little of that during our time together. It wasn't a feeling she was offered many times in her life.

WE'LL NEVER KNOW how many lives have been lost because of the significant inadequacies in our health care and housing systems. Nor will we ever know how many people have felt disrespected and dismissed by the endless wait times. What we do know is that the problems that were there when Margaret desperately needed help all those years ago still exist today.

Without the supports that people need, more will spiral into homelessness and we will continue paying a steep price for them to be there. We are reminded of that every time we walk down the street.

If society is to be judged by the way it treats its most vulnerable, then the way Margaret was treated shows we have failed. The proof of that is in the worn-down faces of the thirty-five thousand people who experience homelessness in Canada every night and in the thousands of others who are one friend's couch away from being homeless.

We owe it to every person who is homeless to speak up and make change happen. We owe it to Margaret.

Margaret, age ten in Antigua. Courtesy of Jacobson family.

Acknowledgements

There are many people I need to thank for helping me unravel the mysteries of Margaret's life and I have to start with the Jacobson family, specifically Margaret's brother David, and her nephews, Brian and David E., who never stopped caring about her and were generous in providing many photos of Margaret. Thank you to Margaret's son, Jeremy, who shared the details of his own life with me as well as his mother's medical files. I hope this book brings more clarity around the mother, sister and aunt you never knew.

Thanks to Bob Dixon for putting up with my endless questions during the hours I spent at his long-term care home where I caught a glimpse of the kindness he showed Margaret. I am so grateful to Rev. Bill MacKinnon, who made sure Margaret was remembered by organizing her memorial services. Your compassion for homeless people is never-ending. A big thank you to the Wesley Centre – had they not permitted me to spend the night there, I would never have met Margaret. And a special thanks to Lynn Ferris and Francine Small, who graciously shared their insights about Margaret. To Claudette Gaudry for talking to me about Margaret's last night and providing me with a copy of the 911 transcript.

To outreach worker Oman Huhad, who allowed me to accompany him on his walks and helped me see the lives of homeless people close up. My thanks to Kasper's family for providing details about his life and for their devotion to Kasper. To Pat Saunders and Helen Kell, thank you for sharing your valuable first-hand insights and observations about Margaret, and for your continuing work to help homeless people.

My undying gratitude goes to the many volunteers, like Jeff Ng, who work in shelters, drive soup vans and feed homeless people night after night. Your acts of kindness show them they matter in a world where they're constantly being told they don't.

My thanks and much affection to *Spectator* librarian Tammie Danciu, who dug through the *Spec* archives for various stories and whose friendly voice made my days in the newsroom even brighter. My heartfelt thanks to Dana Robbins, who was the *Spectator*'s city editor when I met Margaret and trusted me that her story needed to be told. Your support has meant so much to me. Thank you to photographer Barry Gray, who accompanied me on my midnight stakeouts to find Margaret and took such beautiful photos. To Kim Echlin and Gary Barwin, who read parts of my book when they were writer-in-residence at McMaster University; to Alison Wearing, writer-in-residence at the University of Guelph for believing in my book; to Diane Schoemperlen for your support and talented editing skills; and to Cassie White for reigniting my passion to write Margaret's story.

To my close friend Dan Nolan, who has always made me laugh; and to friends who kindly offered suggestions on my book: Heather DeHaan, Deb Wakem, Carol Baldwin, Agnes Bongers, Anne Bokma and Val Neilsen. To my dear friend Allison Barrett for your support; many more trails and tea houses await. To my kayak buddies, the Lillydippers, and to Audrey Johnman, Kathy Garneau and Mary Nolan for sharing many laughs on the water; to my friends in the Elizabeth Gardens Book Club, thanks for the good reads and good times and for supporting my book; and to my awesome high school girlfriends Ursula Vourvoulis, Angelika Kaiser, Jean Greatbatch, Kathy O'Driscoll and Sheila Evans, whose valuable feedback on my book was most appreciated.

A special thank you to Wolsak and Wynn publisher Noelle Allen for guiding me through the process of publishing my first book and believing that Margaret's story was important. Your keen eye, editorial judgment and calm presence made you a dream to work with. Thanks to copy editor Andrew

Wilmot for your meticulous editing skills and to Ashley Hisson for your amazing proofreading skills. To Jennifer Rawlinson for the cover design and Brianna Wodabek for help with publicity.

To my sister, Carol Roe, and brothers, Mark and Drew, and their spouses, Alison and Jackie, for your love and support. To my father, Ken Davy, who has been my sounding board, mentor and friend my whole life. Thank you for showing me the importance of kindness in the way you've lived your life. To my wonderfully brilliant daughters, Emma and Katie, I adore you both beyond words. I hope that through Margaret's story you have learned the importance of caring equally for all of the people you meet in your lives.

Lastly, to Margaret, who shared her story with me on that cold winter night and opened my eyes to the larger story that needed to be told. You are missed.

CHRONOLOGY

August 9, 1911	Abe is born in Midale, Saskatchewan
April 19, 1916	Verna is born in North Seguin, Ontario
April 1943	Abe and Verna marry
July 23, 1943	Abe and Verna move to Barbados and begin missionary work
April 5, 1944	Margaret is born
March 7, 1945	John Morden is born
March 24, 1947	James (Jim) is born
July 15, 1952	David Maurice is born
1954	Abe and Verna contract typhoid fever
1956	Jacobsons return to Canada for two years
January 1958	Jacobsons return to St. John's Pentecostal Church in Antigua
1959	John is in boarding school in Canada
1960	Margaret is hospitalized after two relatives and a friend die
January 1961	Jacobsons leave Antigua and move to Ontario; Abe goes to Springfield, MO
1961	Margaret hospitalized at the Homewood
October 9, 1962	Margaret is admitted to the Ontario Hospital

1964	Verna, David and Jim move to States with Abe; John goes to Vancouver
1967	Jacobson family moves from Wisconsin to New Orleans; Abe teaches
April 1969	Margaret moves to Regina with aunt
August 1969	Margaret moves back to Ontario Hospital in Hamilton
1969	Abe and Verna move to Wiggins, Mississippi
1970	Abe, Verna and David go to Vancouver to see John, then to Hamilton to visit Margaret
March 5, 1972	Margaret gives birth to baby boy, names him Jeffrey
April 27, 1972	Jeffrey is adopted by Hamilton couple; they rename him Jeremy
November 3, 1973	Abe dies of protracted deterioration of his heart; age 62
1984	Margaret now living on the streets
June 16, 1994	Verna dies; age 83
February 25, 1995	Jim dies; age 48
December 6, 1995	Margaret dies after falling in Mr. Sub shop
December 14, 1995	Bob finds out Margaret has died
July 1998	Jeremy and his fiancée visit me in Burlington
February 20, 2008	John dies, age 62
2009	Jeremy is admitted to the Hamilton Psychiatric Hospital
December 6, 2015	Twentieth anniversary memorial for Margaret at Woodland Cemetery

Suggested Reading

Arnold, William. *Shadowland.* New York: Jove, 1978.

Clifford Larson, Kate. *Rosemary: The Hidden Kennedy Daughter.* New York: Mariner Books, 2015.

Crowe, Cathy, and Nancy Baker. *Dying for a Home: Homeless Activists Speak Out.* Toronto: Between the Lines, 2007.

Dear, Michael J., and Jennifer R. Wolch. *Landscapes of Despair: From Deinstitutionalization to Homelessness.* Princeton: Princeton University Press, 1987.

Isaac, Rael Jean, and Virginia C. Armat. *Madness in the Streets: How Psychiatry and the Law Abandoned the Mentally Ill.* New York: Free Press, 1990.

Kesey, Ken. *One Flew Over the Cuckoo's Nest.* New York: Penguin, 1962.

Kozol, Jonathan. *Rachel and Her Children: Homeless Families in America.* New York: Crown Publishing, 1987.

Layton, Jack. *Homelessness: How to End the National Crisis.* Toronto: Penguin Random House, 2000, 2008.

Lopez, Steve. *The Soloist: A Lost Dream, an Unlikely Friendship, and the Redemptive Power of Music.* New York: Berkley Publishing, 2008.

Loue, Sana. *Therapeutic Farms: Recovery from Mental Illness.* Cham, Switzerland: Springer International Publishing, 2016.

Perry, Bruce D. *The Boy Who Was Raised as a Dog: And Other Stories from a Child Psychiatrist's Notebook: What Traumatized Children Can Teach Us*

About Loss, Love, and Healing. New York: Basic Books, 2006.

Plath, Sylvia. *The Bell Jar.* New York: Harper and Row, 1971. First published under a pseudonym in 1963 by Heinemann.

Solomon, Andrew. *The Noonday Demon: An Atlas of Depression.* New York: Touchstone, 2001.

Stote, Karen. *An Act of Genocide: Colonialism and the Sterilization of Aboriginal Women.* Halifax: Fernwood Publishing, 2015.

Torrey, E. Fuller. *Out of the Shadows: Confronting America's Mental Illness Crisis.* New York: Wiley Publishing, 1997.

Whitaker, Robert. *Mad in America: Bad Science, Bad Medicine and the Enduring Mistreatment of the Mentally Ill.* New York: Perseus Publishing, 2001.

Worth, Jennifer. *Call the Midwife: Shadows of the Workhouse.* New York: HarperCollins Publisher, 2005.

Sources

Alberta Secretariat for Action on Homelessness. *A Plan for Alberta: Ending Homelessness in 10 years*. Calgary: Alberta Secretariat for Action on Homelessness, 2008. http://www.humanservices.alberta.ca /documents/PlanForAB_Secretariat_final.pdf.

Austen, Andrea, and Ann Marie Sirko. *The Homelessness Continuum: A Community Plan for Hamilton*. Hamilton: City of Hamilton, 2003.

Canadian Institute for Health Information. *Improving the Health of Canadians: Mental Health and Homelessness*. Ottawa: Canadian Institute for Health Information, 2007.

Centre for Addiction and Mental Health and the Canadian Council on Social Development. *Turning the Key: Assessing Housing and Related Supports for Persons Living with Mental Health Problems and Illness*. Ottawa: Mental Health Commission of Canada, 2016. https:// www.mentalhealthcommission.ca/sites/default/files/PrimaryCare _Turning_the_Key_Full_ENG_0_1.pdf.

Dear, Michael J., and Jennifer R. Wolch. *Landscapes of Despair: From Deinstitutionalization to Homelessness*. Princeton: Princeton University Press, 1987.

Gaetz, Stephen. *The Real Cost of Homelessness: Can We Save Money by Doing the Right Thing?* Toronto: Canadian Homelessness Research Network Press, 2012.

Gaetz, Stephen, Erin Dej, Rim Richter and Melanie Redman. *The State of*

Homelessness in Canada 2016. Toronto: Canadian Observatory on Homelessness Press, 2016.

Khandor, Erika, and Kate Mason. *Street Health Report 2007.* Toronto: Street Health, 2007. www.wellesleyinstitute.com/wp-content/uploads/2007/09/Street-Health-Report-2007.pdf.

Latimer, Eric. *Costs Associated With Homelessness.* Montreal: McGill University, 2017.

Latimer, Eric, Daniel Rabouin, Christian Méthot, Christopher McAll, Angela Ly, Henri Dorvil, Anne Crocker, et al. *At Home/Chez Soi: Montréal Site Final Report.* Calgary: Mental Health Commission of Canada, 2014. https://www.mentalhealthcommission.ca/English/document/24376/national-homechez-soi-final-report.

Mayo, Sara. *Not to be Forgotten: Homeless Women in Hamilton.* Hamilton: Social Planning and Research Council, 2011.

Minister of Public Works and Government Services Canada. *The Human Face of Mental Health and Mental Illness in Canada.* Ottawa: Public Health Agency of Canada, 2006.

Read, Alison. "Psychiatric Deinstitutionalization in BC: Negative Consequences and Possible Solutions." *University of British Columbia Medical Journal* 1, no. 1 (September 2009): 25–26. https://med-fom-ubcmj.sites.olt.ubc.ca/files/2015/11/ubcmj_1_1_2009_25-26.pdf.

Sealy, Patricia, and Paul C. Whitehead. "Forty Years of Deinstitutionalization of Psychiatric Services in Canada: An Empirical Assessment." *Canadian Journal of Psychiatry* 49, no. 4 (April 2004).

Simmons, Harvey G. *Unbalanced Mental Health Policy in Ontario, 1930–1989.* Toronto: Wall & Thompson, 1989.

Thomas, Bethan. *Homelessness Kills: An Analysis of the Mortality of Homeless People in Early Twenty-First Century England.* London: Crisis, 2012.

Trypuc, Bri, and Jeffrey Robinson. *Homeless in Canada: A Funder's Primer in Understanding the Tragedy on Canada's Streets.* King City, ON: Charity Intelligence Canada, 2009. https://www.charityintelligence.ca/images/Reports/homeless-report.pdf.

Organizations

Canadian Alliance to End Homelessness: Leads a growing national movement of individuals, organizations and communities working together to end homelessness in Canada.

Canadian Mental Health Association of Canada: Founded in 1918, the CMHA provides advocacy, programs and resources that help prevent mental health problems and illnesses, support recovery and resilience.

Canadian Observatory on Homelessness (COH), formerly the Canadian Homelessness Research Network (CHRN): A national non-profit, non-partisan research institute based at York University that works with researchers, service providers, policy-makers, students and people who have experienced homelessness.

The Homeless Hub: The largest online research library in the world, developed by the COH; houses nearly thirty thousand resources on homelessness.

Mental Health Commission of Canada: A national non-profit organization created by the Canadian government in 2007 that studies mental health, mental illness and addiction, and recommends improvements to the mental health system on a national level.

DENISE DAVY IS a nationally recognized, award-winning journalist who specializes in writing about mental health, homelessness and gender issues. She worked at the *Hamilton Spectator* for twenty-six years, was twice honoured with the Journalist of the Year award by the Ontario Newspaper Association and is a recipient of a National Newspaper Award, several Ontario Newspaper Association awards and two awards from the Registered Nurses' Association of Ontario. In 1993, the Canadian Association of Journalists awarded her for co-founding the National Women in the Media conference.

She is the recipient of four national journalism fellowships, which allowed her to investigate child prostitution in Thailand, poverty in India and the crisis in children's mental health services in Canada.

She is founder of Purses for Margaret, which provides toiletries to homeless women. She lives in Burlington, ON.